ENGLAND

NICHOLAS HOBBES lives in London and is the author of *Essential Militaria, England: 1,000 Things You Need to Know* and *Stumped! The Sports Fan's Book of Answers.*

ENGLAND

1,000 Things You Need to Know

NICHOLAS HOBBES

Atlantic Books
LONDON

First published in hardback in Great Britain in 2006 by Atlantic Books,
an imprint of Grove Atlantic Ltd.

This paperback edition published in Great Britain in 2008
by Atlantic Books.

3 5 7 9 8 6 4

A CIP catalogue record for this book is available
from the British Library.

ISBN: 978 1 84354 797 6

Text design by Lindsay Nash

Printed in Great Britain by
Clays Ltd, St Ives plc

Atlantic Books
An imprint of Grove Atlantic Ltd
Ormond House
26–27 Boswell Street
London
WC1N 3JZ

Saeed Jaffrey: 'He wants to know, are you Gods?'
Michael Caine: 'Not Gods; Englishmen – which is
the next best thing.'

From the film *The Man Who Would Be King* (1975)

This royal throne of kings, this sceptr'd isle,
This earth of majesty, this seat of Mars,
This other Eden, demi-paradise;
This fortress built by Nature for herself
Against infection and the hand of war;
This happy breed of men, this little world;
This precious stone set in the silver sea,
Which serves it in the office of a wall,
Or as a moat defensive to a house,
Against the envy of less happier lands;
This blessed plot, this earth, this realm, this England...

William Shakespeare,
King Richard II, Act 2 scene 1, (1595–6)

William Shakespeare

Contents

	Acknowledgements	ix
	Note	x
1.	Land and People	1
2.	National Character	35
3.	National Heroes	51
4.	Kings and Queens	79
5.	Crown, State and Law	119
6.	The English Language	143
7.	Literature and Letters	155
8.	Stage and Screen	201
9.	Music	231
10.	Art and Architecture	255
11.	Food and Drink	275
12.	Symbols and Institutions	313
13.	Science and Technology	331
14.	Industry, Agriculture and Commerce	349
15.	The Church	375
16.	Legends and Folklore	387
17.	Warfare	403
18.	Sports and Pastimes	421
	Appendix	457

Acknowledgements

Special thanks go to Penny Gardiner, Angus MacKinnon and Toby Mundy for their work in editing and overseeing this book. Thanks also go to Charlotte Foley, Raj Patel, Nicola Perrin and Richard Wood-Wilson for additional help with material and sources, and to Sheila Oakes for 'The Man Who Would Be King'.

Note

Individuals are counted as English if they were born in England or if they were born abroad to English parents and subsequently migrated to England.

1
LAND AND PEOPLE

'England is the paradise of women, the purgatory of men, and the hell of horses.'

John Florio (c. 1553–1625)

England at a Glance

Population: The 2001 census counted 49,138,831 people, of whom 23,922,144 were male and 25,216,687 female.

Area: 50,363 sq. miles (130,439 sq. km)

Highest point: Scafell Pike 3,210 ft (978 metres)

Lowest point on land: Holme Fen, Cambridgeshire 9 ft (2.75 metres) below sea level

Coastline: 2,000 miles (3,200 km)

Furthest place from the sea: Coton in the Elms, Derbyshire – 72 miles

Largest lake: Lake Windermere, Cumbria – 6 sq. miles (16 sq. km)

Geographic centre: Traditionally Meriden in Warwickshire. However, the Ordnance Survey's Gravitational Method of Mapping, which includes the nation's small islands, gives Fenny Drayton in Leicestershire as the centre.

Highest recorded temperature: 38.5°C (101.3°F) on 10 August 2003 in Kent

Lowest recorded temperature: −26.1°C (−15°F) on 10 January 1982 in Shropshire

Principal crops: Wheat, barley, potatoes, sugar beet, oilseed rape–

Natural resources: Coal, petroleum, natural gas, tin, limestone, iron ore, salt, clay, chalk, gypsum, lead, silica

Literacy: 99 per cent

Mobile phone ownership: 81 per cent of adults (defined as 15+)

Home Internet access: 56 per cent

National motto: '*Dieu et mon droit*' ('God and my right')

Coat of arms: Three Lions

Urban population: 89 per cent

Life expectancy: Men 75.3 years, women 80.1 years

Number of times the average citizen is captured on CCTV each day: 300 (600 in Central London)

Percentage who identified themselves in 2003 as 'English' or 'More English than British': 36 per cent (up from 24 per cent in 1997, *Source:* IPPR)

———

The Four Corners of England

———

Most northerly point — Marshall Meadows, Northumberland
Most southerly point — Lizard Point, Cornwall
Most easterly point — Lowestoft Ness, Suffolk
Most westerly point — Land's End, Cornwall

Nomenclature

'England' derives from 'Land of the Angles', the Germanic tribe from Angeln in the south of the Danish peninsula.

'Albion' stems either from the Latin *albus* for 'white', meaning the White Cliffs of Dover, or the Celtic word for the whole of Britain.

'Blighty' originated with soldiers serving in India and derives from *bilayati*, the Urdu for 'foreign land'.

The Anglo-Saxon Heptarchy

The Heptarchy were the seven kingdoms that ruled Anglo-Saxon England for three hundred years until Wessex gained supremacy around AD 829:

East Anglia	Northumbria*
Essex	Sussex
Kent	Wessex
Mercia	

* Northumbria was divided for the most part into two warring kingdoms, Deira and Bernicia.

Modern Regions

England is divided into nine Government Office Regions, which also serve as European Parliament constituencies:

London
South-East
South-West
West Midlands
North-West

North-East
Yorkshire and the Humber
East Midlands
East

Four Regional Monikers

COCKNEYS

A 'cockney' was traditionally someone born within earshot of the bells of St Mary-le-Bow in Cheapside, East London. This meant a 3-mile (5 kilometres) radius that included the City, Bethnal Green, Finsbury, Hackney, Shoreditch, Stepney and Whitechapel. The term stems from the Old English word 'cocena', meaning 'cock's egg' – or, in other words, the runt of a clutch, which came to be applied to unhealthy city dwellers.

GEORDIES

The most plausible origin for the term 'Geordie' is that it stems from Newcastle's support for George III during the Jacobite Rebellion of 1745. It was traditionally applied to anyone born within sight of the River Tyne, for those who lived further out in Northumbria were more likely to have supported the Jacobites. Geordies use the derogatory term 'Mackems' for the residents of Sunderland, referring to their shipbuilding industry – 'they make them and we take them' becomes 'make them and take them'. Geordies refer to their Hartlepool neighbours as 'monkey-hangers' after the incident during the Napoleonic Wars when a shipwrecked monkey was hanged as a French spy.

SCOUSERS

Liverpool natives acquired the name from 'lobscouse', a mutton and hard-tack stew once popular with sailors and their families.

TYKES

Every Yorkshireman is proud to call himself a 'Tyke', which was an Old Norse word introduced by Viking settlers to refer to a vicious dog. An alternative, though no kinder, explanation is that it derives from the Welsh 'taeog', meaning rogue before it was used to refer to farmers.

The Traditional Counties

The number of English counties and their names have changed several times, but thirty-seven traditional counties still exist in some administrative form:

Bedfordshire	Cambridgeshire	Cumbria
Berkshire	Cheshire	Derbyshire
Buckinghamshire	Cornwall	Devon

Dorset	Leicestershire	Staffordshire
County Durham	Lincolnshire	Suffolk
Essex	Norfolk	Surrey
Gloucestershire	Northamptonshire	Sussex
Hampshire	Northumberland	Warwickshire
Herefordshire	Nottinghamshire	Wiltshire
Hertfordshire	Oxfordshire	Worcestershire
Isle of Wight	Rutland	Yorkshire
Kent	Shropshire	
Lancashire	Somerset	

The largest is Yorkshire. Rutland is the smallest.

Former counties: Cumberland and Westmoreland (now Cumbria), Huntingdonshire (now part of Cambridgeshire), Middlesex (now part of Greater London), Monmouthshire (now part of Wales).

The Home Counties

These border London and comprise:

Berkshire	Hertfordshire
Buckinghamshire	Kent
Essex	Surrey

London Boroughs

There are thirty-two boroughs in Greater London, not including the City of London ('The Square Mile'):

Barking and Dagenham	Islington
Barnet	Royal Borough of
Bexley	Kensington & Chelsea*
Brent	Royal Borough of
Bromley	Kingston upon Thames*
Camden	Lambeth
Croydon	Lewisham
Ealing	Merton
Enfield	Newham
Greenwich	Redbridge
Hackney	Richmond upon Thames
Hammersmith & Fulham	Southwark
Haringey	Sutton
Harrow	Tower Hamlets
Havering	Waltham Forest
Hillingdon	Wandsworth
Hounslow	City of Westminster

* The 'Royal' title denoting the patronage of the crown is shared with only one other borough in England – the Royal Borough of Windsor and Maidenhead.

National Parks

There are nine:

The Broads	Northumberland
Dartmoor	North York Moors
Exmoor	Peak District
Lake District	Yorkshire Dales
New Forest	

The status of the South Downs National Park is pending in 2006.

The Ten Largest Cities
And their populations according to the 2001 Census

1.	London	7,172,091
2.	Birmingham	977,087
3.	Leeds	715,402
4.	Sheffield	513,234
5.	Bradford	467,665
6.	Liverpool	439,477
7.	Manchester	392,819
8.	Bristol	380,615
9.	Coventry	300,848
10.	Leicester	279,921

The Cathedral Towns

Possession of a cathedral does not automatically confer city status, as in the case of the following:

Blackburn	Rochester*
Bury St Edmunds	Southwark
Chelmsford	Southwell
Guildford	

* Rochester lost its city status in 1998, when the local authorities of Rochester and Gillingham became Medway.

The Ten Best English Beaches
According to The Rough Guide to England (2006)

1. Par Beach, St Martin's, Isles of Scilly
2. Porthcurno, Cornwall
3. Polzeath, Cornwall
4. Woolacombe, North Devon
5. Blackpool Sands, South Devon
6. Studland Bay, Dorset
7. Holkham, Norfolk
8. Bamburgh, Northumberland
9. Blackpool, Lancashire
10. Whitby, North Yorkshire

The Mongrel Race

'From a mixture all kinds began, that heterogeneous
thing – an Englishman.'

Daniel Defoe, *The True-Born Englishman* (1701)

The eleven chief sources of the English gene pool, along with the
date of first large-scale immigration:

CELTS – PRE ROMAN

THE GERMANIC TRIBES ('ANGLO-SAXONS')

Jutes	Jutland Peninsula	late fourth century
Frisians	Northern Germany	fifth century
Saxons	Northern Germany	fifth century
Angles	Southern Denmark	sixth century

NORSEMEN

Vikings	Norway, Sweden, Denmark	ninth century
Normans	Northern France	eleventh century

JEWS – ELEVENTH CENTURY

Encouraged to settle by William the Conqueror to aid trade and com-
merce. Most were expelled by Edward I in 1290. Jews did not return
in significant numbers until the late seventeenth century under
Charles II. (Responsibility for the new tolerance is often erroneously
awarded to Oliver Cromwell, who was petitioned without success by
the Jews of Amsterdam.)

French – SEVENTEENTH CENTURY

Huguenots fleeing religious persecution under Louis XIV.

Africans – SEVENTEENTH CENTURY

There were around 14,000 black people in England by 1770, many of them working as servants, though the first were slaves accompanying West Indian planters' children to school in the homeland. Black African legionnaires manned Hadrian's Wall in AD 250, but there is no evidence that they remained in England.

Irish – NINETEENTH CENTURY

Fleeing poverty and famine between 1830 and 1850.

Poles – TWENTIETH CENTURY

157,000 settled in England after the Second World War.

West Indians – TWENTIETH CENTURY

First arrived at Tilbury Docks on HMS *Empire Windrush* in 1948.

Asians

Small-scale immigration from the Indian subcontinent began with servants and businessmen in the nineteenth century and gathered pace in the twentieth: 28,000 African Asians were admitted in two months in 1972 after they were expelled from Uganda by the tyrant, Idi Amin.

East Europeans

Over 350,000 have registered for work permits since 2004.

Population since 1066
And comparisons with modern nations

All medieval figures for England's population are estimates, while official censuses are slight underestimates of the real total. Up to 250,000 went uncounted in the first census in 1801. More recently, large-scale unrecorded immigration has led the government to suggest that current figures may be out by up to 400,000 people.

1066	1,100,000	(comparable to Trinidad and Tobago in 2006, US Census Bureau)
1215	2,500,000	(Kuwait)
1348	3,750,000	(Lebanon)

The Black Death

1350	2,500,000	(Kuwait)
1570	4,800,000	(Eritrea)
1630	5,800,000	(Libya)
1700	6,500,000	(Paraguay)
1801	8,308,000*	(Haiti)
1811	9,496,000	(Guinea)
1821	11,158,000	(Cuba)
1831	12,993,000	(Malawi)
1841	14,866,000	(Kazakhstan)
1851	16,769,400†	(Netherlands)
1861	18,776,300	(Syria)
1871	21,298,000	(Yemen)
1881	24,402,700	(Malaysia)
1891	27,230,200	(Uzbekistan)

| 1901 | 30,515,000 | (Afghanistan) |
| 1911 | 33,651,600 | (Morocco) |

First World War

| 1921 | 35,230,200 | (Kenya) |
| 1931 | 37,359,000 | (Tanzania) |

Second World War

1951	41,042,200	(Sudan)
1961	43,983,300	(Colombia)
1971	45,870,100	(South Africa)
1981	46,623,500	(Ukraine)
1991	48,067,300	(Burma)
2001	49,138,831	(South Korea)

* The first census.

† Beginning of regular censuses.

————

England's Demographics
Three key factors

————

BIRTH RATE

The highest birth rate since records began in 1924 was in 1964, when the average woman had 2.93 children. The average number of children per woman in England today is just 1.64 – the lowest since records began. The 'replacement rate' which is required to maintain the population at its current level is 2.1 children per woman. However, the population is expected to continue to increase rather than dwindle due to immigration.

Couples in the north-east have the fewest children, with an average of 1.58 per woman, compared with a high of 1.74 in the West Midlands. This is despite the region having the highest teenage birth rate in the country, with 32.5 births per 1,000 to girls aged between 15 and 19, compared with 22.1 per 1,000 in the south-east.

Londoners are most likely to abort a pregnancy. Around a third (32.5 per cent) of all conceptions in the capital are terminated, compared with less than a fifth (19.1 per cent) in the east of England.

The number of births outside marriage rose from 30 per cent in 1991 to 40 per cent in 2001.

Women are waiting on average until the age of 27 before starting a family.

AGE BREAKDOWN, 2001

0–14	18.9 per cent
15–29	18.8 per cent
30–44	22.6 per cent
45–59	18.9 per cent
60–74	13.3 per cent
75+	7.5 per cent

Source: 2001 Census

ETHNICITY

White:	90.9 per cent
Indian:	2.1 per cent
Pakistani:	1.4 per cent
Mixed:	1.4 per cent
Black Caribbean:	1.1 per cent
Black African:	0.9 per cent

| Chinese: | 0.4 per cent |
| Black other: | 0.2 per cent |

Source: 2001 Census

The Ten Worst Crime Hotspots
By recorded offences per 1,000 residents, 2004–2005

1.	Nottingham	156
2.	North East Lincolnshire	132
3.	Kingston upon Hull	130
4.	Manchester	128
5.	City of Westminster	127
6.	Islington	121
7.	Middlesbrough	121
8.	Bristol	112
9.	Peterborough	111
10.	Liverpool	110

Source: Urban Crime Rankings, Reform 2006

Population Density
People per square kilometre in 2002

England at large 380

CITIES AND TOWNS

Greater London	4,679	Birmingham	3,697
Portsmouth	4,671	Manchester	3,652
Southampton	4,438	Nottingham	3,619
Luton	4,295	Reading	3,574
Blackpool	4,065	Bournemouth	3,547
Liverpool	3,947	Bristol	3,482
Leicester	3,868	Wolverhampton	3,447
Southend-on-Sea	3,802	Kingston-upon-Hull	3,379
Watford	3,751	Sandwell	3,329
Slough	3,725	Norwich	3,117

INNER LONDON BOROUGHS

Kensington & Chelsea	13,609	Westminster	8,875
Islington	12,181	Southwark	8,710
Hackney	11,027	Wandsworth	7,859
Hammersmith & Fulham	10,566	Haringey	7,609
Tower Hamlets	10,462	Lewisham	7,220
Lambeth	10,136	Newham	7,013
Camden	9,948	City of London	2,694

COUNTIES (NON-METROPOLITAN)

Surrey	638	Oxfordshire	233
Hertfordshire	631	County Durham	221
Lancashire	393	Gloucestershire	214
Essex	381	Cambridgeshire	183
West Sussex	380	Suffolk	177
Kent	378	Dorset	155
Nottinghamshire	361	Somerset	146
Hampshire	338	Cornwall	143
Cheshire	324	Norfolk	139
Bedfordshire	323	Wiltshire	134
Worcestershire	314	Lincolnshire	111
Staffordshire	309	Devon	108
Buckinghamshire	306	Rutland	91
Leicestershire	295	Shropshire	89
Derbyshire	290	Cumbria	72
East Sussex	289	North Yorkshire	71
Northamptonshire	270	Northumberland	62
Warwickshire	260		

Source: Office for National Statistics

———

The Ten Longest Rivers

———

1. Severn   220 miles (354km)
2. Thames   215 miles (346km)*
3. Trent   185 miles (297km)
4. Great Ouse   150 miles (240km)

5. Wye	130 miles (208km)
6. Tweed	97 miles (156km)
7. Avon	96 miles (154km)
8. Tees	80 miles (130km)
9. Ribble	75 miles (120km)
10. Mersey	70 miles (112km)

* The Thames is the longest river that lies wholly within England – parts of the Severn lie in Wales.

Land Usage

Grasses and rough grazing	37 per cent
Crops and fallow	30 per cent
Urban/developed	19 per cent
Forest and woodland	9 per cent
Other	5 per cent

Source: Defra 2004

Forest and Woodland Cover

6,000 BC	80 per cent
AD 100	20 per cent
1086	15 per cent
1350	10 per cent
1800	8 per cent

1905	5.2 per cent
1924	5.1 per cent
1947	5.8 per cent
1965	6.8 per cent
1980	7.3 per cent
2005	8.6 per cent

Source: Forestry Commission

Tree Species
Three phases of colonization

INDIGENOUS SPECIES

Alder	Elder	Maple
Ash	Elms	Oaks
Beech*	Hawthorn	Rowan
Birch	Hazel	Service
Black poplar	Holly	Whitebeam
Box	Hornbeam	Willow
Cherry	Juniper	Yew
Crab apple	Lime	

* Julius Caesar reported that beech trees could not be found in Britain in the first century AD, but modern botanists disagree.

ROMAN IMPORTS

Stone pine	Sycamore
Sweet chestnut	Walnut

Sixteenth-century Imports

Horse chestnut – from the Balkans. 'Conkers' was originally played in England with hazelnuts or snail shells.

Norway spruce (Christmas Tree) – native before the Ice Age, reintroduced in 1500s from Germany and Scandinavia.

Source: Royal Forestry Society

———

The Cinque Ports

———

The confederation of the Cinque Ports ('Five Ports') provided the backbone of the English Royal Fleet between the eleventh and fourteenth centuries in return for tax and trading privileges. Some of the latter lasted into the early nineteenth century.

The Ports

Hastings (the chief port)
Dover
Hythe
New Romney
Sandwich

They were supported by the 'Ancient Towns' of Winchelsea and Rye.

As several of the Cinque Ports' harbours became silted, further ports were added as 'Limbs' including:

Deal	Lydd	Tenterden
Faversham	Margate	
Folkestone	Ramsgate	

The Royal Parks

1. Richmond Park, Surrey   2,500 acres
2. Bushy Park, Middlesex   1,099 acres
3. Hampton Court Park and Gardens, Surrey   669 acres
4. Regent's Park and Primrose Hill, London NW1   487 acres
5. Hyde Park, London W1/W2   350 acres
6. Royal Botanic Gardens at Kew, Surrey   300 acres
7. Kensington Gardens, London W2/W8   275 acres
8. Greenwich Park, London SE10   183 acres
9. St James's Park, London SW1   93 acres
10. Green Park, London W1   40 acres

The Royal Palaces

1. Buckingham Palace, London (the monarch's official London residence since 1837)
2. Windsor Castle, Windsor (the world's largest occupied castle)
3. Frogmore House, Windsor (the site of Queen Victoria and Albert's mausoleum)
4. Palace of Holyrood House, Edinburgh
5. Balmoral Castle, Aberdeenshire
6. Sandringham House, Norfolk (the Queen's Christmas retreat)
7. Clarence House, London (the official residence of the Prince of Wales)
8. St James's Palace, London (the sovereign's 'senior palace')

9. Kensington Palace, London
10. Hampton Court Palace, Surrey
11. Banqueting House, London (part of the old Whitehall Palace)
12. Hillsborough Castle, County Down, Northern Ireland
13. Kew Palace, Richmond (the smallest royal palace)

The English Rain

'In England all they ever do is talk about the weather.
But no one does a damn thing about it.'

George Axelrod

The wettest month, on average, is November with 3.4 inches (84mm). The driest are March and June with 2 inches (50mm).

The Lake District is England's wettest region, with 130 inches (330cm) each year.

2000 was the wettest year since records began in 1776.

The Eleven Grand English Waterfalls

1. Aira Force, Lake District
2. Aysgarth Falls, Yorkshire Dales
3. Cauldron Snout, County Durham*
4. Cautley Spout, Yorkshire Dales

5. Gaping Gill, Yorkshire Dales
6. Hardraw Force, Yorkshire Dales
7. High Force, County Durham
8. Kisdon Force, Yorkshire Dales
9. Lady Exmouth Falls, Dartmoor
10. Low Force, County Durham
11. Scale Force, Lake District

* Cauldron Snout is considered to be England's highest at 150 feet (45 metres), though there are disputes over whether to measure the height above ground or sea level and whether to include horizontal stretches.

England's Sixteen UNESCO World Heritage Sites

1. Blenheim Palace
2. Canterbury Cathedral, St Augustine's Abbey and St Martin's Church
3. City of Bath
4. Derwent Valley Mills (Derbyshire)
5. Dorset and East Devon Coast
6. Durham Castle and Cathedral
7. Frontiers of the Roman Empire (Hadrian's Wall)
8. Ironbridge Gorge (Shropshire)
9. Liverpool – Maritime Mercantile City
10. Maritime Greenwich
11. Royal Botanic Gardens, Kew
12. Saltaire (West Yorkshire)
13. Stonehenge, Avebury and associated sites

14. Studley Royal Park including the ruins of Fountains Abbey
    (Yorkshire)
15. Tower of London
16. Westminster Palace, Westminster Abbey and
    St Margaret's Church

Famous Standing Stones

England's earliest stone circles from around 3000 BC predate the
Druids by several centuries.

STONEHENGE (c. 3100–1500 BC), WILTSHIRE

The eighty or so 'Bluestones' erected in the second phase of building
in around 2100 BC, each weighing 4 tons, were somehow transported from the Preseli Mountains in South Wales, 250 miles
(402km) away. Parts of Stonehenge were scavenged for building
materials in the Middle Ages.

AVEBURY STONE CIRCLE (c. 3000 BC), WILTSHIRE

The largest stone circle in the world consists of two circles enclosed
by a larger circle a quarter of a mile in diameter that encompasses 28
acres (0.405 hectares) and part of the village of Avebury. Twenty-
seven stones remain out of what could once have been up to a
hundred.

CASTLERIGG STONE CIRCLE (c. 3000 BC), CUMBRIA

A ring of thirty-eight boulders, 100 feet (30 metres) in diameter, set
in the natural amphitheatre of the Keswick Hills.

The Rollright Stones (c. 2500 bc), Oxfordshire

The site consists of the seventy-seven heavily weathered stones in the Kings' Men circle, the King Stone, and the Whispering Knights stones. The King Stone has been chipped away at in recent centuries to make lucky charms.

Long Meg and her Daughters (c. 2500 bc), Cumbria

Long Meg is a 12-foot high (3.5 metres) piece of red sandstone that stands outside the circle of her 'daughters'. According to local legend, they were a coven of witches turned to stone by the Scottish wizard Michael Scott. He is said to have cast another spell to make the stones uncountable, but there is little dispute today that twenty-seven remain out of what was once around seventy. They also inspired a Wordsworth poem.

Famous Hill Figures

Giant figures were cut into chalk hills in various parts of the country by persons unknown. Just as strange as who created them and why is the fact that they must have been rescoured every few years, sometimes for millennia, despite the absence of interested tourist boards until relatively recently. A single break in the tending would allow the turf to overgrow the figure and erase it forever. This fate befell giants in Oxford, Cambridge and Plymouth Hoe, where a figure was first referred to in 1486. The three most famous surviving hill figures are:

THE CERNE ABBAS GIANT

The Dorset figure stands, or lies, 180 feet tall (55 metres), carries a giant club and boasts a penis 26 feet long (8 metres) erect. The phallus has been 'improved' at least once over the years during successive rescourings. It probably dates only to the seventeenth century, as there are no extant references to it before 1694. Sleeping on the giant is said to boost fertility.

THE WHITE HORSE OF UFFINGTON

Various explanations have been cited, including it being a memorial to Alfred the Great's victory over the Danes in 871, or a picture of the horse St George was riding when he slew the dragon. All theories were refuted in the 1990s, however, after silt dating suggested that it was created as early as 1000 BC. It is said that a wish made while standing within the horse's eye will come true.

THE LONG MAN OF WILMINGTON

A naked giant holding two poles dates back to at least 1710. He is said to be the 'crime scene' outline of a monster who died on the hillside.

There are over fifty figures in total, seventeen of which are horses (the most recent being created in Folkestone in 2003). The others include the Bulford Kiwi, the Mormond Stag, the Tan Hill Donkey, the Whipsnade Lion, the Laverstock Panda and the regimental badges of several army units.

Eight Historic Mazes

The view that the English were descended from the Trojans was popular in Elizabethan England. This is reflected in the names of some of the country's eight surviving turf labyrinths.

1. City of Troy, c. 1860 – Dalby, North Yorkshire
2. Julian's Bower, 1170 – Alkborough, Lincolnshire
3. The Old Maze, c. 1634 – Wing, Rutland
4. The Maze, 1660 – Hilton, Cambridgeshire
5. Troy Town, c. 1700 – Somerton, Oxfordshire
6. The Maze, 1699 – Saffron Walden, Essex
7. The Mizmaze, late 17th century – Winchester, Hampshire
8. The Mizmaze, medieval – Breamore, Hampshire

Four Literary Landscapes

1. Brontë Country: the West Yorkshire and East Lancashire Pennines
2. Austen Country: Hampshire
3. Hardy Country: Dorset
4. Wordsworth Country: the Lake District

The Last English Wolf, and Other Extinct Animals

In 1281, Edward I decided that wolves should be eradicated to protect the wool trade that was an increasing source of English wealth. He enlisted Peter Corbet to oversee the extermination of all wolves in the counties of Worcestershire, Herefordshire, Gloucestershire, Shropshire and Staffordshire. According to myth, the task was completed by the young Lady Jane Grey in the 1540s, who used a hunting knife and a stick to dispatch a wolf that attacked her. However, the truth is that Edward's wish had been fulfilled by no later than 1500.

Where the last English wolf was killed depends upon which local tourist board is to be believed. A vigorous claim has been pursued by Cumbria, which insists that John Harrington shot the last animal after a long chase at Humphrey Head, the largest limestone cliff in the region some time in the late fifteenth century. The event is commemorated by a wolf's head on the weathervane of the nearby Cartmel Priory. Rival claimants include Wolverstone in Devon and Stittenham in Yorkshire.

OTHER EXTINCTIONS

10th century	Lynx
c. 1200	Beaver
16th century	Wild boar (though several farmed boars have escaped in recent years)
17th century	Roe deer (reintroduced in 18th century)
1935	Muskrat (eradicated after being unwisely introduced from North America)
1955	Horned dung beetle

1957	Norfolk damselfly
1972	Burbot fish
1987	Coypu (exterminated as a pest after being introduced from South America)
1990	Mouse-eared bat, the largest bat in the UK
1994	Pine marten

Dinosaurs

A bone from a megalosaurus was discovered in a quarry near Oxford in 1676, when it was thought to be the thighbone of a giant.

The existence of dinosaurs was confirmed in England in 1822 when Mary Ann Mantell found a fossilized tooth in Tilgate Forest in Cuckfield. It looked like an iguana's tooth, only much larger, so her husband Gideon named the creature Iguanadon from the ancient Greek word for tooth, 'odontos'. The dinosaur is a favourite of schoolchildren, who know it as 'the one with the spiky thumbs' and lived 121 million years ago. The thumb was at first mistakenly thought to be a horn. Other beasts that once roamed the land that became England (or swam around what became her shores) include:

Dimorphodon
Eotyrannus
Ichthyosaurus*
Megalosaurus
Plesiosaurus*
Pteranodon*
Pterodactyl*

Scelidosaurus

Titanosaurus

* Not a 'true' dinosaur, but related.

English Dog Breeds

Border Terrier
Bull Mastiff
Bull Terrier
Cavalier King Charles Spaniel
Clumber Spaniel
English Boodle
English Bulldog
English Bullen Bordeaux Terrier
English Cocker Spaniel
English Coonhound
English Foxhound
English Pointer
English Setter
English Shepherd
English Springer Spaniel
English Toy Spaniel
Field Spaniel
Flat-coated Retriever
Fox Terrier (Smooth)

Fox Terrier (Wire)
Harrier
Jack Russell Terrier
Lakeland Terrier
Manchester Terrier
Mastiff
Miniature Bull Terrier
Norfolk Terrier
Norwich Terrier
Old English Sheepdog
Otter Hound
Rat Terrier
Staffordshire Bull Terrier
Sussex Spaniel
Toy Fox Terrier
Toy Manchester Terrier
Whippet
Yorkshire Terrier

Migratory Birds

SUMMER VISITORS

Arctic Tern
Common Crane
Cuckoo
Curlew Sandpiper
Fulmar
Gannet
Garden Warbler
Garganey
Golden Oriole
Grasshopper
  Warbler
Guillemot
Hobby
Honey Buzzard
Housemartin
Kittiwake
Lesser Whitethroat

Little Ringed Plover
Little Tern
Manx Shearwater
Marsh Harrier
Marsh Warbler
Montagu's Harrier
Nightingale
Nightjar
Pied Flycatcher
Puffin
Quail
Razorbill
Redstart
Reed Warbler
Ring Ouzel
Roseate Tern
Sand Martin

Sandwich Tern
Savi's Warbler
Sedge Warbler
Serin
Spotted Crake
Spotted Flycatcher
Stone Curlew
Swallow
Swift
Tree Pipit
Turtle Dove
Wheatear
Whinchat
Whitethroat
Willow Warbler
Wood Warbler
Yellow Wagtail

WINTER VISITORS

Barnacle Goose
Bar-tailed Godwit
Bean Goose
Bewick's Swan
Black-tailed Godwit
Brambling

Brent Goose
Fieldfare
Glaucous Gull
Goldeneye
Great Northern
  Diver

Green Sandpiper
Greenshank
Grey Plover
Jack Snipe
Knot
Lapland Bunting

Little Auk
Little Gull
Long-tailed Duck
Mealy Redpoll
Pink-footed Goose
Purple Sandpiper
Red-necked Grebe
Redwing

Sanderling
Scaup
Slavonian Grebe
Smew
Snow Bunting
Spotted Redshank
Turnstone
Velvet Scoter

Water Pipit
Waxwing
White-fronted
 Goose
Whooper Swan
Wigeon

2

NATIONAL CHARACTER

'The English, of any people in the universe, have the least of a national character; unless this very singularity may pass for such.'

David Hume, *Of National Character* (1742)

National Characteristics

'Solidity, caution, integrity, efficiency. Lack of imagination, hypocrisy. These qualities characterize the middle classes in every country, but in England they are national characteristics.'

E. M. Forster, *Notes on the English Character* (1920)

'Here are a couple of generalisations about England that would be accepted by almost all observers. One is that the English are not gifted artistically. They are not as musical as the Germans or Italians, painting and sculpture have never flourished in England as they have in France. Another is that, as Europeans go, the English are not intellectual. They have a horror of abstract thought, they feel no need for any philosophy or systematic "world view". Nor is this because they are "practical", as they are so fond of claiming for themselves. One has only to look at their methods of town-planning and water-supply, their obstinate clinging to everything that is out-of-date and a nuisance, a spelling system that defies analysis and a system of weights and measures that is intelligible only to compilers of arithmetic books, to see how little they care about mere efficiency.'

George Orwell, *England, Your England* (1941)

Internationally recognized characteristics of the English include:

THE CULT OF THE AMATEUR

> 'The English think incompetence is the same thing as
> sincerity.'

Quentin Crisp

In *The Character of England* (1947) the political scientist Sir Ernest
Barker wrote, 'It is perhaps a true economy of effort which has
inspired us to be the lovers of activity (for the amateur is by definition
a lover) rather than its servants.' Rather less kindly, it might be attributed to an attempt on the part of the upper classes to retain
precedence in activities in which they had been far outstripped by the
lower orders. Athletics is a case in point, with the times set by
nineteenth-century runners conveniently forgotten by the gentlemen
of the British Olympic Commission. Qualities of sportsmanship were
valued over monetary concerns by those who had no need to worry
about their income. The Cult of the Amateur arguably exacerbated
the decline of British industry in the post-war years and before them
it undoubtedly had a catastrophic effect on England's performance
on the battlefield against anyone who was equally well equipped.

FAIR PLAY

Fair play was part of the code of honour of the Knights of the Round
Table in Thomas Malory's *Le Morte d'Arthur*. Such chivalry filtered
through to the general population to an extent, but it has always been
the particular preserve of the nobility. When Henry V ordered the
French prisoners on the battlefield at Agincourt to be executed, his
knights demurred and the archers carried out the task. In the film

The Charge of the Light Brigade (1968), John Gielgud's Lord Raglan intones: 'I do not like to see an officer who knows too well what he is doing – it smacks of murder.' The results are well known, but as late as 1939, when Sir Kingsley Wood, the head of the Air Ministry, was instructed to fire-bomb German munitions stores in the Black Forest, he replied, 'Are you aware that it's private property? Why, you'll be asking me to bomb Essen next!'

English sportsmanship is counterbalanced by the phenomenon of the English 'rotter', 'cad' or 'bounder', personified by the actor Terry-Thomas. The classic rotter has lately been replaced by the more democratic 'love rat' in the tabloid press. But there was far more to rotters than merely cheating on their partners. The rotter was an anti-hero who bent the rules of English fair play and got away with it through his charm. He did it with style, a plummy accent and a thin moustache, and then he drove away in a vintage sports car.

ANTI-INTELLECTUALISM

> 'Always in England if you had the type of brain that was capable of understanding T. S. Eliot's poetry or Kant's logic, you could be sure of finding large numbers of people who would hate you violently.'
>
> D. J. Taylor, *Guardian*, 14 September 1989

England is the land of common sense. Terms like 'Clever Dick' and 'Egghead' have few equivalents in continental Europe, where intellectuals are respected celebrities. The attitude has inoculated the English against the various forms of political extremism that have destroyed other nations.

POLITENESS

> 'In no country inhabited by white men is it easier to
> shove people off the pavement.'

> George Orwell, *The Lion and the Unicorn* (1941)

The English are obsessed with the word 'sorry'. According to the novelist Will Self, 'It is even rumoured that some Englishmen say "sorry" at the point of orgasm...'

STOICISM

Examples range from Winston Churchill climbing on to his roof to watch the Blitz, to Lord Uxbridge's famous exchange with the Duke of Wellington at the Battle of Waterloo: 'By God, sir, I've lost my leg.' – 'By God, sir, so you have.' A useful trait in wartime has become a millstone today. The English public is willing to accept high taxation, poor public services and the erosion of their rights and liberties so long as, in the words of an Indian tourist, 'there is beer in the pubs and football on the television'.

RESERVE

> 'Smile at us, pay us, pass us; but do not quite forget.
> For we are the people of England, that never have
> spoken yet.'

> G. K. Chesterton, *The Secret People* (1915)

> 'My father and he had one of those English friendships
> which begin by avoiding intimacies and eventually
> eliminate speech altogether.'
> Jorge Luis Borges

Modesty does not need to be defended, but English politeness, which started life as a noble virtue, is often mistaken for diffidence, aloofness or even effeminacy. Americans privately remark that, to their ears, all Englishmen sound gay – even James Bond.

GOOD HUMOUR

English humour is as old as the V-sign lofted by archers in the Hundred Years War to show off the tools of their trade to opposing forces. The French did not find this funny and would cut off the first two fingers of captured bowmen's right hands.

English comedians are aided by the grammar of their language. Unlike most other modern European languages, the meaning of a sentence in English is conferred by word order rather than case endings, which means that punchlines can be hidden from the listener.

The modern English sense of humour flows naturally from other national characteristics acquired in the meantime. Stoicism becomes laughter in the face of adversity, while reserve leads to a fondness for double meanings.

ECCENTRICITY

> 'The English like eccentrics. They just don't like them living next door.'
>
> Julian Clary

Eccentrics have to be unusually talented if they are not to be regarded more plainly as twits. If they cannot be talented, then they must be rich. The famous eccentrics of the past tended to be upper-class and male, for if they were not, it would have been difficult for many of them to avoid being sent to an asylum. The English affection for eccentrics is part of the national sense of humour, but to a cynic it amounts to an elitist contempt for the ordinary, coupled with the hypocritical attitude that forgiveness can be bought.

––––

The Public Schools

––––

'I wish I had been born early enough to have been called a "Little Englander". It was a term of sneering abuse, but I should be delighted to accept it as a description of myself. That little sounds the right note of affection. It is little England I love. And I considered how much I disliked Big Englanders, whom I saw as red-faced, staring, loud-voiced fellows, wanting to go and boss everybody about all over the world, and being surprised and pained and saying, "Bad show!" if some blighters refused to fag for them.'

J. B. Priestley in English Journey (1934)

KEY STATISTICS

In England, 7 per cent of pupils attend independent schools. They produce 38 per cent of all candidates gaining three A grades or better at A-level.

Independent schools save the state £2 billion every year that would otherwise be spent on educating over 600,000 children in state schools.

Public schools receive around £90 million a year in fiscal benefits from their charitable status. They pay out around £300 million annually in scholarships and bursaries.

THE TEN MOST EXPENSIVE INDEPENDENT SCHOOLS

In order of fees per term for boarding pupils, and their alumni

Charterhouse, Surrey (1611): £7,985. William Makepeace Thackeray, Sir Anthony Caro, Peter Gabriel

Tonbridge School,* Kent (1553): £7,928. Frederick Forsyth, E. M. Forster, Aleister Crowley

Eton College,* Berkshire (1440): £7,896. Shelley, Aldous Huxley, John Maynard Keynes, George Orwell, nineteen prime ministers including the Duke of Wellington

Harrow School,* Middlesex (1572): £7,875. Sir Winston Churchill, Lord Byron, Anthony Trollope, nineteen recipients of the Victoria Cross

Bedales, Hampshire (1893): £7,845. Daniel Day-Lewis, Minnie Driver, Sophie Dahl

Winchester College,* Hampshire (1382): £7,833. Arnold Toynbee, Oswald Mosley, George Mallory, Freeman Dyson

The King's School, Canterbury, Kent (597): £7,760. W. Somerset Maugham, Carol Reed, David Gower

Marlborough College, Wiltshire (1843): £7,720. Sir John Betjeman, Nick Drake, Rab Butler

Wycombe Abbey,† Buckinghamshire (1896): £7,700. Penelope Fitzgerald, Rachel Stirling

Westminster, London (1560): £7,682. Ben Jonson, John Locke, Christopher Wren, Kim Philby, John Gielgud

* Denotes all-boys school.   † Denotes all-girls school.

Perspectives on English Drunkenness

'The English are noted among foreigners for their persistent drinking.'

John of Salisbury (c. 1115–1180)

'Everyone is drunk, but drunk joylessly, gloomily and heavily, and everyone is strangely silent. Only curses and bloody brawls occasionally break that suspicious and oppressively sad silence... Everyone is in a hurry to drink himself into insensibility... wives in no way lag behind their husbands and all get drunk together, while children crawl and run about among them.'

Fyodor Dostoevsky, *Winter Notes on Summer Impressions* (1863)

'Before the Roman came to Rye or out to Severn strode,
The rolling English drunkard made the rolling English
   road.'

G. K. Chesterton, *The Rolling English Road* (1922)

'England is nothing but the last ward of the European madhouse, and quite possibly it will prove to be the ward for particularly violent cases.'

Leon Trotsky, *Diary in Exile*, entry for 11 April 1935

'Terrified drinkers ducked for cover as a group of around sixty West Bromwich Albion fans attacked the Little Crown on Saturday afternoon. Innocent bystanders were caught in the mêlée as fighting raged out of control until the police stepped in with batons. The damage would cost £1,000 to fix, with numerous doors and windows smashed. Landlord Peter Coady was disgusted: "The smell was awful, people were heaving as they walked past. What kind of people would come prepared to fight with pigs' intestines?"'

Great Barr Observer, February 2003

According to the Office for National Statistics (ONS), two-fifths of English men and a quarter of women exceed the recommended amount of alcohol (defined as more than four units a day for men, and three units for women) on at least one day a week.

———

Sex and the English

———

VITAL STATISTICS

The average age for first sex is 16. (The global average is 17.)

The average number of partners is thirteen for men and seven for women, or ten overall. (The global average is nine.) Researchers claim that the gender disparity is due to respondents' dishonesty – even in anonymous surveys.

9 per cent of women and 14.6 per cent of men are engaged in re-lationships with more than one person at the same time.

51 per cent are happy with their sex lives (compared with 36 per cent in Italy and 38 per cent in France).

5 per cent report a 'monotonous' sex life (compared with 6 per cent in Italy and 8 per cent in France).

10.8 per cent of men and 12.6 per cent of women report ever having had a sexually transmitted infection. (The global average is 13 per cent.)

4 per cent of Londoners claim to have made love on an aeroplane and 15 per cent on public transport.

Bondage is most popular in the Midlands, where 40 per cent of men and women have experimented with handcuffs, blindfolds, restraints or whips. Midlanders are also the least likely to suffer from an STI (9 per cent).

People in the north-west engage in the most risky behaviour, with 56 per cent prepared to have unprotected sex without knowing a partner's sexual history. 57 per cent of the region's women are satisfied with their sex lives, compared to only 42 per cent of men.

Men and women in the north-east make the least faithful partners: 16 per cent confess to cheating.

20 per cent of people in London, Yorkshire and the north-east have filmed themselves or taken photos during sex.

Yorkshire natives are the most fulfilled – 57 per cent reporting satisfaction with their sex lives. They have more sex on average than anyone else in the country, and 40 per cent have had sex in their parents' bedroom.

Sources: National Survey of Sexual Attitudes and Lifestyles (Natsal 2000), Durex Report 2006, Durex Report 2005

Sex: Average Number of Times Per Year, By Region

Yorkshire   128
South-West   124
North-East   124
Midlands   123
London   119
South   117
East Anglia   116
North-West   115

(The average across the UK is 118 times a year)

Source: Durex Report 2006

Pornography Consumption

Residents of Birmingham undertake more internet searches for pornography than the inhabitants of any other city in the world. Manchester residents take second place worldwide. No other English city appears in the top ten.

The ten most porn-addicted places in the country, rated by frequency of internet searches, are:

1. West Bromwich
2. Solihull
3. Milton Keynes
4. Birmingham
5. Portsmouth
6. Thames Ditton
7. Reading
8. Ipswich

9. Sheffield
10. Basildon

Source: Google Trends 2006

THE 'ENGLISH VICE'

According to the French, *le vice anglais* is flagellation, although it can refer to homosexuality.

Homosexuality

In 1991, the *Observer* newspaper published an interview in which the French Prime Minister, Edith Cresson, claimed that a quarter of all Englishmen were gay. The 57-year-old explained, 'I remember from strolling about in London and French girls still make the same observation that the men in the streets don't look at you. In Paris, the men look at you. A workman, or indeed any man, looks at passing women. The Anglo-Saxons are not interested in women as women; for a woman arriving in an Anglo-Saxon country, it is astonishing.' Conservative MP Tony Marlow responded by attempting to pass a motion in the House of Commons titled, 'This House does not fancy elderly French women'.

Sado-masochism

England is nevertheless noted for sado-masochistic sexual practices, as can be gathered from the numerous advertisements placed in London telephone boxes. The demise of 'fagging' and corporal punishment in England's public schools has done nothing to end the 'English Vice'.

Notable Vice Pioneers

Theresa Berkley (c. 1780–1836)

Brothel-keeper to the aristocracy from her premises in Hallam Street, London, she invented an automatic wheel for flogging clients and the 'Berkley Horse' – a padded rack to which a client would be strapped and then whipped.

Henry Spencer Ashbee (1834–1900)

Compiled the *Index Librorum Prohibitorum* of 1877, a catalogue of London brothels offering sado-masochistic services. He is also suspected to be the author of *My Secret Life*, an anonymous diary in eleven volumes detailing sex with 1,200 prostitutes over a forty-year whoring career.

George Mountbatten, Second Marquess of Milford Haven (1892–1938)

Prince Philip's uncle and surrogate father amassed one of Europe's largest collection of sado-masochistic pornography. He bequeathed it, along with a smaller but still impressive collection of sex toys, to the British Museum.

Two Views of English Conversation

'Lady C— took me into the rose garden, and, having qualified her remarks with: "Look here. You're a very good boy, and I like you very much", forbade me peremptorily to talk to Beatrice about "things". It bewildered me a little at the time because, I suppose, not being to the English manner born, I did not know just what "things" were. And it harassed me a little for the future, because I did not know at the time, so it appeared to me, what else to talk about but "things". Nowadays I know very well what "things" are; they include, in fact, religious topics, questions of the relations of the sexes; the conditions of poverty-stricken districts – every subject from which one can digress into anything moving. That, in fact, is the crux, the Rubicon that one must never cross. And that is what makes English conversation so profoundly, so portentously, troublesome to maintain. It is a question of a very fine game, the rules of which you must observe. It is as if one were set on making oneself interesting with the left hand tied behind one's back.'

Ford Madox Ford, in *The Spirit of the People* (1907)

'In France it is rude to let a conversation drop; in England it is rash to keep it up. No one there will blame you for silence. When you have not opened your mouth for three years, they will think: "This Frenchman is a nice quiet fellow." Be modest. An Englishman will say, "I have a little house in the country"; when he invites you to stay with him you will discover that the little house is a place with three hundred bedrooms. If you are a world tennis-champion, say, "Yes, I don't play too badly." If you have crossed the Atlantic alone in a small boat, say, "I do a little sailing."'

André Maurois, in *Three Letters on the English* (1938)

3

NATIONAL HEROES

Sir Francis Drake (1540–96)

PIRACY AND EXPLORATION

Drake was the son of a Devon yeoman and joined the family pirate fleet of Jack Hawkins when he was 18. The interference of the Spanish authorities in his business dealings gave him a lifelong hatred of Spain and a thirst for retribution against the country's king.

His first captaincy was command of a slave trading ship, but he made his fortune by ambushing Spanish silver trains in 1572, helped by a band of escaped slaves who sought revenge on Spain. Elizabeth I gave him a privateering commission in 1572, giving him licence to plunder Spanish shipping.

In 1577, Drake set out with five ships to explore the Pacific coast of the Americas and raid any Spanish interests he came across. After sacking several cities in the West Indies, it is thought that he landed near what is now San Francisco in 1579 and claimed the lands of Nova Albion (New England) for Elizabeth I. The exact location was hidden and the records in England later burned to frustrate Spanish spies. On Drake's return in 1580, after he had circumnavigated the globe, the queen knighted him aboard his ship, *The Golden Hind*. He was the first man to survive a circumnavigation, Magellan having died. The queen's share of the booty was £300,000 – more than the crown's annual income.

John Cooke, Drake's companion on his circumnavigation of the globe, described him as a 'tyranous and cruell tirant', guilty of 'murder... venome... conceyved hatred' and 'moaste tyranicall blud spilling'.

DRAKE'S WAR

The mission that 'singed the King of Spain's beard' was the raid on Cadiz in 1587. Drake destroyed twenty-six enemy ships and thousands of tons of stores set aside for the invasion of England. He occupied one of Spain's main ports for three days and delayed the attempted invasion by a year.

Drake was Vice Admiral of the fleet that defeated the Spanish Armada in 1588, famously joining his ship after finishing his game of bowls. While Philip II lamented that 'God is an Englishman' upon hearing of the Armada's destruction, it was widely believed in Spain that Satan helped Drake win his battles. The devil is also supposed to have helped Drake build a barn at one point, as well as create a stream by diverting water from a Dartmoor river along the course to Plymouth followed by his horse, but apparently he could not save him from yellow fever. Drake died at Puerto Bello in Panama and was buried at sea in 1596.

THE LEGEND OF DRAKE'S DRUM

A drum he took on his circumnavigation and on his final voyage when he died of a fever now hangs on the wall of Buckland Abbey at Yelverton, near Plymouth. According to legend, the instrument begins to beat all by itself at times when England is in danger. In 1940, several seamen on the boats that evacuated the troops from Dunkirk and officers stationed on the Hampshire coast claimed to have heard 'a very incessant beat, pause, two sharp beats in succession, one sharp beat'.

The Duke of Marlborough (1650–1722)

MARLBOROUGH'S EARLY BATTLES

John Churchill was the son of a Member of Parliament, Sir Winston Churchill. He first learned military strategy and field tactics from books in the library at St Paul's School in London and went on to become Europe's pre-eminent military commander prior to the rise of Napoleon.

In 1672 he was sent to help the French king Louis XIV in his war against the Dutch. Louis appointed him colonel of the English regiment, but despite his exploits he was able to forge a friendship with the Dutch prince William of Orange, who later came to the English throne as William III. In 1691 he was imprisoned in the Tower of London for several months under suspicion of treason. His crime was to object to the patronage William bestowed on so many Dutchmen in preference to English candidates.

Marlborough returned to favour in 1701, when he was needed to oppose the ambitions of his old comrade Louis XIV, who sought to swallow Spain and the remains of her empire. The newly created Duke was as slippery on the battlefield as he was in politics. He became famous for his feints and surprise attacks, and often gave his allies the same misinformation he gave his foes.

AFTER BLENHEIM

At the Battle of Blenheim in 1704 Marlborough saved Germany and Austria from French rule by inflicting around 40,000 casualties on Louis's force at a cost of 12,000 of his own men. At Ramillies, in 1706, the ratio of casualties was even greater, at more than 5:1. It was there that he was being helped on to his horse when a cannonball flew between his legs and blew off his equerry's head.

In 1710, Marlborough had advanced into France, capturing Lille and Bouchain, and was on the verge of invading Picardy when he fell from power. Back in England, his wife Sarah quarrelled with her close friend Queen Anne, and was banished from the court. The Duke subsequently admitted to embezzling £150,000 from the aid sent to Austria, and accepting bribes to the total of £60,000 from the army's suppliers.

In 1705 he was granted the Royal Manor of Woodstock in Oxfordshire with 16,000 acres (6,475 hectares) of land, on which he built Blenheim Palace. He died from a stroke before it was finished.

The town of Churchill in Manitoba, Canada, gets its name from the Duke's stint as a governor of the Hudson Bay Company.

The Duke of Wellington (1769–1852)

EARLY LIFE

Arthur Wellesley was born in Dublin to the Earl and Countess of Mornington. After his father died, his mother wanted a military career for her son, but his first ambition was to study music.

He went to school at Eton but received his military education in France at the Royal Academy of Equitation in Angers.

FIRST ENGAGEMENTS

Wellesley became Tory MP for Newport on the Isle of Wight in 1806, a role he combined with his duties as a field commander. He was made a duke in 1814.

Napoleon mocked him as a 'Sepoy General' after his exploits in the Indian subcontinent, yet in 1803 Wellesley, outnumbered and outgunned in artillery, led just 10,000 men to victory over the 40,000-strong army of the Marathas.

After routing the French at the Battle of Vitoria in 1813 during the Peninsular War, Wellesley's troops became so drunk on wine looted from the captured baggage that they were unable to pursue the enemy across the Pyrenees. He was moved to describe his men as 'the scum of the earth'. Wellington himself would drink half a dozen glasses of wine during dinner and a pint of claret afterwards, but without ill effects.

THE BATTLE OF WATERLOO, 1815

He described Waterloo as 'the nearest run thing you ever saw in your life'. The outcome was settled by the arrival in the early evening of 40,000 Prussian troops in support of Wellington's force. Austrians, Dutch and Russians were also involved.

When the day was over, Marshal Blücher suggested that the engagement be called 'The Battle of La Belle Alliance', referring to the inn where the two Allied commanders met and where Napoleon had had his command post, but Wellington preferred 'Waterloo', the site of his own headquarters.

After his victory at Waterloo in 1815, he was awarded an estate in Hampshire and a fortune of £500,000. King William of Holland also gave him 2,600 acres (1052 hectares) of land and the title 'Prince of Waterloo', which today comes with an annuity of £150,000. In 2001, a Belgian senator launched a legal campaign against the arrangement, estimating that the duke's heirs have received around £33 million since 1815.

The story that the Duke of Wellington claimed that the Battle of Waterloo was 'won on the playing fields of Eton' is a myth. The duke felt little affection for the school, which in any case had no playing fields or team sports in his day. The first recorded use of the phrase was three years after his death.

Wellington boots were named after the duke, but during his lifetime there were also coats, hats, pairs of trousers, apples and pine trees named in his honour, along with the famous recipe for cooking beef.

THE POLITICIAN

Wellington became Prime Minister in 1828. After his first Cabinet meeting, he remarked, 'It was an extraordinary affair. I gave them their orders and they wanted to stay and discuss them.' He spent much of his time in office suppressing democratic reforms and favoured elitism over greater enfranchisement. This made him so unpopular that a mob attacked his London home. Contrary to popular belief, he acquired his nickname 'The Iron Duke' from the metal shutters he subsequently had fitted to protect his windows.

The one exception to Wellington's conservatism was his granting of civil rights to Catholics in 1829, which prompted Lord Winchelsea to accuse him of treachery. The two fought a duel, but deliberately missed each other. In the end, Wellington was able to push through the Catholic Emancipation bill only by threatening to resign.

Harriette Wilson, London's greatest courtesan, tried to blackmail Wellington with the threat of publishing her memoirs and his letters unless he gave her £200 or a pension. He famously replied, 'Publish and be damned!' Harriette retaliated by describing him in her book as a bore with the looks of a 'rat-catcher'.

The duke once passed a small boy crying in the street because no one would take care of his pet toad while he was away at boarding school. Wellington decided there and then to adopt the creature.

In his seventies, Wellington armed himself with a brace of pistols and patrolled the streets on horseback, looking for Spring-Heeled Jack, a serial attacker who preyed on women and slashed his victims with metal claws.

On 18 November 1852, over a million people lined the route of Wellington's funeral procession from Horse Guards to St Paul's Cathedral, where he is buried.

Admiral Lord Nelson (1758–1805)

ILL HEALTH

Horatio Nelson was born in Burnham Thorpe in Norfolk. He was such a sickly child that when his uncle, Maurice Suckling, was asked to take the 12-year-old boy into the Royal Navy, he answered, 'What has poor Horace done, who is so weak, that he should be sent to rough it out at sea?' Even as a famous commander, Nelson would suffer seasickness throughout his life. He was also a victim of dysentery, yellow fever, depression, scurvy and malaria. By the time he fought Trafalgar he had lost most of his teeth, his right arm below the elbow and the sight in one eye.

FRANCOPHOBIA

Nelson once advised a new midshipman: 'There are three things, young gentleman, which you are constantly to bear in mind. First, you must always implicitly obey orders, without attempting to form any opinion of your own respecting their propriety. Secondly, you must consider every man your enemy who speaks ill of your king; and, thirdly, you must hate a Frenchman as you do the devil.' The third instruction was clearly more important than the first, for when the Channel fleet mutinied over pay and conditions at Spithead in 1797, he called it 'the most manly thing I ever heard of, and does the British sailor infinite honour'.

Nelson thought the French despots and hypocrites for boasting of 'rights' and 'liberty' while committing mass murder. In 1799 he wrote: 'Down, down with the damned French villains. Excuse my warmth, but my blood boils at the name of a Frenchman. I hate them all – Royalists and Republicans.' He once took a holiday in France because, he said, 'I want to be proficient in the language, which is my only reason for returning there. I hate their country and their manners.'

Character Flaws

Nelson's insecurity led to a fixation with etiquette. Any failure to fire the correct number of guns to acknowledge His Britannic Majesty's flag was taken as an insult to the nation. In 1784, Nelson even fired upon the British fort at Barbados for neglecting to salute a schooner leaving port under the flag of France.

He humiliated his wife Fanny by conducting public tours with his married lover Emma Hamilton, with whom he had a daughter, Horatia. Nelson asked the government to make provision for Emma in the event of his death, but she received nothing and died shortly after a stay in a debtors' prison.

Nelson's Four Greatest Victories

Commemorated in bas-reliefs at the base of Nelson's Column in Trafalgar Square, London:

Cape St Vincent, 1797

Fought aboard HMS *Captain* against the Spanish off the southern coast of Portugal.

Nelson and his boarding party captured the *San Nicolas*, and from there boarded and took the *San Josef* that had drawn up alongside her. It was the first case of 'double boarding' in naval history.

The Nile, 1798

Aboard HMS *Vanguard* against the French in the Bay of Aboukir on Egypt's Mediterranean coast.

During the battle, the French captain Dupetit-Thouars had first one arm blown off, then another, then a leg and continued to bark orders from the deck while propped up in a grain barrel.

Copenhagen, 1801

Aboard HMS *Elephant* against the Danes.

It was here that he famously disobeyed an order to retreat, though he never said, 'Ships? I see no ships.' Instead, he remarked, 'I have only one eye. I have a right to be blind sometimes.' Raising his telescope to his blind eye, he added, 'I really do not see the signal.' He pressed on and broke the enemy's defensive line.

Fourth and finally...

Trafalgar 1805

Aboard HMS *Victory* against the French and Spanish at the mouth of the Mediterranean.

On the eve of Trafalgar, Napoleon declared, 'A nation is very foolish when it has no fortifications and no army to lay itself open to seeing an army of 100,000 veteran troops land on its shores... It is necessary for us to be masters of the sea for six hours only, and England will have ceased to exist.'

Twenty-seven British warships were opposed by thirty-three French and Spanish with 2,640 guns to Nelson's 2,150. Yet at the end of hostilities not a single British ship had surrendered, compared with seventeen enemy vessels captured.

Late in the battle, the French Rear Admiral Dumanoir – after failing to respond to his commander's orders to join the fighting – ordered his division to fire upon captured French and Spanish ships. This prompted one outraged Spanish crew, of the *Argonauta*, to offer to change sides. The Spanish officers were given their arms back and their sailors manned the lower gun deck while their English captors manned the upper. The people of Cadiz contrasted the treachery of their French allies with the kind treatment the British accorded to wounded Spanish sailors.

NELSON'S DEATH

Nelson was fatally wounded late in the battle, shot through the back. His body was preserved in a cask of brandy for the voyage home – some of which was said to have been drunk by sailors on the way. He was interred below the central dome of St Paul's Cathedral in a coffin made from the planks of the French flagship *L'Orient*, destroyed at the Battle of the Nile in 1798.

Captain Hardy won a reward of over £3,000 and a baronetcy for his part in the victory at Trafalgar, while Nelson's brother William was created an earl and granted £90,000 to buy an estate. The ordinary seaman who survived the battle received £5 for his efforts.

Before the statue of Nelson was placed on its Corinthian column in Trafalgar Square, fourteen of the stonemasons who had worked on the column held a dinner party at the top.

William Wilberforce (1759–1833)

England began trading in slaves under Elizabeth I, but the nation ended the practice in 1807 thanks to the son of a rich merchant from Hull. Wilberforce was sent to study at St John's College, Cambridge, of which he wrote, 'I was introduced on the very first night of my arrival to as licentious a set of men as can well be conceived. They drank hard, and their conversation was even worse than their lives.' He found them much to his liking and he spent his university years in the pursuit of pleasure. A few years afterwards, he regretted his indolence and became an evangelical Christian.

Wilberforce became an MP for Hull at the age of 21 in 1780. From 1788 he spent eighteen years annually introducing abolitionist bills to Parliament.

In 1792, he was horrified to be made an honorary citizen of the revolutionary French Republic, fearing that this would damage the image of the abolitionist cause.

In 1805, Wilberforce's friend Lord Melville faced impeachment as First Lord of the Admiralty for condoning the misappropriation of funds. Although many MPs urged support for Melville due to his important role in the war with France, Wilberforce voted against him because, he said, 'We are now on trial before the moral sense of England.' The impeachment was successful by one vote. Fortunately, Melville's successor Lord Barham proved even more effective for the war effort.

Wilberforce's 1807 bill abolished slave trading in the British West Indies, but the trade was not abolished throughout the British Empire until 1833, a month after Wilberforce's death. The bans were enforced by the Royal Navy. Wilberforce was buried in Westminster Abbey.

Florence Nightingale 1820–1910

Nightingale was named after her birthplace, Florence in Italy, and grew up in Derbyshire, Hampshire and London, where her father taught her Greek, Latin, French, German and Italian. She also studied philosophy and mathematics.

Throughout her life, Florence would periodically fall into trances. During one instance when she was 16, she heard the voice of God, who told her that she had a mission to accomplish. However, He omitted to tell her what it was. She waited many years for the Almighty to contact her again, in the meantime falling in love but refusing to marry lest she be called upon. Florence suspected that her task was to care for the sick, but her parents forbade her to study as a nurse since this was a job for poor, disabled war veterans.

In 1850 her family believed she was ill and sent her to Egypt to recover. However, God 'followed' her and explained what she was to do in a half-hour conversation shortly before her thirtieth birthday. She wrote in her diary, 'Now no more childish things. No more love. No more marriage. Now Lord let me think only of Thy Will, what Thou willest me to do.' The issue of caring for the sick was settled and Florence enrolled with the Lutheran deaconesses at a hospital in Germany, but she found that God was not as exacting as she expected, asking that she devote five minutes of every hour to thinking of Him. A devoted wife, she remarked, 'does not give five minutes every hour to the thought of her husband. She thinks of him every minute, spontaneously.'

Back in England, she invented a valve-driven system of bells so that invalid patients could summon a nurse, who would know exactly which bed she was being called to.

When the Crimean War broke out in 1854, Florence volunteered for service and was put in charge of nursing care at military hospitals in Turkey. She soon transformed the foul and unsanitary conditions she had discovered on her arrival at Scutari, where patients' clothes and bedding were never washed and the wards were infested with rats and fleas. More soldiers were dying from infections contracted at the hospital than from wounds sustained on the battlefield.

When the officers obstructed her reforms, she went over their heads and appealed directly to Queen Victoria. By this means she established an official system for soldiers to send money home to their families. She also encountered problems with her fellow nurses and had to dismiss several. The problem was not the ten Roman Catholics or the fourteen Anglicans, she said, but the fourteen who 'worshipped Bacchus'.

She would allow no woman to enter the wards after 8 p.m., when she began her nightly patrol with an oil lamp. The wounded soldiers gave her the nickname 'The Lady with the Lamp'.

Her work made her a national hero, but she evaded a public reception on her return and proceeded to campaign for better conditions in army hospitals. She conducted her arguments through a statistical analysis of casualty lists that proved the importance of good sanitation. Her chief ally throughout was the enlightened secretary of state for war, Sidney Herbert. When he died in 1861, she asked God to raise him from the dead and was shocked to have her request declined.

In 1907 she became the first woman ever to receive the Order of Merit. She refused the offer of a burial in Westminster Abbey and ordered that her tombstone be inscribed simply 'F. N. 1820–1910'.

Emmeline Pankhurst (1858–1928)

THE SUFFRAGETTE

'Mrs Pankhurst', as she was popularly known, was the daughter of a radical Manchester industrialist and developed a taste for abolitionist literature as a child.

In 1903, she and her daughters founded the Women's Social and Political Union, which she described as 'a suffrage army in the field', and set about leading the militant wing of the emancipation movement. Violent protests began two years later when Christabel Pankhurst and Annie Kenney were removed from a public meeting for heckling Sir Edward Grey, and responded by kicking and spitting at a policeman. Civil disobedience soon escalated into acts of arson and window smashing, culminating in a riot in 1910 when over a hundred suffragettes, including Mrs Pankhurst, tried to force their way into Parliament.

Pankhurst believed that the participation of women in politics and the victory of 'female' values would bring about a worldwide moral renewal. She explained, 'The militancy of men, through all the centuries, has drenched the world with blood. The militancy of women has harmed no human life save the lives of those who fought the battle of righteousness.'

The novelist Rebecca West said of Pankhurst's oratory, 'Trembling like a reed, she lifted up her hoarse, sweet voice on the platform, but the reed was of steel and it was tremendous.'

In 1912, at the age of 54, she was sent to prison twelve times under the 'Cat and Mouse Act', which allowed for the release of hunger strikers for long enough for them to recover before they were re-interned.

The Patriot

Pankhurst suspended her work during the Great War and initiated a campaign for factory owners to permit women to do 'men's work' in order to help the war effort. The government rewarded her patriotism by releasing all suffragettes from prison and awarding her organization a grant of £2,000.

Towards the end of the war in 1918, women over 30 were given the right to vote, while women over 21 could stand for Parliament.

Winston Churchill (1874–1965)

'There is a forgotten, nay almost forbidden word,
which means more to me than any other. That word
is ENGLAND.'

Sir Winston Churchill

'After meeting Hitler, people felt that he, the Führer,
could achieve anything. But when people met
Churchill, they felt that they themselves could achieve
anything. Genuine inspiration beats artificially created
charisma.'

Andrew Roberts, *Hitler and Churchill:*
Secrets of Leadership (2003)

Early Life

Churchill's mother was American, and her family claimed that his great-great grandmother was a Native American Indian. He was also a direct descendant of John Churchill, First Duke of Marlborough.

Churchill was a poor student at Harrow, where he suffered from a lisp and claimed to have finished bottom of the school. This was an exaggeration – he did well in those subjects he enjoyed. However, he left early to attend Sandhurst, where he passed the entrance exam at the third attempt.

In 1894, the Empire Theatre in Leicester Square was closed temporarily by the Licensing Board for running risqué skits and allowing prostitutes to operate at the back of the dress circle. On its reopening night, an exuberant crowd stormed the stage in celebration. A young Winston Churchill boasted to his brother: 'It was I who led the rioters and made a speech to the crowd. My cry was, "Ladies of the Empire! I stand for liberty!"'

Churchill became a war correspondent in India, Africa and Cuba, where he took up cigar smoking. He first won fame by helping to rescue an armoured train during the Boer War, where he was captured and escaped in 1899.

POLITICAL CAREER

Churchill became Tory MP for Oldham in 1900, but switched to the Liberals between 1904 and 1924 because of their advocacy of free trade.

In January 1911, Churchill was serving as Home Secretary when he took personal charge of the Siege of Sydney Street, the police operation to catch a gang of anarchists wanted for several murders. He called in the Scots Guards for extra firepower, and when the building in which the suspects were hiding caught fire, he refused the fire brigade access. The anarchists were faced with a choice between surrender and burning to death, and opted for the latter.

Churchill became First Lord of the Admiralty in 1911, but he lost his post in 1915 after his idea to knock Turkey out of the war in the

Dardanelles campaign ended in disaster. In penance, he volunteered for active service and commanded a battalion of the Royal Scots Fusiliers on the Western Front.

He once proposed marriage to the Hollywood actress Ethel Barrymore, but she turned him down.

Churchill created the nation of Iraq out of the remains of the defeated Turkish Empire when he was Colonial Secretary in 1921–2.

In 1925, he was Chancellor of the Exchequer, and his decision to return the country to the Gold Standard led to deflation, higher unemployment and subsequently the General Strike of 1926.

Neville Chamberlain's first choice to succeed him as Prime Minister in 1940 was Lord Halifax, but the latter stood aside to allow Churchill to become the nation's saviour.

Churchill's KGB codename was 'Boar'.

LITERARY SUCCESS

Churchill received the Nobel Prize for Literature in 1953. *Savrola*, his only published novel, was a Ruritanian romance judged to be devoid of literary merit. However, the prize committee decided to make the award 'for his mastery of historical and biographical description as well as for brilliant oratory in defending exalted human values'. Churchill said he modelled his speaking style on that of Bourke Cockran, an American Congressman whom he met in 1895. In 1940 he also helped write the script for *That Hamilton Woman* in which Laurence Olivier and Vivien Leigh portrayed Admiral Nelson and his mistress Emma Hamilton for an American audience.

He appears as a fictional character in several books, including Rupert Catskill in *Men Like Gods* (1923) by H. G. Wells; Tom Hogarth in *Lord Raingo* (1932) by Arnold Bennett; Algernon Woodstock in *Eleven Were Brave* (1941) by Francis Beeding; Walter Chancel in *Storm in* the West (1963) by Sinclair Lewis; and spymaster 'Winnie the Pooh' in *The Paladin* (1980) by Brian Garfield.

When Churchill's grandson Nicholas Soames was 6 years old, he inveigled himself into the old man's study and asked, 'Grandpapa, is it true that you are the greatest man in the world?' Churchill answered, 'Yes, and now bugger off.'

ESSENTIAL QUOTATIONS

'A modest man with much to be modest about.'
(On Clement Attlee)

'In defeat indomitable; in victory unbearable.'
(On Bernard Montgomery)

'If Hitler invaded Hell, I would at least make a favourable reference to the Devil in the House of Commons.'
(Following the invasion of the Soviet Union in June 1941)

'Writing a book is an adventure. To begin with it is a toy, an amusement; then it becomes a mistress, and then a master.'

'I would make all boys learn English... But the only thing I would whip them for is not knowing English.'

'Each one hopes that if he feeds the crocodile enough, that the crocodile will eat him last.'
(On nations following the policy of appeasement)

'I like pigs. Dogs look up to you; cats look down on you; pigs treat you as equals.'

'History will judge me kindly, for I intend to write it myself.'

English Nobel Prize Winners

PHYSICS

1904: Lord Rayleigh (John William Strutt) – for the discovery of Argon

1906: John Joseph Thompson – for investigating the conduction of electricity in gases

1915: Sir William Henry Bragg and William Lawrence Bragg – for X-ray analysis of crystal structure. (Lawrence Bragg was 25 years old and remains the youngest ever recipient of a Nobel Prize.)

1917: Charles Glover Barkla – for the discovery of the characteristic Röntgen radiation of the elements

1928: Owen Willans Richardson – for work on the thermionic phenomenon and discovery of Richardson's Law

1935: James Chadwick – for the discovery of the neutron

1937: George Paget Thomson (shared with Clinton Joseph Davisson of the USA) – for the discovery of the diffraction of electrons by crystals

1947: Sir Edward Victor Appleton – for the discovery of the Appleton layer in the upper atmosphere

1948: Patrick M. S. Blackett – for the development of the Wilson cloud chamber method

1950: Cecil Powell – for the development of the photographic method of studying nuclear processes

1951: Sir John Douglas Cockcroft (shared with Ernest Walton of Ireland) – for work on the transmutation of atomic nuclei by artificially accelerated atomic particles

1974: Sir Martin Ryle and Antony Hewish – for research in radio astrophysics

1977: Sir Nevill Francis Mott (shared with Philip Warren Anderson and John Hasbrouck van Vleck of the USA) – for investigations of the electronic structure of magnetic and disordered systems

2003: Anthony J. Leggett (shared with Alexei A. Abrikosov and Vitaly L. Ginzburg of the USA and Russia) – for contributions to the theory of superconductors and superfluids

CHEMISTRY

1921: Frederick Soddy – for investigations into the origin and nature of isotopes and the chemistry of radioactive substances

1922: Francis Aston – for the discovery, by means of his mass spectrograph, of isotopes in various non-radioactive elements

1929: Arthur Harden (shared with Hans von Euler-Chelpin) – for investigations on the fermentation of sugar and fermentative enzymes

1937: Walter Haworth (shared with Paul Karrer of Switzerland) – for investigations on carbohydrates and vitamin C

1947: Sir Robert Robinson – for investigations on plant products of biological importance, especially the alkaloids

1952: Archer Martin and Richard Synge – for the invention of partition chromatography

1956: Sir Cyril Hinshelwood (shared with Nikolay Semenov of the USSR) – for researches into the mechanism of chemical reactions

1958: Frederick Sanger – for work on the structure of proteins, especially that of insulin

1962: John Kendrew (shared with Max Perutz of Austria) – for studies of the structures of globular proteins

1964: Dorothy Hodgkin – for determinations by X-ray techniques of the structures of biochemical substances

1967: Ronald Norrish and George Porter (shared with Manfred Eigen of the Federal Republic of Germany) – for studies of extremely fast chemical reactions

1969: Derek Barton (shared with Odd Hassel of Norway) – for contributions to the development of the concept of conformation

1973: Geoffrey Wilkinson (shared with Ernst Fischer of the Federal Republic of Germany) – for work, performed independently, on the chemistry of the organometallic, so-called sandwich compounds

1978: Peter Mitchell – for his contribution to the understanding of biological energy transfer through the formulation of the chemiosmotic theory

1980: Frederick Sanger (shared with Paul Berg and Walter Gilbert of the USA) – for contributions concerning the determination of base sequences in nucleic acids

1993: Michael Smith (shared with Kary Mullis of the USA) – for contributions to the establishment of oligonucleotide-based, site-directed mutagenesis and its development for protein studies

1996: Sir Harold Kroto (shared with Robert Curl and Richard Smalley of the USA) – for the discovery of fullerenes

1997: John Walker (shared with Paul Boyer of the USA and Jens Skou of Denmark) – for the elucidation of the enzymatic mechanism underlying the synthesis of adenosine triphosphate (ATP)

1998: John Pople (shared with Walter Kohn of the USA) – for the development of computational methods in quantum chemistry

PHYSIOLOGY OR MEDICINE

1922: Archibald Hill (shared with Otto Meyerhof of Germany) – for the discovery relating to the production of heat in the muscle

1929: Sir Frederick Hopkins (shared with Christiaan Eijkman of the Netherlands) – for the discovery of the growth-stimulating vitamins

1932: Sir Charles Sherrington and Edgar Adrian – for discoveries regarding the functions of neurons

1936: Sir Henry Hallett Dale (shared with Otto Loewi of Austria) – for discoveries relating to chemical transmission of nerve impulses

1960: Peter Medawar (shared with Sir Frank Burnet of Australia) – for the discovery of acquired immunological tolerance

1962: Francis Crick (shared with James Watson of the USA and Maurice Wilkins of New Zealand) – for discoveries concerning the molecular structure of nucleic acids and its significance for information transfer in living material

1963: Alan Hodgkin and Andrew Huxley (shared with Sir John Eccles of Australia) – for discoveries concerning the ionic mechanisms involved in excitation and inhibition in the peripheral and central portions of the nerve cell membrane

1972: Rodney Porter (shared with Gerald Edelman of the USA) – for discoveries concerning the chemical structure of antibodies

1982: John Vane (shared with Sune K. Bergström and Bengt I. Samuelsson of Sweden) – for discoveries concerning prostaglandins and related biologically active substances

1993: Richard Roberts (shared with Phillip Sharp of the USA) – for the discovery of split genes

2001: Timothy Hunt and Sir Paul Nurse (shared with Leland Hartwell of the USA) – for the discovery of key regulators of the cell cycle

2002: John Sulston (shared with Robert Horvitz of the USA and Sydney Brenner of South Africa) – for discoveries concerning 'genetic regulation of organ development and programmed cell death'

2003: Sir Peter Mansfield (shared with Paul Lauterbur of the USA) – for discoveries concerning magnetic resonance imaging

LITERATURE

1907: Rudyard Kipling

1932: John Galsworthy

1950: Bertrand Russell

1953: Winston Churchill

1983: William Golding

2005: Harold Pinter

PEACE

1925: Sir Austen Chamberlain – for the Locarno Pact between Germany, France, Belgium, Britain and Italy

1933: Sir Norman Angell – for work with the League of Nations

1937: Viscount Robert Cecil – for the International Peace Campaign

1959: Philip J. Noel-Baker – for lifelong work towards international cooperation

1977: Amnesty International – founded by Peter Benenson in 1961

ECONOMICS

1984: Richard Stone – for the development of systems of national accounts

1991: Ronald Coase – for discovering the significance of transaction costs and property rights for the functioning of the economy

----

Twelve Explorers and their Discoveries

JOHN CABOT (c. 1450–c. 1499)

Explored Newfoundland, Novia Scotia and Labrador in 1497. Cabot was actually an Italian named Giovanni Caboto, who emigrated to England during the reign of Henry VII and claimed the waters around the new lands for his adopted nation.

SIR MARTIN FROBISHER (c. 1535–94)

Discovered Resolution Island in Canada and brought back 'gold ore' from Baffin Island that turned out to be fool's gold.

SIR HUMPHREY GILBERT (c. 1539–83)

Obtained from Queen Elizabeth a charter to explore 'remote heathen and barbarous lands' and founded the first English colony in North America at St John's, Newfoundland. However, the colonists mutinied and returned to England.

SIR FRANCIS DRAKE (1540–96)

First captain to survive circumnavigation of the globe. Discovered California, and that Tierra del Fuego was an island rather than part of a continent.

SIR WALTER RALEGH (1554–1618)

Explored what is now North Carolina and searched for El Dorado, the City of Gold, in Venezuela. He failed to find it, but he introduced the potato and tobacco to Europe from the Americas.

HENRY HUDSON (c. 1556–1611)

Discovered Hudson Bay in Canada in 1610 while searching unsuccessfully for the North-west Passage.

JAMES COOK (1728–79)

Sailed around the world twice and discovered Hawaii (which he named the 'Sandwich Islands') and Australia.

John Speke (1827–64)

In 1858, he discovered Lake Victoria and, with Sir Richard Burton (1821–90), Lake Tanganyika. His claim that Lake Victoria was the source of the Nile was accepted for many years.

Sir Henry Stanley (1841–1904)

Traced the Congo River from its source.

Robert Scott (1868–1912)

The first person to explore Antarctica by land in 1901–1904. In 1911 he set out for the South Pole, but was beaten to it by the Norwegian Roald Amundsen. Scott and his party died on their return journey.

Neil McGrigor (b. 1961)

Co-led the expedition that found the true source of the Nile in Rwanda's Nyungwe Forest in March 2006. He journeyed 4,163 miles (6,700km) in eighty days on his second attempt, the first being abandoned when his team mate Steve Willis was murdered by rebels.

4
KINGS AND QUEENS

A Brief Guide to Queen Elizabeth II

She made her first radio broadcast in 1940 at the age of 14, speaking to evacuated children during the Blitz.

She is the only female member of the royal family to have served in the armed forces rather than merely receive honorary rank. Before the end of the Second World War in 1945, No. 230873 Second Subaltern Elizabeth Windsor joined the Auxiliary Territorial Service as a driver.

On VE Day in London, she disguised herself and slipped into the celebrating crowds.

She speaks fluent French, but not German.

Both the Queen and her husband Prince Philip are great-great-grandchildren of Queen Victoria. They are third cousins.

She heard of her succession while staying in the Treetops Hotel in Kenya – a genuine tree house – leading her biographer William Shawcross to write that Elizabeth was 'the only woman known to have gone up a tree a Princess and come down a Queen'.

She does not have a passport.

She is the fifteenth richest woman and the 180th richest individual in Britain, with a personal fortune of £270 million according to the *Sunday Times* Rich List 2005.

Her full official title is: 'Elizabeth the Second, by the Grace of God, of the United Kingdom of Great Britain and Northern Ireland and of Her other Realms and Territories Queen, Head of the Commonwealth, Defender of the Faith'.

The Queen is the Head of State for sixteen independent territories: Antigua and Barbuda, Australia, the Bahamas, Barbados, Belize,

Canada, Grenada, Jamaica, New Zealand, Papua New Guinea, the Solomon Islands, St Kitts-Nevis, St Lucia, St Vincent and the Grenadines, Tuvalu and the United Kingdom.

Her lost titles are: Queen of Ghana (1960), Tanganyika (1962), Nigeria (1963), Uganda (1963), Kenya (1964), Malawi (1966), The Gambia (1970), Guyana (1970), Sierra Leone (1971), Malta (1974), Trinidad and Tobago (1976), Fiji (1987) and Mauritius (1992).

No journalist has ever been granted a full interview with the Queen.

THE QUEEN IN HER OWN WORDS

'It's inevitable that I should seem a rather remote figure to many of you – a successor to the kings and queens of history; someone whose face may be familiar in newspapers and films but who never touches your personal lives. But now, at least for a few minutes, I welcome you to the peace of my own home.'
First televised Christmas address, 25 December 1957

'The upward course of a nation's history is due in the long run to the soundness of heart of its average men and women.'
Christmas address, 1954

'I cannot lead you into battle. I do not give you laws or administer justice but I can do something else – I can give my heart and my devotion to these old islands and to all the peoples of our brother-hood of nations.'
Christmas address, 1957

'They are not royal. They just happen to have me as their aunt.'
On the children of Princess Margaret and Lord Snowdon,
Daily Mail, 4 October 1977

Henry VIII (1491–1547, reigned 1509–47)

HENRY'S RULE

Henry succeeded to the throne because his elder brother Arthur died in 1502. His first wife, Catherine of Aragon, was Arthur's widow.

He was so pious that he took mass three times a day.

Henry increased the size of the navy from five to fifty-three ships. His flagship, the *Mary Rose*, was named after his sister. He was watching from Southsea when it sank in the Solent after leaving Portsmouth Harbour in July 1545 with the loss of seven hundred lives. The remains of the *Mary Rose* were raised in 1982 and are now on display at Portsmouth Dockyard Naval Museum.

He made sodomy illegal for the first time with the Buggery Act of 1533.

During his reign the Laws in Wales Acts (1535–42) formally united England and Wales.

His dissolution of the monasteries between 1536 and 1540 was the largest act of expropriation in English history.

He would sometimes scare his ministers for amusement by pretending that he was thinking of having them executed. He would amuse himself still further by sometimes carrying out his threat...

LOVE-LIFE

He had eleven children with three of his six wives, though only three survived beyond childhood. His first wife, Catherine of Aragon, bore him six children in eight years. She was married to him for over twenty.

In 1519, Henry's teenage mistress Elizabeth Blount bore him a son, Henry FitzRoy, who was made Duke of Richmond and

Somerset. He died in 1536 while an Act of Parliament was being passed that would have made him heir to the throne. FitzRoy was the only bastard the king acknowledged, but there were rumoured to be several more.

Seventeen love letters Henry wrote to his second wife Anne Boleyn found their way to the Vatican Library. At her trial for treason in 1536, Anne was falsely accused of witchcraft, adultery, incest, plotting to murder her husband and poisoning Henry FitzRoy. Her brother George and four other supposed sexual partners were executed. Anne was beheaded by a swordsman after her marriage to the king was annulled.

Henry did not divorce any of his wives. Two marriages were annulled.

TALENTS

Henry played the lute, organ, harp, viola and virginal (a small English harpsichord). An enthusiastic composer of songs, his work is available on a CD, *If Love Now Reigned*, and includes 'Pastime With Good Company' and 'Departure is my Chief Pain'. The Isaak Ensemble, the German group who perform his works, also reads out his love letters to Anne Boleyn on the recording in a thick German accent. The notion that Henry wrote 'Greensleeves' is a myth.

He spoke fluent French, Latin and Spanish.

Henry wrote the *Defence of the Seven Sacraments*, a best-selling book attacking Martin Luther that was published in twenty editions in England and Europe. The Pope rewarded him with the title 'Defender of the Faith'. Henry also penned a riddle: 'What is it that being born without life, head, lip, or eye, yet doth run roaring through the world til it die?' The answer: a fart. The Pope excommunicated Henry in July 1533.

He was 6 feet in height, which was very tall for his day, and was famous for his physique as a young man. He continued to take part in sporting events even when he was long past his prime. In 1536, when he was 44, he was once knocked unconscious for two hours after a jousting accident.

He was so fat in his later years, with a waist of 54 inches, that he had to be carried everywhere on a sedan chair and winched into his saddle when he rode a horse.

The king's corpse exploded while it was being transported to Windsor for burial. The lead-lined casket split and, during a halt on the journey, dogs were seen licking the blood falling on to the ground under the carriage.

The Other Henries

HENRY I (1069–1135, REIGNED 1100–35)

Conan's Tower in Rouen gets its name from Conan Pilatus, the town burgher who led a rebellion against Henry's elder brother, Duke Robert Curthose, in 1090. The young Henry dragged Conan up the staircase to the highest window, told him to admire the lands he had tried to conquer, and then threw him to his death.

Henry was the youngest son of William the Conqueror. On the death of the oldest, William Rufus, the second son, Duke Robert, had not yet returned from the Crusades and so could not take up the succession. Henry seized power, and when Robert invaded England to take his rightful crown, the king bought him off by giving him his lands in Normandy, only to later win back the region through force. He then kept his brother prisoner for the rest of his life.

He was called Henry Beauclerc because of the fine education he received. He was also the first Norman ruler to speak English fluently.

His Archbishop of Canterbury was the philosopher St Anselm, with whom he quarrelled several times.

He founded the department of the Exchequer for the management of royal finances.

Henry died from a surfeit of lampreys that gave him food poisoning. After the death of his son, the king had prepared his daughter Matilda to be his successor. The absence of a male heir precipitated the first English civil war, as Henry's nephew Stephen fought for the crown against Matilda and her husband, Geoffrey Plantagenet.

HENRY II (1133–89, R. 1154–89)

Henry II reigned for thirty-four years, but spent only fourteen of them in England.

Thomas Becket was Henry II's Chancellor before the king made him Archbishop of Canterbury, even though he had never been a priest. Henry fell out with his close friend over the issue of whether secular courts could try members of the clergy and, later, the coronation of the king's son Henry. The king was prone to ranting at the archbishop and one day asked aloud, 'Who will rid me of this turbulent priest?' He denied that he meant it, but four of his knights answered the call and journeyed to Canterbury, where they murdered Becket inside the cathedral, four days after Christmas 1170.

As penance for Becket's death, Henry ordered that monks whip him in public.

He crowned his son Henry king in 1170, but he died before his father and 'Henry the Younger', as he is known, is not counted as one of the monarchs of England.

He controlled more of France than the King of France.

He had eight children with his wife, Eleanor of Aquitaine, four of whom survived to adulthood.

His mistress was Rosamond Clifford, the legendary beauty known as 'Fair Rosamond'. He acknowledged her after imprisoning Eleanor, a famous beauty in her own right, for supporting their sons in a rebellion. Later storytellers fancied that the jealous king kept Rosamond hidden in a labyrinth in the woods at Woodstock in Oxfordshire, where Eleanor eventually tracked her down and poisoned her.

Henry's sons rose in revolt against him over their meagre pocket money, since he refused to grant them estate revenues. They allied with the kings of France and Scotland and several powerful barons, but Henry defeated them all soundly.

Pope Alexander gave official approval to Henry's invasion of Ireland in 1171. The Vatican thought that English rule would put an end to abuses of the Catholic Church, such as bishops who married and passed on their posts to their offspring. The Pope was so pleased with Henry's campaign that he asked him to lead a crusade and become King of Jerusalem.

HENRY III (1207–72, R. 1216–72)

Henry III inherited the throne when he was 9 years old.

His reign lasted fifty-six years, making it the longest of any English monarch.

Henry III is regarded by historians as the most nondescript of English kings. He appears in Purgatory in Dante's *Divine Comedy* as a late-repentant outside the gates of Hell: 'There, alone, sits Henry of England, the king of the simple life.'

Henry was notorious for bringing in foreigners to run the country. The Savoy Hotel gets its name from the London house of one of them, Peter of Savoy, who was created Earl of Richmond.

He defeated his longstanding enemy and brother-in-law, Simon de Montfort, Earl of Leicester, at the Battle of Evesham, near Worcester, during a thunderstorm on 4 August 1265. The head, hands, feet and genitals were severed from de Montfort's corpse.

Henry was obsessed with the cult of Edward the Confessor, to the point of dressing like him, sleeping beneath a mural of the saint and naming a son after him. He rebuilt Westminster Abbey and had Edward's body reburied there, personally helping to carry the casket to the saint's new shrine.

He amassed a large collection of holy relics, including items claimed to be bones from St George, St Jerome and St Augustine, fragments of the golden gate at Jerusalem and the Holy Sepulchre, a twig from the burning bush through which God spoke to Moses and a sample of blood shed by Jesus at the Crucifixion.

After Henry was buried, a beggar claimed to have been cured of blindness after praying at his tomb. Henry's widow Eleanor believed the story, but his ruthless son Edward I scoffed at the idea and dismissed the beggar as a fraud.

HENRY IV (1366–1413, R. 1399–1413)

Henry Bolingbroke (named after his Lancashire birthplace) usurped the throne from Richard II, when his estate was confiscated on the death of his father, John of Gaunt. John was the First Duke of Lancaster, from whom the Lancastrian line gets its name.

Henry's coronation on 13 October 1399 was the first occasion after the Norman Conquest when the monarch made an address in English. On the same day, he doubled Geoffrey Chaucer's pension.

He passed legislation under which heretics could be burned at the stake.

Henry's wife Joan of Navarre was widely believed to have practised necromancy. She was convicted of witchcraft in 1419.

He suffered from epilepsy and leprosy, which might, in fact, have been the symptoms of syphilis. Many thought this was divine punishment for the king's execution of Richard Scrope, the Archbishop of York.

Henry was told a prophecy that he would die in Jerusalem, which he took to mean a crusader's death. He eventually expired in the Jerusalem Chamber of Westminster Abbey.

HENRY V (1387–1422, R. 1413–22)

Henry V was the first English king who could read and write easily in English.

He was 14 years old when he fought in his first battle against Owen Glendower's Welsh. In 1403, at the age of 16, he led an army against Harry Hotspur at Shrewsbury, where he was shot in the face with an arrow that penetrated 6 inches into the base of his skull. The arrowhead was removed over the course of several days, but Henry was disfigured for life and his portrait painters took care to feature their king in profile.

The Shakespearian character Falstaff was based upon Henry's early friend Sir John Oldcastle, the Lollard conspirator burned alive for heresy in 1417.

Henry assembled a fleet for the invasion of France comprising 1,500 ships – twelve times the size of the Spanish Armada. This was achieved by commandeering every ship over 20 tons currently in English ports, whether they were English or foreign owned. Foreign visitors also helped with the financing, though some needed encouragement. Ten partners in Italian merchants' houses were thrown into a debtors' prison for declining to grant the Crown loans totalling £2,000.

He proposed to avoid bloodshed on both sides by challenging the French dauphin to single combat. The offer to take on the lethal English king was declined.

When he accidentally rode past the village selected for his lodgings by his scouts on the road to Agincourt, Henry refused to turn back since he was wearing his coat of arms and this would count in his own mind as a retreat. Exhausted by three weeks of marching, the half-starved, dysentery-racked army spent the night before the battle out in the open under torrential rain. Henry's 6,000 were outnumbered by 6:1 or more. Over 10,000 Frenchmen died in the battle.

HENRY VI (1421–71, R. 1422–61, 1470–71)

Henry succeeded to the throne when he was only 9 months old.

He was crowned King of France at Notre Dame in Paris on 16 December 1431.

He lost the English claim to all French soil except for Calais.

A lord once arranged for a troupe of bare-breasted dancing girls to entertain the young king. Henry was horrified and averted his eyes, crying, 'Fy, fy, for shame, forsoothe ye be to blame!'

He inherited mental illness through the line of his mother, Catherine of Valois.

He founded Eton College in 1440, originally a charitable institution where boys from poor backgrounds would be educated at the king's expense. Henry also founded King's College Cambridge, where they could go on to receive a university education.

Henry was murdered in the Tower of London a few days after the Yorkists' victory in the Wars of the Roses at Tewkesbury.

HENRY VII (1457–1509, R. 1485–1509)

His mother, Margaret Beaufort, was only 14 years old when she gave birth to Henry Tudor.

He gained the throne when he defeated and killed Richard III at the Battle of Bosworth in 1485.

He was a Lancastrian descended from John of Gaunt via an extramarital affair, but he united the two houses of the Wars of the Roses by marrying Edward IV's daughter, Elizabeth of York.

After Henry defeated the pretender Lambert Simnel's rebel army in 1487, he put Simnel to work in the royal kitchens.

Henry's greatest threat was Perkin Warbeck, who pretended to be Richard, Duke of York – the younger of the two princes murdered in the Tower of London.

He made peace with Scotland and married his sister, Margaret Tudor, to James IV, a move that led eventually to the Stuart line taking over the English throne and the union of the two nations.

Henry kept a tight grip on revenues and examined the royal account books every day. He trebled the royal income during his reign and handed over a solvent crown to his son, Henry VIII. His personal fortune when he died was over a million pounds, at a time when the average weekly wage was around 5p.

Alfred the Great and The House of Wessex

THE DARK AGES

Due to the scarcity of sources from the fifth and sixth centuries – the 'Dark Ages' – it cannot be established whether the Romans decided to leave Britain or the Britons rebelled against them. But after the end of imperial rule at the beginning of the fifth century, pagan Germanic peoples migrated to the British Isles in significant numbers. Britain was re-Christianized after the arrival of St Augustine in AD 597.

The kings of the West Saxons gradually won the power struggle to rule the lands that became England. They then faced waves of Viking invasion and incursions. Most of the Wessex kings suffered persistent ill-health or were dogged by physical pain and discomfort, yet they were compelled to spend much of their reigns in the field.

EGBERT (c. 770–839, R. 802–39)

Egbert, ruler of the West Saxons, is regarded as the first king of England by virtue of his conquering or subduing the other six Anglo-Saxon kingdoms under the crown of Wessex. He was proclaimed 'Bretwalda' – the ruler of all Britain.

In 789, he was driven into exile by the Mercian king Offa and the West Saxon king Beorhtric. He spent several years at the court of Charlemagne.

ÆTHELWULF (c. 800–58, R. 839–58)

(The prefix 'Æthel-' or 'Ethel-' was used in Anglo-Saxon to denote noble birth.)

Æthelwulf was very religious and completed a pilgrimage to Rome with his youngest son Alfred (later Alfred the Great).

Four of his sons became king: Æthelbald, Æthelbert, Æthelred and Alfred.

ÆTHELBALD (c. 834–60, R. c. 855–60)

Rebelled while his father was away on pilgrimage, reducing Æthelwulf to ruler of Kent on his return.

When Æthelwulf died, Æthelbald married his young widowed stepmother, Judith, who the old king had brought back from the Frankish court. However, the church forced him to have the marriage annulled.

ÆTHELBERT (c. 835–66, R. 860–66)

Under his reign the Danes laid waste to much of Kent and destroyed Æthelbert's capital, Winchester. However, the invaders were cut off and massacred on their way back to the sea.

ÆTHELRED (c. 837–71, R. 866–71)

Æthelred had earlier stood aside to allow his brother Æthelbert to take the crown.

Aided by his younger brother Alfred, he spent his entire reign fighting Viking incursions, and died of wounds sustained in the Battle of Merton in 1871.

ALFRED THE GREAT (849–99, R. 871–99)

Alfred was the youngest of five brothers and never expected to become king. He spent his early life as a scholar.

He made two trips to Rome as a boy, the first at the age of 4, when the Pope made him an honorary Roman Consul.

After buying time with the Danegeld tribute, he built a chain of forts to protect his kingdoms against the Vikings. The Anglo-Saxon name for the forts, 'burh', became the place name suffix '-bury'.

He also personally designed large fighting ships to take the battle to the Vikings at sea. Although there was a fleet before his reign, both the Royal Navy and the United States Navy recognize him as their spiritual founder. The first ship ever commissioned in the United States Navy was the USS *Alfred*.

In 878 Alfred was forced to retreat to a fort in the Somerset marshes when the Danes took Wessex – most of his kinsmen having surrendered. It was at this point that according to legend a peasant woman let the king into her hovel and set the stranger to watch over her cakes, scolding him when he let them burn. She apologized, aghast, when she realized his identity, but he insisted that he was the one who should apologize.

He was said to have disguised himself as a harpist to slip into the Danish king Guthrun's camp on spying missions.

Alfred mustered an army in secret and with it defeated the Danes decisively at the Battle of Edington in 878, after which Guthrun was baptized.

Alfred enforced a code of laws based on an amalgam of the Book of Exodus and earlier English codes. This was designed to protect the weak, enforce oaths and reduce blood feuds. His sense of justice also extended to the defeated Danes, who were allowed to remain in their settlements and be treated on equal footing with the English before the law.

Alfred was a noted scholar who gathered learned Europeans to his court. He believed that the Vikings were divine punishment for the decline in virtue, which was the result of ignorance. He decreed that all free men of means had to learn to read English. To encourage them, he personally translated several works of philosophy and theology from Latin into Anglo-Saxon and instigated the *Anglo-Saxon Chronicle* – the story of the English people that would be written over centuries.

He patronized the arts and crafts, creating a fashion for elaborate gold and silver jewellery and illuminated manuscripts.

EDWARD I, 'THE ELDER' (c. 871–924, R. 899–924)

Alfred's son Edward conquered the areas of England administered by the Vikings under the Danelaw.

He was thought to have received the submission of Constantine II of Scotland, setting a precedent for future English claims to the country.

ATHELSTAN (c. 895–939, R. 924–39)

Edward the Elder's son Athelstan was the first of the West Saxon kings to exercise uncontested authority over the whole of England.

He won a famous victory over a combined army of Danes, Scots and Irish at Brunanburh, Cumbria, in 937, in which large numbers died.

He forced the Welsh to pay tribute.

EDMUND I (921–46, R. 939–46)

The son of Edward the Elder, he was also called 'Edmund the Deed-Doer' and '*Edmundus Magnificus*' ('Edmund the Magnificent').

He helped start a monastic revival by appointing Dunstan Abbot of Glastonbury. Edmund had earlier expelled the monk from his court, but while out hunting one day his horse almost ran over a precipice, upon which Edmund silently promised to make amends to Dunstan if his life was spared.

Edmund was murdered by a thief in his palace in Pucklechurch, Gloucestershire.

EADRED (c. 923–55, R. 946–55)

When an exiled Norwegian, Eric Bloodaxe, made himself King of Northumbria in 948, Edmund I's son Eadred and his army pillaged the region until the Northumbrians rejected the Norseman.

Eadred suffered ill-health throughout his life and could not swallow solid food.

EADWIG (C. 941–59, R. 955–9)

On the day of his coronation at the age of 15 or 16, St Dunstan dragged Eadwig from the bed of a girl to a meeting of state, earning the young king's enmity thereafter. The girl, Ælgifu, was described as a 'strumpet', but Eadwig went on to marry her.

Two years into his reign, Eadwig was deposed from the regions north of the Thames in favour of his brother Edgar.

EDGAR (943/4–75, R. 959–75)

Edgar was called 'Edgar the Peaceable' for his unusually tranquil reign.

He made it a legal obligation to pay tithes and Peter's Pence, the subsidy paid to the Vatican each year.

He made St Dunstan Archbishop of Canterbury.

EDWARD II 'THE MARTYR' (C. 963–78, R. 975–8)

Edward was crowned at 12 and murdered at 15 by the household of his younger brother Æthelred, at Corfe Castle.

He was canonized after his remains were said to heal the sick.

ÆTHELRED II (968–1016, R. 978–1013, 1014–16)

Called 'Æthelred the Unready', which meant ill-advised.

He followed a policy of appeasement towards the marauding Danes, who ravaged most of the country while taking ever larger tribute.

When the Danes ceased their pillaging and settled in English towns, Æthelred provoked a further invasion by having them slaughtered in the St Brice's Day Massacre of 13 November 1002.

EDMUND II (c. 993–1016, R. 1016)

He was nicknamed 'Edmund Ironside' for his steadfast resistance to King Canute's Danish invasion.

He was defeated by Canute at Ashingdon, Essex, in 1016 and limited to the core kingdom of Wessex in the peace settlement.

The Danish Line

After gorging on Danegeld for several years, Svein Forkbeard decided to take the whole kingdom of England rather than merely its proceeds.

SVEIN I (c. 960–1014, R. 1013–14)

Svein Forkbeard, father of Canute, forced Æthelred the Unready into exile and seized the throne for a short period prior to his death.

CANUTE I (c. 955–1035, R. 1016–35)

Canute's reputation for arrogance and madness stems from the legend of how he sat in his throne on the beach at Bosham and forbade the tide from coming in. However, his intention was not to demonstrate his authority but quite the reverse. Canute was so successful in fostering trade and keeping the peace that his courtiers fawned over him. Sick of their flattery, he attempted to command the sea in order to prove his impotence. As he scampered back to dry land he said, 'Let all men know how empty and worthless is the power of kings.'

'Canute the Great' also had a reputation for murdering and mutilating prisoners.

In 1019 he took an English army back to his homeland to help him secure the Danish throne.

He gave generously to the church and was buried in Winchester Cathedral.

HARALD I (B. UNKNOWN, D. 1040, R. 1035–40)

The illegitimate son of Canute, Harald Harefoot became regent upon his father's death.

In 1036, he had Æthelred's son Alfred murdered and Canute's widow Emma exiled before getting himself declared king.

HARDECANUTE (C. 1018–42, R. 1040–42)

Canute's legitimate son by Emma, Hardecanute had Harold I's body exhumed and thrown into a swamp.

He sent an army to torch Worcester in punishment when two of his tax collectors were murdered there.

The *Anglo–Saxon Chronicle* records him as an oath-breaker because he gave the Earl of Northumbria safe passage and then took the opportunity to have him killed.

The Wessex Restoration

EDWARD III, 'THE CONFESSOR' (1003–66, R. 1042–66)

The oldest son of Æthelred the Unready, Edward grew up in Normandy. After he returned to England he placed his trust in Normans and appointed them to several high offices, to the chagrin of both English and Danish noblemen.

He confined his wife Edith to a nunnery to spite her father,

Godwin, the powerful Earl of Wessex. It was during the exile of Godwin's family that Edward invited William of Normandy to his court and supposedly promised to make him his heir. If the story is true, he went back on his word shortly before his death, when he named Godwin's son Harold as his successor.

In the 1050s Edward lost interest in ruling the kingdom and concentrated on religious observance and building Westminster Abbey, which at that point lay outside London.

Edward became the subject of a religious cult in the twelfth century and was canonized in 1161. He was called 'The Confessor' because, although he was made a saint, he had not been martyred but had died of natural causes.

HAROLD II (c. 1020–66, R. 1066)

After a shipwreck in 1064, Harold was handed over to William of Normandy, who forced him to swear an oath of allegiance. It was said that the oath was given over a box that unbeknownst to Harold contained the bones of a saint. William later used this incident as further grounds for his claim to the English throne.

He was the last English king to be defeated by a foreign invader.

He ruled for nine months before he was killed at the Battle of Hastings, apparently shot through the eye with a Norman arrow.

According to twelfth-century conspiracy theorists, Harold survived the battle. After recovering from his grievous wounds, he spent most of his remaining years wandering in Germany before returning home to die as a hermit.

The Normans

WILLIAM I, 'THE CONQUEROR' (1028–87, R. 1066–87)

The illegitimate 'William the Bastard' had a violent childhood. Three of his guardians were killed and his tutor was murdered. He revelled in soldiering throughout his life and eventually died after a riding accident sustained while campaigning.

He was crowned King of England in Westminster Abbey on Christmas Day 1066. The shouts of celebration were misinterpreted by the Norman guards outside to mean that there was infamy at play. They responded by setting fire to neighbouring buildings. In the ensuing chaos, the crowd rushed out of the abbey to engage in a looting spree.

William left England a year after his victory at Hastings, but he had to return swiftly to face a series of rebellions running from 1067–71. This put him off the country and thereafter he stayed away in France as much as possible. England, for its own part, was put off William by his ruthlessness, which included engineering a famine in Yorkshire by burning the granaries. He was remembered by contemporaries as cruel and grasping, although highly efficient.

Almost the entire ruling class of England was replaced by the Norman nobility, with a new language introduced that was spoken at court for the next three hundred years.

William ordered the construction of a series of fortresses that included the Tower of London.

He commissioned the Domesday Book – a thorough survey of the use of land in England in 1085.

William grew obese in his later years, and when he died in Caen in

1087 he was too fat for his coffin. The assembled bishops tried to force the body in, only for the abdomen to burst open and set off a stampede among the mourners, desperate to escape the stench.

WILLIAM II 'RUFUS' (1056–1100, R. 1087–1100)

The third son of William the Conqueror, he was named 'Rufus' for his ruddy complexion.

He was even more brutal than his father, and subjugated Scotland, Wales and his brother Robert's territory in Normandy during his reign.

Churchmen hated Rufus for a long list of grievances that included over-indulgence in concubines, the introduction of the risqué fashion for long hair at court, and extravagance funded at their expense. He would delay appointing abbots and bishops for long periods, while he helped himself to the revenues they would have accrued. The see of Canterbury itself was kept vacant for four years to this end.

Rufus died after he was shot in the back by a supposedly stray arrow during a hunt in the New Forest. Since his younger brother Henry was in the area and quickly seized power, many thought that the king had in fact been assassinated.

HENRY I

(See 'The Other Henries'.)

STEPHEN (C. 1097–1154, R. 1135–54)

Stephen, a grandson of William the Conqueror, was, by 1130, the richest man in England and Normandy, thanks to the generosity of King Henry. By the end of his reign he had spent his entire fortune on mercenaries.

Henry had promised the throne to Stephen's cousin, Matilda, but she was in Anjou when the king died. Stephen took power, claiming that Henry had changed his mind on his deathbed.

Stephen was said to be very handsome, but his royal portrait shows him to have been cross-eyed.

Stephen was brave with his own life, but was loath to risk the lives of others. He did everything in his power to avoid warfare, allowing his barons to seize royal land without punishment, buying off the Scots with generous grants of land, and accepting an unfavourable treaty with Geoffrey of Anjou in Normandy. Royal authority was so weakened that Matilda invaded England in 1139. Instead of meeting her with an army, Stephen magnanimously had her escorted to Bristol, from where she fomented a rebellion across western England.

Matilda was briefly crowned queen before Stephen regained power. The final treaty of the wars permitted Stephen to remain on the throne until his death, after which the crown would be transferred to the House of Anjou.

EMPRESS MATILDA (1101–67, R. 1141)

England's first female monarch.

She made two daring escapes during the war with Stephen: from Devizes disguised as a corpse and more famously from Oxford across the snows in the night, wearing a white cape.

The Angevin Plantagenets

HENRY II
(See 'The Other Henries'.)

RICHARD I (1157–99, R. 1189–99)

In various wars, Richard the Lionheart fought with his brothers in a rebellion, with his father against his brothers and with the King of France against his father.

At around 6 feet 4 inches he was extremely tall for his day.

He only spent six months of his reign in England.

His wife, Berengaria of Navarre, is the only English queen never to have set foot in England.

On the day of his coronation, Jews were banned from the festivities. Londoners rioted and massacred those who attended in defiance. Richard had the perpetrators executed and allowed a forcibly converted Jew to return to his faith.

He left for the Third Crusade in 1190, during which he conquered Cyprus and made two narrowly unsuccessful attempts on the city of Jerusalem. His truce with Saladin gave Christian pilgrims access to holy sites.

On his return journey from the crusades, Richard was forced to defend his 'Saucy Castle', Château-Gaillard in Normandy, against Philip II of France. Philip is said to have claimed, 'I would take that castle though its walls were made of iron!' to which Richard replied, 'I would hold it though its walls were made of butter!'

JOHN (1167–1216, R. 1199–1216)

John was nicknamed 'John Lackland' as he was a fourth son with no inherited lands.

He spent his life making enemies, first as overlord of Ireland and then in failing to overthrow Richard's administrators while the Lionheart was imprisoned in Germany. As king, he was excommunicated and the entire country was placed under a papal interdict which ordered a halt to public worship and the withdrawal of the sacraments.

John lost England's French territories after arranging the murder of his nephew, Arthur of Brittany, which sparked a rebellion. The heavy taxation required to fund John's doomed attempts to recover Normandy led to the Barons' Revolt, that ended with the signing of Magna Carta in 1215.

He lost the Crown Jewels to an incoming tide in the Wash.

The Tudor line was descended from his illegitimate daughter, Joan, who married Llewellyn the Great of Wales.

HENRY III

(See 'The Other Henries'.)

EDWARD I (1239–1307, R. 1272–1307)

Known as 'Edward Longshanks' for his height (6 feet 2 inches) and 'Hammer of the Scots' for his conquest of Scotland. He may as well also have been christened 'Hammer of the Cockneys' for his slaughter of Londoners during the civil war of the 1260s.

He fathered nineteen legitimate children.

He defeated William Wallace at the Battle of Falkirk in 1298. Wallace was captured and executed in 1304.

Edward taxed the Jews and borrowed from them heavily until they could no longer pay. He forced them to wear yellow stars for identification and finally banished them from England in 1290.

He committed England's worst-ever massacre – the sack of Berwick in 1296. His army spent three days killing almost every man, woman and animal in the town. Edward only called off his troops after he saw them hacking a pregnant woman to death: seven to eight thousand people died.

EDWARD II (1284–1327, R. 1307–27)

Edward was prone to be manipulated by his favourites. One of his first acts as king was to make his homosexual lover, Piers Gaveston, Earl of Cornwall. Edward's barons murdered Gaveston in 1312. In 1322, he made the notoriously corrupt Hugh Despenser Earl of Winchester, but he proved no more popular with the barons and was executed in his turn in 1326.

In 1314, the English lost power over Scotland with Robert the Bruce's victory at Bannockburn. Rebellion in Ireland reduced England's dominion to the territory known as the 'Pale'.

Edward sent his queen, Isabella, on a diplomatic mission to her brother Charles IV of France in 1325, but there she fell in love with the exiled baron, Roger Mortimer. The pair invaded England the following year and forced Edward to abdicate in favour of his son.

It was rumoured that Edward was murdered while in captivity by having a red-hot poker inserted into his anus through a tube. This was reportedly so as to leave no marks. Though suffocation would have achieved the same effect, it was thought that his murderers had symbolism in mind.

EDWARD III (1312–77, R. 1327–77)

For the first three years of his reign, Edward was beholden to his mother and her lover, Roger Mortimer. He threw off their influence by having Mortimer executed.

He initiated the Hundred Years War with victories at Crécy (1346), Calais (1347) and Poitiers (1356) and controlled much of northern and western France before the Black Death depleted his armies and reduced his territories to Calais, Bordeaux and Bayonne.

His son Edward, the Black Prince, was instrumental in England's success in France, but the king outlived his famous son and believed his death to be a punishment from God for usurping Edward II's crown. He did not think it had anything to do with his son's massacre of three thousand civilians at Limoges in 1370.

RICHARD II (1367–1400, R.1377–99)

Richard was the son of the Black Prince.

He insisted that courtiers address him as 'Your Majesty' or 'Your Highness' rather than simply 'My Lord'. He took great pleasure in the reverence with which he was greeted in Ireland, and a trip to that country gave Henry Bolingbroke the chance to invade and usurp the crown. Richard was murdered in prison.

The Lancastrian Plantagenets

HENRY IV
(See 'The Other Henries'.)

Henry V
(See 'The Other Henries'.)

Henry VI
(See 'The Other Henries'.)

———

The Yorkist Plantagenets

———

EDWARD IV (1442–83, R. 1460–70, 1471–83)

Warwick the Kingmaker sought to procure a French princess as Edward's bride, but he married Elizabeth Woodville in secret. He married for love, as Elizabeth was a commoner, but he later became notorious for his many mistresses and debauched lifestyle.

Edward had his rebellious brother, the Duke of Clarence, executed in the Tower of London. According to legend, he was drowned in a butt of Malmsey wine.

Highly intelligent, handsome and imposing, Edward was thought to have the potential to become a truly great king, but self-indulgence and heavy drinking ruined his physique and dulled his imagination and he died at the age of 40.

(See 'Wars of the Roses' in **Warfare** for further information.)

EDWARD V (1470–83, R. 1483)

Edward reigned for only two months before his uncle, Richard, had him and his younger brother imprisoned in the Tower of London and declared illegitimate. The boys were never seen again, and the skeletons of two children were uncovered at the Tower in 1674.

Richard III (1452–85, R. 1483–5)

Richard was the last English king to die in battle.

His reputation suffered from a concerted propaganda campaign following his death. He was probably not the hunchback of Shakespearian legend.

Richard stayed in the White Boar Inn in Leicester before he met his end at the Battle of Bosworth. The sign was subsequently repainted as The Blue Boar Inn – the symbol of one of Henry VII's supporters, the Earl of Oxford. The king left his travelling royal bed behind, and in 1605, the landlady was murdered and robbed of £300 in gold coins hidden in the mattress.

Richard's remains were dug up and thrown over a bridge during Henry VIII's dissolution of the monasteries.

(See 'Wars of the Roses' in **Warfare** for further information.)

The Tudors

Henry VII

(See 'The Other Henries'.)

Henry VIII

(See earlier section.)

Edward VI (1537–53, R. 1547–53)

Edward was the son of Jane Seymour. He died of tuberculosis aged 16, having come to the throne when he was just 9 years old. He was England's first Protestant monarch and his reign was marked by -

religious persecution, court intrigue and countrywide rebellion. The changes he instigated in the church and state, however, still endure to this day.

LADY JANE GREY (1537–54, R. 1553)

Jane was a great-granddaughter of Henry VII. Her father, the Duke of Suffolk, and John Dudley, Duke of Northumberland, plotted to make her queen and marry her to the latter's son, who would become king.

She reigned for nine days at the age of 15. Jane was a reluctant queen, and her father failed to win public support for her claim to the throne. She was sent to the Tower and later beheaded for treason, having refused Mary's offer of a pardon if she converted to Catholicism.

MARY I (1516–58, R. 1553–8)

Mary was given her own court at Ludlow Castle as a child, but after her parents' marriage was annulled she was declared illegitimate. Her father, Henry VIII, separated her from her mother and forced her to act as a lady-in-waiting to her half-sister, Elizabeth. She was forbidden to attend her mother's funeral in 1536.

Her husband, Philip II of Spain, refused to sleep with her and she suffered several phantom pregnancies. Philip left England after a year.

Mary is the title character in the nursery rhyme 'Mary, Mary, Quite Contrary', according to one interpretation. Her 'growing garden' is said to be the graveyard of the Protestants martyred during her reign. The 'silver bells' and 'cockleshells' represent instruments of torture, while the 'pretty maids' refer to the Maiden – an early incarnation of the guillotine.

ELIZABETH I (1533–1603, R. 1558–1603)

Elizabeth was fluent in French, Greek, Latin, Spanish and Welsh by the age of 11.

One in four girls born during her reign were named after her.

Ivan the Terrible of Russia asked Elizabeth to grant him political asylum in the event of revolution in his homeland. She consented, but politely declined Ivan's offer to reciprocate should circumstances ever be reversed.

She had a laboratory built for Cornelius Lannoy, a Dutchman who promised that he could turn base metals into gold. Elizabeth sent him to the Tower of London when he failed to produce.

Elizabeth's advisor Sir Francis Walsingham created the nation's first organized secret service.

In middle age, Elizabeth applied heavy white lead make-up to her face and painted blue veins on her forehead to mimic the skin of a younger woman. Lead is now known to be a poison, and the paint would have damaged her skin and required ever thicker layers.

Elizabeth owned over two thousand dresses.

She used wads of cotton to puff out her cheeks – sunken with the loss of her teeth caused by her habit of chewing on sugar cane. She was once too frightened to have a rotten tooth pulled out until John Aylmer, the Bishop of London, had one of his own teeth pulled out by the surgeon to show her how painless it would be.

Well into her old age, Elizabeth attempted to charm foreign ambassadors by pulling down the front of her dress and leaning forwards to expose part of her bosom. Her habit found its way into several official reports.

The US state of Virginia was named after England's 'Virgin Queen'.

Elizabeth's Illustrious Suitors
Philip II of Spain
Archduke Charles of Austria
Erik XIV of Sweden
Henry, duc d'Anjou (later King of France)
François, duc d'Alençon
Robert Dudley, Earl of Leicester

The Stuarts and the House of Orange

JAMES I (1566–1625, R. 1603–25)

James was the first Scottish ruler of England and the first to call himself 'King of Great Britain'.

He was the son of Mary, Queen of Scots. She left Scotland when he was an infant and he never saw her again.

James had been King of Scotland for twenty-nine years when he acceded to the English throne and was overjoyed to inherit his new kingdom's finances. He alienated Parliament with his lavish spending on fripperies such as expensive interior décor, and awarded over two hundred peerages to buy support.

Henri IV called him 'The wisest fool in Christendom'.

He fell in love with George Villiers and made him the Duke of Buckingham. The king called Villiers his 'sweet child and wife' and wrote to him, 'I naturally so love your person, and adore all your other parts, which are more than ever one man had.'

James's Archbishop of Canterbury, George Abbot, was notorious for his punishments. He once sent 140 Oxford University undergraduates to prison for neglecting to remove their hats in his presence.

Churchmen who offended him risked having their noses and ears cut off, being lashed to a stake and flogged, branded with an iron or imprisoned for life.

CHARLES I
(See **Warfare**.)

CHARLES II
(See **Warfare**.)

JAMES II (1633–1701, R. 1685–8)

James was 15 when his father Charles I was executed. He escaped to France in 1648, disguised as a girl.

New Amsterdam was renamed 'New York' in his honour when as Lord High Admiral he ordered it to be seized from the Dutch in 1664.

Following Monmouth's Rebellion in 1685, James had 320 people executed in the 'Bloody Assizes', many by being hanged, drawn and quartered.

He was deposed in the Glorious Revolution of 1668–9.

James's corpse was dismembered and the heart, brain, hair, entrails, blood and part of his right arm were preserved as religious relics.

(See 'Notable Revolts and Rebellions' in **Crown, State and Law** for more information.)

WILLIAM III (1650–1702, R. 1689–1702) AND MARY II (1662–94, R. 1689–94)

William of Orange and Mary ruled jointly until her death from small-pox in 1694.

Mary had been an unwilling bride and found William physically repulsive when they were first introduced, yet she was deeply offended by his infidelities.

Several series of ballads to Mary were printed during her reign. They featured illustrative woodcuts depicting the queen with exposed breasts, and sold in great numbers.

The English public adored Mary, but they never took to William, who spent much of his reign abroad fighting the French. In 1705, Daniel Defoe wrote that their dislike 'ate into his very soul, tired it with serving an unthankful nation, and absolutely broke his heart'.

Anne (1665–1714, r. 1702–14)

Anne was the last English sovereign to perform the ceremony of 'touching for the King's Evil' to cure scrofula.

She drank so much brandy that she was known as 'Brandy Nan'.

Anne and the Duke of Marlborough's wife, Sarah, were inseparable friends for many years. They fell out after the duchess began to take her influence at court for granted and persisted in scolding the queen in public. 'I believe,' complained Anne, 'nobody was ever so used by a friend as I have been since my coming to the Crown. I desire nothing but that she would leave off teasing and tormenting me.'

The House of Hanover

George I (1660–1727, r. 1714–27)

The first German King of England made little effort to learn the language and customs of the country and communicated with his ministers in French. He left the Cabinet to rule while he spent much of his reign in Hanover.

George arrived in England without his wife Sophia, who had been imprisoned for adultery. Instead he brought two mistresses. One was tall and thin and the other was short and fat. The public called them the 'Maypole' and the 'Elephant'.

GEORGE II (1683–1760, R. 1727–60)

George lived in Hanover until he was 30 but spoke fluent English, albeit with a heavy German accent.

George II was the last English king to appear on the battlefield – against the French at the Battle of Dettingen in 1743. It was a significant victory, with 2,354 Allied casualties against around 8,000 on the French side.

GEORGE III (1738–1820, R. 1760–1820)

George III was the first Hanoverian monarch born in England.

The king's famous bouts of insanity were caused by the disease porphyria. His symptoms ranged from charming eccentricity (such as addressing a speech to 'My Lords and peacocks') to violent rages that saw him confined to a straitjacket.

His son was appointed Prince Regent in 1811 and the king spent his last decade at Windsor Castle deaf, blind and irretrievably unhinged.

GEORGE IV (1762–1830, R.1820–30)

George was a lifelong hedonist who grew so grossly overweight that he was too embarrassed to be seen out in public.

In a time of poverty following the Napoleonic Wars, he courted resentment by running up hundreds of thousands of pounds in debts. The money went on gambling, pet architectural projects and the lavish entertainment of a succession of mistresses.

When he died, *The Times*'s obituarist concluded, 'There never was an individual less regretted by his fellow creatures than this deceased king.'

WILLIAM IV (1765–1837, R. 1830–37)

As Duke of Clarence, William led the House of Lords' opposition to the abolition of slavery.

He had ten illegitimate children with the Irish actress Dorothea Jordan.

VICTORIA (1819–1901, R. 1837–1901)

She was christened 'Alexandrina Victoria'. Her family nickname was 'Drina'.

She slept in her mother's room until she became queen. Under the influence of the scheming Sir John Conroy, her mother became convinced that the royal dukes (George IV and William IV – the 'Wicked Uncles') would try to murder Victoria and so never let her be left alone. Neither was she allowed to hold a conversation with anyone without a third person being present.

She called her grandson, Kaiser Wilhelm II of Germany, 'Willy'.

She survived seven assassination attempts.

She was the first English monarch to visit France without an invading army since the coronation of Henry VI in 1431.

In 1876, Disraeli crowned her 'Empress of India'. He referred to her in conversation as 'the Faery Queen', while she called him 'Dizzy'.

She was a carrier of haemophilia, which her daughters transmitted to the royal houses of Spain and Russia.

She created the Victoria Cross after visiting soldiers wounded in the Crimean War. She later knitted scarves for veterans of the Boer War.

She had nine children with her cousin, Albert. After Albert died of typhoid in 1861, Victoria wore black for the rest of her life and would still have his washbasin filled with hot water each day for his morning shave. She was dressed, according to her instructions, in a white gown and her wedding veil for her funeral.

House of Saxe-Coburg-Gotha/Windsor

EDWARD VII (1841–1910, R. 1901–10)

Albert and Victoria were ashamed of their son, 'Bertie'. He was lazy and stupid, incapable of remembering commands as an army officer, and an arrogant bully to his servants. He was addicted to drink, gambling and women, and was implicated in several divorce cases.

However, the public forgot their own hardships and took pity on him when he suffered a bout of polio in 1871. Thereafter, his misadventures were viewed as an amusing antidote to Victorian austerity. As monarch, he proved helpful in cementing the Grand Alliance with France and Russia.

GEORGE V (1865–1936, R. 1910–36)

George changed the family name from Saxe-Coburg-Gotha to Windsor during the First World War.

He began the sovereign's Christmas Day radio broadcasts in 1932.

EDWARD VIII (1894–1972, R. 1936)

Edward abdicated so that he could marry the American divorcee, Wallis Simpson.

During the Second World War, he was appointed Governor of the Bahamas, but had to be reprimanded by Churchill for his 'defeatist and pro-Nazi' views. He also requested that his servants be released from military service and asked for several thousand pounds to refurbish his official residence in 1940. Churchill was appalled and replied that the money would be better spent on Spitfires.

Adolf Hitler considered reinstalling him as a puppet ruler should he have succeeded in conquering Britain.

GEORGE VI (1895–1952, R. 1936–52)

George founded the Duke of York's Camp to bring together public schoolboys and working-class youngsters.

He suffered from knock-knees, chronic gastric problems and a severe stammer, which he overcame through speech therapy.

During the Blitz, he insisted on remaining in Buckingham Palace, which was bombed nine times over the course of the war.

5

CROWN, STATE AND LAW

'The English people believes itself to be free; it is
gravely mistaken; it is free only during election of
members of parliament; as soon as the members are
elected, the people is enslaved; it is nothing. In the
brief moment of its freedom, the English people
makes such a use of that freedom that it deserves to
lose it.'

Jean-Jacques Rousseau, *The Social Contract* (1762)

England and the United Kingdom
England's legal relationship with the other home nations

STATUTE OF RHUDDLAN 1284

Formalized Edward I's conquest of Wales, annexing the country and dividing it into two political and administrative areas. The Principality, defended by fourteen castles, was under the king's control, while the Marcher Lordships retained much of their independence.

ACTS OF UNION 1535–42

Under Henry VIII, English criminal law was extended into Wales, where the Acts were popular because they gave the Welsh equality with the English under the law. English became the language of the courtroom and all Welsh political representatives were to be able to speak it.

ACTS OF UNION 1707

Created the Kingdom of Great Britain, with a common monarch and a common parliament to meet on the site of the old English parliament. Scottish law was to be maintained, though Catholics were barred from the throne. The Acts led to civil unrest and the declaration of martial law in Edinburgh.

ACT OF UNION 1800

Merged the kingdoms of Great Britain and Ireland. Created a united Church of England and Ireland and sent Irish MPs and peers to the

Westminster Parliament. The Union flag was unveiled, with the Cross of St Patrick representing Ireland.

GOVERNMENT OF IRELAND ACT 1920

Gave Home Rule to Southern Ireland.

ANGLO-IRISH TREATY 1921

Created the Irish Free State as a dominion within the British Empire.

Notable Revolts and Rebellions

REBELLION OF 1069

Three years after the Norman invasion, Northumbria revolted, as it had done twice against Tostig and Harold in the previous two years. Separatists massacred the Norman garrison at Durham and besieged York. The rebellion spread to the rest of northern England before it was crushed by William's army. The king's revenge was 'The Harrying of the North', in which crops were burned, houses demolished and the populace slaughtered until there were no inhabited villages left between York and Durham.

THE BARONS' REVOLT 1215

After King John imposed extortionate taxes and inheritance duties to finance his unsuccessful wars in France, a group of barons captured London and demanded a meeting at Runnymede on pain of civil war. They presented the king with 'The Articles of the Barons', a list of demands that would place formal limits on the abuse of feudal powers. This became Magna Carta (the Great Charter) and heralded the beginning of the Rule of Law in England.

PEASANTS' REVOLT 1381

The revolt in East Anglia and the south-east was sparked by the imposition of a poll tax. Rebels under Wat Tyler marched on London, where they murdered Flemish merchants and destroyed the palace of the king's uncle, John of Gaunt. They then took the Tower of London and beheaded the architects of the tax – Archbishop Simon of Sudbury and Sir Robert Hales. King Richard II promised the rebels land and gave the false assurance that he would abolish serfdom, but when he met their leaders to parley, his companion the Mayor of London killed Wat Tyler on the spot.

MONMOUTH'S REBELLION 1685

The Duke of Monmouth was the illegitimate son of Charles II who rose to become the commander of the English armed forces. He was banished by his father so that he could not interfere in the succession of his Catholic brother, James. When James acceded to the throne in 1685, Monmouth landed at Lyme Regis with eighty-two followers and quickly raised an army of 4,000 peasants. However, he failed to gain the support of the gentry and he was captured and beheaded after his men were defeated on Sedgemoor Plain. The so-called 'Bloody Assizes' followed at which 320 people were executed, many by being hanged, drawn and quartered.

THE GLORIOUS REVOLUTION 1688–9

After the wife of the Roman Catholic King James II produced a male heir, a cross-party group of MPs panicked and petitioned the king's nephew and son-in-law William of Orange to invade England and save Protestantism. James fled the country as William's army approached London, throwing the Great Seal of England into the River Thames on the way. The Palace of Westminster took this as an abdication and crowned William and his wife Mary, James's daughter, king and queen. The most significant effect was to limit the monarch's powers and establish the primacy of Parliament.

THE GORDON RIOTS 1780

The Protestant MP Lord George Gordon led a mob to Parliament to demand the repeal of the Catholic Relief Act of 1778, which had absolved Catholics from taking the religious oath on joining the army. He so inflamed the protesters with fears of papism and treachery that they spent a week burning and looting the homes of prominent London Catholics, vandalizing churches and attacking prisons to release inmates. George III eventually called in troops to put down the riots, leaving around five hundred dead or wounded. Gordon was found not guilty of treason and went unpunished. He converted to Judaism in 1786. He later died in Newgate Prison, where he was sent for libelling the Queen of France.

CAPTAIN SWING AND THE TOLPUDDLE MARTYRS 1830–34

'Captain Swing' was the signatory of the letters sent to several large landowners in 1830 threatening grave consequences if they failed to increase wages for farm workers. The introduction of the threshing machine in the southern counties had pushed many workers to destitution, and riots followed in which farm buildings were torched and agricultural machinery destroyed. (Captain Swing became so infamous that the boys at Eton wrote a letter to their headmaster in his name, complaining about excessive use of the 'thrashing machine'.) Nineteen people were executed as a result of the disturbances, 644 were imprisoned and over five hundred were transported to Australia, but Captain Swing was never caught, probably because he did not exist. The Tolpuddle Martyrs were six Dorset farm labourers sentenced to transportation in 1834 for organizing a trade union in the village of Tolpuddle. There were popular protests in London and around the country in support of the men, but the government did not remit their sentences until 1846.

The Last Executions

Hanging, drawing and quartering: 1820. The five 'Cato Street Conspirators', who planned to murder several members of the Cabinet, were executed on 1 May.

Beheading: 1747. Simon Fraser, Lord Lovat, executed on Tower Hill on 9 April for his part in the Highland Rising of 1745.

Burning at the stake: 1789. Catherine Murphy at Newgate on 18 March for High Treason (counterfeiting).

Firing squad: 1944. American soldier Benjamin Pyegate on 28 November, for stabbing a fellow soldier to death.

Hanging: 1964. Convicted murderers Peter Allen and Gwynne Evans were hanged simultaneously at 8 a.m. on 13 August at Liverpool and Manchester Prisons respectively. The last woman to be hanged was Ruth Ellis on 13 July 1955.

Last execution for witchcraft: 1686. Alice Molland was hanged in Exeter.

Last execution for High Treason: 1946. William Joyce, aka 'Lord Haw Haw' was hanged in Wandsworth Prison.

Last public execution: 1875. Joseph Le Brun, hanged on 11 August in Jersey for murder. The last on the English mainland was the hanging of Michael Barrett at Newgate in 1868 for the Fenian bombing at Clerkenwell which killed seven people.

Last execution of a juvenile: 1833. Thomas Knapton, aged 17, hanged on 26 July for rape.

Inns of Court

The Four Inns of Court have the sole right and responsibility to call barristers to the Bar. Law students can become advocates only after completing a period of vocational training, known as a 'pupillage', at one of the courts and acquiring the degree of Barrister-at- Law. All the Inns are located in London. They are equal in rank and have their origins in the Middle Ages, when they were originally hostels for students which sprang up after Edward I placed barristers and solicitors under the control of the judges rather than the church in 1292. The exact dates of inception are lost, but it is thought that they were all well established by the mid fourteenth century. Each Inn's full name is 'The Honourable Society of...'

LINCOLN'S INN

Named after Henry de Lacy, the third Earl of Lincoln who died in 1311, Lincoln's Inn has the oldest continuous formal records. The Inn's 'Black Books' date from 1422. When Charles II came to visit in

1672, none of the senior benchers were physically capable of rising to propose the Loyal Toast, upon which the king granted the Inn in perpetuity the privilege to drink the Loyal Toast sitting down. Lincoln's Inn Fields is the largest square in central London, comprising twelve acres laid out by Inigo Jones in the seventeenth century. Members include Sir Thomas More, John Donne, Lord Denning, Lord Hailsham, Horace Walpole and Rider Haggard.

INNER TEMPLE

Inner Temple occupies the eastern half of the twelfth-century London headquarters of the Knights Templar. Many of its original buildings were destroyed either in the Great Fire of London of 1666 or by Luftwaffe bombing during the Second World War. It was first referred to officially as a separate society in 1440, though it appears in Chaucer's *Canterbury Tales*. Members include Clement Attlee, Bram Stoker, John Mortimer, Mahatma Gandhi, Jawaharlal Nehru, John Maynard Keynes and A. J. P. Taylor.

MIDDLE TEMPLE

Middle Temple occupies the western half of the old Templar headquarters. The 'Cup Board', the table at which newly called barristers stand to enter their names in the Inn's books, is made from the forehatch of Sir Francis Drake's flagship, the *Golden Hind*, and until it was destroyed by German bombing in 1941, the ship's lantern hung in the entrance to the Hall. Members include Sir Walter Ralegh, William Congreve, Edmund Burke and Richard Sheridan.

GRAY'S INN

Gray's Inn had an Elizabethan heyday when the queen became its Patron Lady. Her advisors Lord Burleigh, Sir Francis Walsingham and the Lord High Admiral of England, Howard of Effingham, were members. The 'Armada' screen in the Hall was made partly from the timbers of the Spanish ship *Nuestra Señora del Rosario*. Shakespeare's patron, the Earl of Southampton, was also a member, and his *Comedy of Errors* was first performed in the Hall in 1594. In the early nineteenth century Charles Dickens spent eighteen months there as a clerk, and the Inn features in *David Copperfield* and *Pickwick Papers*. Other members include Lord Macaulay, Hilaire Belloc and Edward Heath.

Notable Differences Between
the Scottish and English Legal Systems

TERMINOLOGY

England	Scotland
Barrister	Advocate
Injunction	Interdict
Arbiters	Arbitrators
County Courts	Sheriff's Courts

Scottish juries have fifteen members rather than twelve.

Scottish juries can give a verdict of 'Not proven' as well as 'Guilty' or 'Not guilty' in cases where the prosecution has provided substantial but not conclusive proof of the defendant's guilt. The 'not proven' verdict is returned in around one-third of all acquittals in trials by jury in Scotland.

In Scotland, there is no distinction between 'crimes' and 'offences'.

A breach of the peace in England results in a magistrate's court order, whereas in Scotland it is an arrestable offence.

In England, a defamatory statement comes in two forms: libel and slander. Both forms of defamation are regarded as one in Scottish law.

English courts are guided by precedents set by older cases to produce like-for-like judgments. In Scotland, precedent is used only to help divine the principle which justifies a law.

Mock Mayors

The election of local officials was once often accompanied by a ballot to elect a figure who would ridicule the local mayor or Member of Parliament. Sometimes the election would be a shoo-in for the individual who had made the biggest fool of himself in public over the past year. The successful candidate would be carried through the streets issuing bizarre decrees, rewards and punishments while he and his supporters drank heavily. In coastal towns and villages he would usually be thrown into the sea at some point. Though proceedings often descended into drunken violence, the 'mock' elections of the eighteenth and nineteenth centuries were more democratic than the real thing, being freer, fairer and allowing a wider suffrage. The most famous was the Mayor of Garratt, elected at the Leather Bottle pub in Garratt Lane, Wandsworth, after each General Election from 1747 to 1796 following unpopular land closures in the area.

Surviving mock mayors can be found at:

Abingdon, Oxfordshire
Barton, Gloucester
Penzance, Cornwall
Woodstock, Oxfordshire

Parliament

HISTORY

Westminster was the world's first parliament. The oldest surviving part of the old Palace is Westminster Hall, built by William Rufus between 1097 and 1098. The rest of the original Palace of Westminster was destroyed by a fire in 1834. Until an earlier fire in 1512, it had been the king's main residence. The current structure, designed by Sir Charles Barry, was begun in 1840 and completed in 1870. The Commons Chamber itself was destroyed by German bombing in May 1941 and rebuilt after the war by Sir Giles Gilbert Scott.

'Big Ben' refers to the Great Bell inside the clock tower rather than to the tower itself. The 13.8 tonne bell was named after Sir Benjamin Hall, the Welshman who was First Commissioner of Works between 1855 and 1858.

The clock tower has 393 steps, leading to the Ayrton Light, the lantern lit whenever Parliament is sitting after nightfall.

The first representative Parliament was summoned by Edward I in 1295 and comprised two knights from each county, two burgesses from each borough and two citizens from each city, along with arch-bishops, bishops, abbots, earls and barons. Parliament was divided into the House of Commons and the House of Lords during the reign of Edward III in the fourteenth century.

The original five conspirators in the Gunpowder Plot of 1605 were Thomas Winter, Thomas Percy, John Wright, Guy 'Guido' Fawkes and the ringleader Robert Catesby. They were later joined by Robert Keyes. They planned to restore the Catholic faith in England by blowing up the House of Lords during the State Opening of Parliament on 5 November, when the Lords, the Commons and the king would all be present in the chamber. Fawkes – originally a Protestant from York who had converted and enlisted in the Spanish army – was caught red-handed in a cellar after the Catholic Lord Monteagle received an anonymous letter warning him not to attend the ceremony.

The last time Parliament met outside London was in 1681 in Oxford.

Transcribing the debates in the House of Commons was once a punishable offence, but in the eighteenth century reports were published, thinly disguised as the proceedings of imaginary clubs such as The Lower Room of the Robin Hood Society, or The Senate of Lilliputia. William Cobbett began to publish parliamentary debates in 1806, but he received a two-year sentence for seditious libel after revealing that British soldiers had been flogged for mutiny. He sold his publication to his printer, T. C. Hansard, who received a lighter sentence. Official parliamentary reports bear Hansard's name to this day. Television coverage of debates began in 1989.

The first non-white MP was Dadabhai Naoroji, a University College London professor from Bombay, elected for Finsbury Central in London in 1892. He won the support of the press and local people after the Conservative Prime Minister Lord Salisbury played the race card against him during the campaign, questioning whether 'a black man' should stand for Parliament.

The first female MP was Countess Constance Markiewicz, elected to St Patrick's, Dublin, in 1918. Along with other members of Sinn Féin, she did not take up her seat. In 1919, Viscountess Nancy Astor became the first woman to actually take her seat when she won Plymouth Sutton. In 2001, four Sinn Féin MPs joined the Commons after restrictions on the use of facilities were lifted for those who had not taken their oath of allegiance.

Until 1948, Oxford and Cambridge Universities had their own seats in the House of Commons.

When the House of Commons rises, a member of the police shouts, 'Who Goes Home?' The tradition began when members retiring to the same part of London were called to form groups for safety en route.

Snuff is provided at public expense to Members and Officers of the House. It is kept in a box by the entrance to the Chamber.

Until 1998, MPs could interrupt and delay debates by shouting, 'I spy strangers.' Proceedings would be brought to a halt while a motion to clear the visitors' galleries was considered. In the 1870s, an Irish Nationalist MP removed the Prince of Wales thus.

WHILE IN THE COMMONS CHAMBER, MEMBERS MUST NOT:

Smoke.

Eat or drink (except for the Chancellor, who may drink alcohol while delivering the Budget speech. Several chancellors have taken advantage of this privilege: Ken Clarke slugged whisky, Benjamin Disraeli drank brandy with water – Churchill did likewise without the water – while William Gladstone took sherry with a beaten egg. Geoffrey Howe preferred gin and tonic and Derick Heathcoat Amory mixed milk, honey and rum.)

Read books, magazines or letters.

Read pre-prepared speeches, though they may refer to notes.

Wear hats, military decorations or swords. There are loops of ribbon for each Member to leave their swords, which today are used for umbrellas.

Bring in dogs, except for guide dogs.

Refer to each other by name. (see 'Terms of Address'.)

Have their hands in their pockets. (Conservative MP Andrew Robathan was censured for doing this in 1994.)

Die. (As the House is a Royal Palace where commoners are not allowed to die, any Member who expires there is said to have died at St Thomas's Hospital.)

TERMS OF ADDRESS IN THE COMMONS

'The Honourable Member for...' – a backbench MP

'The Right Honourable Member...' – a Privy Councillor (current or past senior minister or member)

'The Noble Lord, the Member...' – an MP with a courtesy title, such as the son of a duke or earl

'The Gallant Member...' – a Member who has been a commissioned officer in the armed forces

'The Learned Member...' – MPs who are senior barristers

'My Honourable Friend...' – a member of the same party

Prime Ministers
And their parties

18th Century

Sir Robert Walpole (1721–42)	Whig
Spencer Compton (1742–3)	Whig
Henry Pelham (1743–54)	Whig
Thomas Pelham-Holles (1754–6, 1757–62)	Whig
William Cavendish (1756–7)	Whig
John Stuart, Earl of Bute (1762–3)	Tory
George Grenville (1763–5)	Whig
Charles Wentworth (1765–6, 1782)	Whig
William Pitt 'The Elder' (1766–8)	Whig
Augustus Henry Fitzroy (1768–70)	Whig
Lord North (1770–82)	Tory
William Petty (1782–3)	Whig
William Bentinck (1783, 1807–1809)	Whig

19th Century

William Pitt 'The Younger' (1783–1801, 1804–1806)	Tory
Henry Addington (1801–1804)	Tory
William Wyndham Grenville (1806–1807)	Whig
Spencer Perceval (1809–12)	Tory
Robert Banks Jenkinson (1812–27)	Tory
George Canning (1827)	Tory
Frederick Robinson (1827–8)	Tory
Arthur Wellesley (1828–30)	Tory
Earl Grey (1830–34)	Whig
William Lamb (1834, 1835–41)	Whig

Sir Robert Peel (1834–5, 1841–6)	Tory
Earl Russell (1846–51, 1865–6)	Liberal
The Earl of Derby (1852, 1858–9, 1866–8)	Conservative
Earl of Aberdeen (1852–5)	Tory
Viscount Palmerston (1855–8, 1859–65)	Liberal
Benjamin Disraeli (1868, 1874–80)	Conservative
William Gladstone (1868–74, 1880–85, 1886, 1892–4)	Liberal
Robert Gascoyne-Cecil (1885–6, 1886–92, 1895–1902)	Conservative
The Earl of Rosebery (1894–5)	Liberal

20th Century

Arthur James Balfour (1902–1905)	Conservative
Henry Campbell-Bannerman (1905–1908)	Liberal
Herbert Henry Asquith (1908–16)	Liberal
David Lloyd George (1916–22)	Liberal
Andrew Bonar Law (1922–3)	Conservative
Stanley Baldwin (1923, 1924–9, 1935–7)	Conservative
James Ramsay MacDonald (1924, 1929–35)	Labour
Arthur Neville Chamberlain (1937–40)	Conservative
Sir Winston Churchill (1940–45, 1951–5)	Conservative
Clement Richard Attlee (1945–51)	Labour
Anthony Eden (1955–7)	Conservative
Harold Macmillan (1957–63)	Conservative
Sir Alec Douglas-Home (1963–4)	Conservative
Harold Wilson (1964–70, 1974–6)	Labour
Edward Heath (1970–74)	Conservative
James Callaghan (1976–9)	Labour
Margaret Thatcher (1979–90)	Conservative

| John Major (1990–97) | Conservative |
| Tony Blair (1997–) | Labour |

Pageantry

STATE OPENING OF PARLIAMENT

The Yeomen of the Guard and the police search the cellars of the Houses of Parliament in remembrance of the Gunpowder Plot of 1605. Black Rod, the queen's messenger, then bangs on the door to the House of Commons. The door is slammed in his face, to remind him of Parliament's rights. He knocks again, whereupon the door is opened for him to convey the sovereign's summons to the Speaker.

CHANGING OF THE GUARD

The Foot Guards at Buckingham Palace are changed daily at 11.30 a.m. during the summer months, and on alternate days during the winter, in a 45-minute ceremony accompanied by a Guards band.

TROOPING THE COLOUR

In the seventeenth century during the reign of Charles II, regimental colours would be regularly paraded in front of the troops so that they could recognize their standard on the battlefield. The Household Division has performed the Trooping of the Colour annually since 1748 on the sovereign's official birthday. Seventeen-year-old Marcus Sarjeant fired six blank shots at the Queen during the parade in 1981. He was unable to procure live ammunition, but became the first person to be tried for treason since 1966 and sentenced to five years' imprisonment.

CEREMONY OF THE KEYS

The ceremony has been performed nightly just before 10 p.m. at the Tower of London since the fourteenth century. The Chief Warder and the Escort of the Key secure the main gates and take the keys inside while the Last Post is sounded. The ceremony has only been delayed twice: by an air raid during the Second World War, whereupon an official letter of apology was written to George VI, who issued a royal pardon, and in 2003 when the Escort fell asleep on duty.

SWAN UPPING

Since the twelfth century the Crown has retained ownership of all unmarked mute swans in the country's open waters. The royal Swan Marker and the Swan Uppers of the Vintners' and Dyers' livery companies carry out a census of swans on the River Thames every July in full regalia.

The Honours System

ACTIVE ORDERS OF CHIVALRY AND THEIR ABBREVIATIONS

Most Noble Order of the Garter (founded 1348)*: Knight of the Garter/Lady of the Garter (KG/LG)

Most Ancient and Most Noble Order of the Thistle (1687)*: Knight of the Thistle/Lady of the Thistle (KT/LT)

Most Honourable Order of the Bath (1725): Grand Cross of the Bath, Knight Commander of the Bath/Dame Commander of the Order of the Bath, Companion of the Bath (GCB, KCB/DCB, CB)

Most Distinguished Order of St Michael and St George (1818): Grand Cross of St Michael and St George, Knight Commander of St Michael and St George/Dame Commander of the Order of St Michael and St George, Companion (of the Order of) St Michael and St George (GCMG, KCMG/DCMG, CMG)

Royal Victorian Order (1896)*: Grand Cross of the (Royal) Victorian Order (Knight), Knight Commander of the Royal Victorian Order/Dame Commander of the Royal Victorian Order, Commander of the Royal Victorian Order, Lieutenant of the Royal Victorian Order, Member of the Royal Victorian Order (GCVO, KCVO/DCVO, CVO, LVO, MVO)

Order of Merit (1902)*: (OM)

Most Excellent Order of the British Empire (1917): Grand Cross of the British Empire (Knight or Dame), Knight Commander of the Order of the British Empire/Dame Commander of the Order of the British Empire, Companion of the Order of the British Empire, Office/Officer of the Order of the British Empire, Member of the Order of the British Empire (GBE, KBE/DBE, CBE, OBE, MBE)

Order of the Companions of Honour (1917): (CH)

* Conferred on the personal decision of the monarch.

THE ORDER OF MERIT

The Order was founded by Edward VII in 1902 to recognize outstanding contributions to the arts and sciences and the military. It is limited to twenty-five members including the monarch, who may confer the honour without reference to the government of the day.

Current Members

HRH The Duke of Edinburgh	Royal Consort
The Revd Owen Chadwick	Theological historian
Sir Andrew Huxley	Physiologist
Dr Frederick Sanger	Biochemist
Baroness Thatcher	Prime Minister (1979–90)
Dame Joan Sutherland	Soprano
Sir Michael Atiyah	Mathematician
Lucian Freud	Painter
Sir Aaron Klug	Biophysicist
Lord Foster of Thames Bank	Architect
Sir Denis Rooke	Engineer
Sir James Black	Pharmacologist
Sir Anthony Caro	Sculptor
Sir Roger Penrose	Mathematical physicist
Sir Tom Stoppard	Playwright
HRH The Prince of Wales	Heir to the Throne
Lord May of Oxford	Ecologist
Lord Rothschild	Philanthropist
Sir David Attenborough	Naturalist and broadcaster
Baroness Boothroyd	First female Speaker of the House of Commons
Sir Michael Howard	Military historian

PEERAGES

Hereditary ranks:

1. Duke
2. Marquess
3. Earl
4. Viscount
5. Baron

Life peerages were introduced in 1876. Hereditary titles no longer confer the automatic right to a seat in the House of Lords.

Baronetcy: This confers the hereditary title 'Sir' or 'Dame' and the suffix 'Bt'.

Knighthood: Confers the title 'Sir' or 'Dame'.

'Lordships of the Manor' are not true titles and only denote a form of property ownership. They cannot be stated on a passport and do not entitle the owner to a coat of arms.

The sale of honours is prohibited under the Honours (Prevention of Abuses) Act, 1925.

The Crown Jewels

King John lost the first Crown Jewels to an incoming tide in the Wash while fighting the French Dauphin Louis's army in 1216.

The second set was melted down by Oliver Cromwell in 1649 as symbols of 'the detestable rule of kings'. The only original items to survive are the Coronation Chair, the Golden Ampulla ('Sacred Eagle'), three swords and a spoon. Many of the gems were later recovered and set into the third Crown Jewels made at a cost of £12,185 for Charles II's coronation in 1661.

The jewels have been pawned twice to pay for wars: by Edward III and by Charles I's queen.

James II spent £12,000 restoring the Crown of England after he discovered that many of its gems had been stolen and replaced by fakes.

The present Crown Jewels are kept in the Tower of London and brought out for coronation ceremonies and other state occasions. They are valued at around £20 million.

In 1671, Colonel Thomas Blood ('Captain Blood') disguised himself as a priest and led three accomplices to steal the Crown Jewels from the Tower. They tricked a guard into showing them the collection and then knocked him unconscious. Blood hammered St Edward's Crown flat and hid it in his clothes, while another man stuffed the Sovereign's Orb down his trousers. Another gang member sawed the Sceptre with the Cross in two. They were caught at the gates, but Charles II was so impressed with their nerve that he granted Blood a reprieve and awarded him an annual pension.

THE COLLECTION

Coronation Chair

St Edward's Crown

Imperial State Crown (inset with the Stuart Sapphire, the Black Prince's Ruby and St Edward's Sapphire)

Imperial Crown of India

George IV State Diadem

Mary of Modena's Crowns

Sceptre with the Cross (represents the sovereign's temporal power)

Sceptre with the Dove (represents the sovereign's spiritual role)

Sovereign's Orb (represents the sovereign as the head of the Church of England)

Jewelled Sword of Offering

Sword of State

Swords of Justice, Spiritual Justice and Mercy

Golden Ampulla and Anointing Spoon (the Ampulla, or 'Sacred Eagle' holds the anointing oil)

Golden Armills (bracelets representing sincerity and wisdom)

The Koh-i-Noor Diamond (106 carats)

Spurs (representing knighthood and chivalry)

6

THE ENGLISH LANGUAGE

Evolution of the Tongue

'Old English', spoken between the fifth and twelfth centuries, was a West Germanic offshoot of the proto-Indo-European tongue spoken in south-east Europe around five thousand years ago. Modern English sentences rely on word order to convey meaning, whereas Old English, like most other European languages today, used different case endings. The most famous Old English work is the epic poem, *Beowulf*.

The 'Middle English' of Chaucer's *Canterbury Tales* was the result of the Norman French influence after 1066.

'Modern English' dates from the late fifteenth century and coincides with the change in pronunciation known as the Great Vowel Shift, before which 'a' was always pronounced 'ah' and 'ea' was pronounced 'ay'. Among other changes, Modern English collapsed the second person pronouns 'thou' and 'thee' and the plural 'ye' and 'you' into one word, 'you'. The language most closely related to modern English is Frisian, which is still spoken in Friesland in the Netherlands.

Dr Samuel Johnson (1709–84)

Johnson was the son of a bookseller from Lichfield in Staffordshire.

As an infant he suffered from scrofula, a tuberculous skin disease known as 'the king's evil' to those who believed it could be cured by the monarch's touch. At the age of 2, he was taken to London to be touched by the queen, but the treatment did not prove to be effective. A succession of quack remedies left him so disfigured that strangers presumed him mentally disabled until he spoke. He also became almost blind in one eye and deaf in one ear, and he would suffer bouts of depression throughout his life. These were compounded by various tics and spasms that have been likened to Tourette's Syndrome.

He was thrashed so brutally by his schoolmaster John Hunter that years afterwards the poet Anna Seward's resemblance to her grandfather made Johnson shake with fear.

In 1735 he married Elizabeth Porter, a widow twenty years older than him.

Johnson opened a school where he taught David Garrick, who became the greatest actor of his day. The two were lifelong friends, despite Garrick regularly performing a cruel impression of Johnson and his wife.

Johnson opined that 'No man but a blockhead ever wrote except for money', yet he gave generous terms to booksellers and wrote several prefaces for books by friends without accepting a penny in return.

He wrote the notorious essay *Taxation No Tyranny*, in which he ridiculed the rebellious American colonies for their hypocrisy, famously adding 'How is it that we hear the loudest yelps for liberty from the drivers of Negroes?' Johnson treated his own black servant Francis Barber like a son and made him his heir.

He was a cat lover who bought oysters for his pets when he could afford it.

Johnson is buried in Westminster Abbey.

Quotations Include

'A cucumber should be well sliced, and dressed with pepper and vinegar, and then thrown out, as good for nothing.'

'A woman's preaching is like a dog's walking on his hind legs. It is not done well; but you are surprised to find it done at all.'

'A second marriage is the triumph of hope over experience.'

'Patriotism is the last refuge of a scoundrel.'

JOHNSON'S DICTIONARY

Samuel Johnson's *Dictionary of the English Language* was published in two volumes weighing 20lbs (9 kilos) in 1755. It was an instant best-seller despite costing £4 10 shillings (over £500 in today's money). The 42,773 entries had taken its author over eight years to compile. Johnson was originally supposed to produce the work in just three years, even though the same task had taken forty scholars of the French Academy forty years. As he remarked, 'Forty times forty is sixteen hundred. As three to sixteen hundred, so is the proportion of an Englishman to a Frenchman.' Johnson was aided by six clerks, but he did most of the work himself and employed them largely out of kindness because they needed the money.

Johnson feared that England was 'deviating towards a Gallick structure and phraseology' that would 'reduce us to babble a dialect of France'. He resolved, 'We have long preserved our constitution, let us make some struggles for our language.' French words such as 'champagne', 'blonde' and 'bourgeois' were banned, but 'ruse' was grudgingly included as 'a French word neither elegant nor necessary'.

It was not the first English dictionary – Robert Cawdrey's *Table Alphabeticall of Hard Words* was published in 1604. But Johnson's was the first to include common usages and was noted for its clear definitions and insistence that the true meaning of a word was given not by its etymology but by how the finest writers in the language used it. Johnson marshalled over 100,000 quotations for the purpose. The *Dictionary* was updated several times in its author's lifetime and gave a chronicle of the language as it developed.

The Personal Touch

The *Dictionary* reflected Johnson's prejudices and sense of humour. Entries included:

Excise: 'a hateful tax levied upon commodities, and adjudged not by the common judges of property, but wretches hired by those to whom excise is paid.'

Lexicographer: 'a writer of dictionaries; a harmless drudge.'

Oats: 'a grain which in England is generally given to horses, but in Scotland supports the people.'

Patron: 'commonly a wretch who supports with insolence and is paid with flattery.' (Johnson's supposed patron was the Earl of Chesterfield, who had been tardy with his aid.)

Pension: 'In England it is generally understood to mean pay given to a state hireling for treason to his country.' (The government later awarded him a pension of £300 a year after he publicly opposed the Seven Years War.)

Stockjobber: 'a low wretch who gets money by buying and selling shares.'

Omissions include: athlete, bang, budge, fuss, gambler, literary, port, shabby and touchy. There were no entries beginning with the letter x.

According to Johnson's preface, the *Dictionary* 'was written with little assistance of the learned, and without any patronage of the great; not in the soft obscurities of retirement, or under the shelter of academick bowers, but amid inconvenience and distraction, in sickness and in sorrow... I have protracted my work till most of those whom I wished to please have sunk into the grave, and success and miscarriage are empty sounds: I therefore dismiss it with frigid tranquillity, having little to fear or hope from censure or from praise.'

Roget's Thesaurus

Peter Mark Roget (1779–1869) was the son of a pastor from Geneva and brought up in London's French Protestant community.

He was elected a fellow of the Royal Society after a long medical career. He also invented the 'log-log' slide rule for calculating the roots and powers of numbers and did the first research on moving images. His paper on the 'Persistence of Vision' – an optical illusion he had noticed while watching the wheels of a horse-drawn carriage through the blinds of a window – laid down the principles that led to cinema and television. Other achievements included inventing a water filtration system still used in London and contributing around 300,000 words to the *Encyclopaedia Britannica*.

Roget's *Thesaurus of English Words and Phrases* began as a list of synonyms he compiled in notebooks to aid his writing and lecturing, starting in 1805. He extended the project after he retired as Secretary of the Royal Society in 1848. The first edition was published in 1852 when Roget was 73. It was revised by three generations of the Roget family.

Thesaurus is Latin for 'treasury' or 'storehouse'.

The *Thesaurus* is divided into six classes of meanings: Abstract Relations, Space, Matter, Intellect, Volition and Emotion. It begins with the entry on Existence and ends with Temple.

The Oxford English Dictionary

In 1857, the Philological Society of London decided to begin a complete re-examination of the language from Anglo-Saxon times onward. A team headed by James Murray began work on the 'New English Dictionary' in 1878, expecting that it would take them ten years to complete. Five years later they were still on the word 'ant'. The first edition of the OED was eventually published in 1928.

The OED is continually updated and contains over 616,500 word-forms. The second edition (1989) runs to 21,730 printed pages over twenty volumes taking up 4 feet of shelf space and weighing 150 lbs.

The longest word is 'Pneumonoultramicroscopicsilicovolcano-coniosis' (45 letters): 'a lung condition caused by the inhalation of very fine silica dust'.

The most quoted author in the OED is William Shakespeare, and the most quoted work is the Bible. George Eliot is the most quoted female author.

The OED lists 464 definitions of the word 'set'. Next come 'run' (396), 'go' (368), 'take' (343), 'stand' (334), 'get' (289), 'turn' (288), 'put' (268), 'fall' (264) and 'strike' (250).

Curiosities

Around forty words of the pre-Indo-European tongue survive. They include apple, bad, gold and tin.

English is the world's most common language taught as a second language: 337 million people speak English as their first language, and 350 million as their second.

There are no English words that rhyme with month, orange, purple or silver.

'Floccinaucinihilipilification' – the act of estimating as worthless – is the longest 'real' word in the English language, not counting scientific terms. In the *Oxford English Dictionary*, it is the longest word that does not contain the letter 'e'.

The highest scoring seven-letter word in Scrabble is 'MUZJIKS' (Russian peasants), worth 79 points (including the 50-point bonus for using all your letters).

Over 80 per cent of the world's electronically stored information is in English.

Foreigners' Favourite English Words
Chosen by a worldwide British Council survey in 2004

Mother	Eternity	Liberty
Passion	Fantastic	Tranquillity
Smile	Destiny	Peace
Love	Freedom	Blossom

Sunshine	Moment	Smashing
Sweetheart	Extravaganza	Whoops
Gorgeous	Aqua	Tickle
Cherish	Sentiment	Loquacious
Enthusiasm	Cosmopolitan	Flip-flop
Hope	Bubble	Smithereens
Grace	Pumpkin	Oi
Rainbow	Banana	Gazebo
Blue	Lollipop	Hiccup
Sunflower	If	Hodgepodge
Twinkle	Bumblebee	Shipshape
Serendipity	Giggle	Explosion
Bliss	Paradox	Fuselage
Lullaby	Delicacy	Zing
Sophisticated	Peekaboo	Gum
Renaissance	Umbrella	Hen night
Cute	Kangaroo	
Cosy	Flabbergasted	
Butterfly	Hippopotamus	
Galaxy	Gothic	
Hilarious	Coconut	

The Global Lingua Franca

Countries and territories where English is one of the official languages:

| Anguilla | Australia | Barbados |
| Antigua and Barbuda | The Bahamas | Belize |

Bermuda
Botswana
British Virgin
    Islands
Cameroon
Canada
Cayman Islands
Christmas Island
Cook Islands
Dominica
Falkland Islands
Fiji
Gambia
Ghana
Gibraltar
Grenada
Guam
Guernsey
Guyana
Hong Kong
India
Jamaica

Jersey
Kenya
Kiribati
Liberia
Lesotho
Malawi
Malta
Marshall Islands
Mauritius
Micronesia
Montserrat
Namibia
Nigeria
New Zealand*
Norfolk Island
Pakistan
Palau
Papua New Guinea
Philippines
Pitcairn Island
Republic of Ireland
Rwanda

St Kitts and Nevis
St Lucia
St Helena
St Vincent and the
    Grenadines
Seychelles
Sierra Leone
Singapore
Solomon Islands
South Africa
Swaziland
Trinidad and Tobago
Turks and Caicos
    Islands
Uganda
United Kingdom*
United States*
US Virgin Islands
Vanuatu
Zambia
Zimbabwe

* De facto only.

The Plain English Campaign

The campaign was set up by Chrissie Mayer in 1979 with the ceremonial shredding of incomprehensible government forms in Parliament Square. Mayer describes her battle against official jargon as 'like pushing water uphill with a rake'.

The 'Crystal Mark' is bestowed upon official documents that meet the Campaign's standards of clarity. Since 1990, the badge has been sought by over 1,200 organizations.

The Golden Bull Awards are given annually to the worst instances of gobbledygook. Winners have received a trophy since health regulations put paid to the original practice of sending a pound of tripe through the post.

The worst sentence ever cited was a 630-word example produced by Halton Borough Council on a notice advising the public of its plans to move a path from one place to another in 2005.

7

LITERATURE AND LETTERS

'The true greatness of a nation is not measured by the
vastness of its territory, or by the multitude of its
people, or by the profusion of its exports and imports;
but by the extent to which it has contributed to the life
and thought and progress of the world... That is why
the Wycliffes, Shakespeares, Miltons, Newtons,
Wesleys, and Gladstones of English history live, and
will live, in everlasting memory... A great nation is not
one which, like Russia, has an enormous territory; or,
like China, has an enormous population. It is the
nation which gives mankind new modes of thought,
new ideals of life, new hopes, new aspirations; which
lifts the world out of the rut, and sets it going on a
cleaner and brighter road.'

L. E. Blaze, Lecture at Dallas Baptist University Hall,
26 November 1926

Geoffrey Chaucer (c. 1342–1400)

Geoffrey Chaucer was born in London and came from a wealthy background, his family having made its fortune in wine and leather. He became a courtier and worked as a diplomat and civil servant under Edward III, Richard II and Henry IV, travelling to France, Spain and Italy.

Chaucer found himself in serious trouble several times. As a teenager he was captured by the French and ransomed. In his thirties he was charged with rape, though the matter was settled out of court. As an old man he was repeatedly robbed and beaten up – twice in the same day on one occasion – while working as comptroller of the petty customs and inspector of the king's buildings.

THE CANTERBURY TALES

The Canterbury Tales was written in the 1390s, about a band of thirty pilgrims who hold a storytelling contest amongst themselves as they travel from the Tabard Inn in Southwark to the shrine of Thomas Becket in Canterbury. There are twenty-four tales within the narrative, orchestrated by the character of the Tabard's landlord, Harry Bailey. However, the book was not completed. Chaucer never got around to covering the pilgrims' return journey, so some of them do not tell stories.

The work begins with 'The General Prologue' and ends with 'Chaucer's Retraction', in which the author asks that all who read the book pray for Christ to have mercy on him. Chaucer himself appears as a character. The tales run as follows:

The Knight's Tale

The Miller's Prologue and Tale

The Reeve's Prologue and Tale

The Cook's Prologue and Tale

The Man of Law's Introduction, Prologue, Tale and Epilogue

The Wife of Bath's Prologue and Tale

The Friar's Prologue and Tale

The Summoner's Prologue and Tale

The Clerk's Prologue and Tale

The Merchant's Prologue, Tale and Epilogue

The Squire's Introduction and Tale

The Franklin's Prologue and Tale

The Physician's Tale

The Pardoner's Introduction, Prologue and Tale

The Shipman's Tale

The Prioress's Prologue and Tale

Chaucer's Prologue, Tale of Sir Thopas and Tale of Melibee

The Monk's Prologue and Tale

The Nun's Priest's Prologue, Tale and Epilogue

The Second Nun's Prologue and Tale

The Canon's Yeoman's Prologue and Tale

The Manciple's Prologue and Tale

The Parson's Prologue and Tale

Chaucer was buried in Westminster Abbey.

William Shakespeare (1564–1616)

LIFE

There are thought to be only two authentic representations of the Bard: his engraved portrait on the title page of the 1623 First Folio and his monument in Stratford's Holy Trinity church.

Shakespeare's birthday is unrecorded but thought to be 23 April, which is also St George's Day.

His father Jonathan was bailiff (mayor) of Stratford-upon-Avon and his mother Mary was an heiress.

According to rumour, Shakespeare had to leave Stratford for London after he was accused of stealing a deer.

Shakespeare wrote his first play, Henry IV Part I, in either 1589 or 1590 when he was around 25 years old.

He was also an actor who performed in his own plays and those of Ben Jonson.

One of his plays, Cardenio, was performed in his lifetime but has since been lost without a trace.

He had three children with his wife Anne Hathaway. He married Anne when he was 18 and she was 26. He bequeathed most of his property to his eldest child Susanna, leaving his wife nothing save his 'second best bed' (which would have been the marital bed).

The character of Sir John Falstaff was based on Sir John Oldcastle, the Lollard leader and friend of Henry V who was condemned for heresy and slowly roasted to death.

No name was inscribed on Shakespeare's gravestone. Instead, the following lines appear, which may have been written by the playwright himself:

> Good friend, for Jesus' sake forbear
> To dig the dust enclosed here.
> Blest be the man that spares these stones,
> And curst be he that moves my bones.

The term 'bowdlerize' was coined in 1936 to refer to the way Thomas Bowdler censored material he thought unsuitable for women and children in his edition of the Bard's works, *The Family Shakespeare*.

Vocabulary

He had a vocabulary of 29,000 words – compared with 15,000 for the average English adult today. The word 'Bible' does not appear in any of his works.

Words invented by Shakespeare include 'assassination', 'bedroom', 'bump' and 'puke'.

Shakespearian Phrases

A fool's paradise – *Romeo and Juliet*
A foregone conclusion – *Othello*
A laughing stock – *The Merry Wives of Windsor*
A plague on both your houses – *Romeo and Juliet*
A sea change – *The Tempest*
A sorry sight – *Macbeth*
As dead as a doornail – *Henry VI*
As good luck would have it – *The Merry Wives of Windsor*
As pure as the driven snow – *The Winter's Tale/Macbeth*
At one fell swoop – *Macbeth*
Beast with two backs – *Othello*
Bloody minded – *Henry VI*
Crack of doom – *Macbeth*

Discretion is the better part of valour – *Henry IV, Part I*
Eaten out of house and home – *Henry V, Part II*
For ever and a day – *As You Like It*
Green-eyed monster – *Othello*
I will wear my heart upon my sleeve – *Othello*
In a pickle – *The Tempest*
In my mind's eye – *Hamlet*
In stitches – *Twelfth Night*
In the twinkling of an eye – *The Merchant of Venice*
Lay it on with a trowel – *As You Like It*
The milk of human kindness – *Macbeth*
More fool you – *The Taming of the Shrew*
Mum's the word – *Henry VI, Part II*
Neither here nor there – *Othello*
Send him packing – *Henry IV*
Set your teeth on edge – *Henry IV*
The game's afoot – *Henry V*
There's method in his madness ('though this be madness, yet there's
method in't') – *Hamlet*
This is the short and the long of it – *The Merry Wives of Windsor*
Too much of a good thing – *As You Like It*
Tower of strength – *Richard III*
Vanish into thin air – *Othello*

SHAKESPEARIAN INSULTS

'Sblood, you starveling, you elf-skin, you dried neat's-tongue, you
bull's pizzle, you stock-fish! O! for breath to utter what is like thee;
you tailor's yard, you sheath, you bow-case, you vile standing-tuck!
(*Henry IV, Part I*)

Away you three-inch fool. (*The Taming of the Shrew*)

Get thee to a nunnery! Why wouldst thou be a breeder of sinners? (*Hamlet*)

Vile worm, thou wast o'erlook'd even in thy birth. (*The Merry Wives of Windsor*)

Thou art a Castilian King Urinal! (*The Merry Wives of Windsor*)

A foul and pestilent congregation of vapours. What a piece of work is man! (*Hamlet*)

You egg! Young fry of treachery! (*Macbeth*)

You ruinous butt, you whoreson indistinguishable cur! (*Troilus and Cressida*)

Your beards deserve not so honourable a grave as to stuff a botcher's cushion or to be entombed in an ass's pack saddle. (*Coriolanus*)

Your peevish chastity is not worth a breakfast in the cheapest country. (*Pericles, Prince of Tyre*)

SHAKESPEARE'S PLAYS

Henry VI, Parts I, II and III	(1589–92)
Richard III	(1592–3)
The Comedy of Errors	(1592–3)
Titus Andronicus	(1593–4)
The Taming of the Shrew	(1593–4)
The Two Gentlemen of Verona	(1594–5)
Love's Labours Lost	(1594–5)
Romeo and Juliet	(1594–5)

Richard II	(1595–6)
A Midsummer Night's Dream	(1595–6)
King John	(1596–7)
The Merchant of Venice	(1596–7)
Henry IV, Parts I and II	(1597–8)
Much Ado About Nothing	(1598–9)
Henry V	(1598–9)
Julius Caesar	(1599–1600)
As You Like It	(1599–1600)
Hamlet	(1600–1601)
The Merry Wives of Windsor	(1600–1601)
Twelfth Night	(1601–1602)
Troilus and Cressida	(1601–1602)
All's Well That Ends Well	(1602–1603)
Measure for Measure	(1604–1605)
Othello	(1604–1605)
King Lear	(1605–1606)
Macbeth	(1605–1606)
Antony and Cleopatra	(1606–1607)
Coriolanus	(1607–1608)
Timon of Athens	(1607–1608)
Pericles	(1608–1609)
Cymbeline	(1609–10)
The Winter's Tale	(1610–11)
The Tempest	(1611–12)
Henry VIII★	(1612–13)
The Two Noble Kinsmen★	(1612–13)

★ The last two were probably co-written with John Fletcher. The Two Noble Kinsmen does not appear in the First Folio of 1623.

The Book of Common Prayer

Introduced in a period of intense religious upheaval, the Book of Common Prayer was the first official liturgy of the Church of England. The original version, written by Henry VIII's Archbishop of Canterbury, Thomas Cranmer, was issued in 1549.

FAMOUS PHRASES FROM THE BOOK OF COMMON PRAYER

'There was never any thing by the wit of man so well devised, or so sure established, which in continuance of time hath not been corrupted.'

'We have left undone those things which we ought to have done; And we have done those things which we ought not to have done; And there is no health in us.'

'Renounce the devil and all his works, the pomps and vanity of this wicked world, and all the sinful lusts of the flesh.'

'An outward and visible sign of an inward and spiritual grace.'

'With this ring I thee wed...'

'Let him now speak, or else hereafter for ever hold his peace.'

'Dearly beloved, we are gathered together here in the sight of God.'

'Those whom God hath joined together let no man put asunder.'

'In the midst of life we are in death.'

'Earth to earth, ashes to ashes, dust to dust.'

'Man that is born of woman hath but a short time to live, and is full of misery. He cometh up, and is cut down, like a flower; he fleeth as it were a shadow, and never continueth in one stay.'

The King James Bible

A church conference of 1604 at Hampton Court decreed that all existing translations of the Bible in English were 'corrupt and not answerable to the truth of the original'. James I took the opportunity to sponsor an alternative to the Puritans' Geneva Bible, which he hated. He added, 'If I mean to live under a presbytery, I will go into Scotland again.'

The King James Bible, otherwise known as the Authorized Version, has been called the only great work of English literature created by committee. The work was divided among forty-seven scholars in Oxford, Cambridge and Westminster who were approved by the king. The result was published in 1611.

Several editions contain notorious misprints. In the 'Vinegar Bible' of 1717, the Parable of the Vineyard in Luke 20 becomes 'The Parable of the Vinegar'. In the 'Wicked Bible' of 1631, Chapter 20, Verse 14 reads, 'Thou shalt commit adultery'. The printers were fined £300.

CONTRIBUTIONS TO THE LANGUAGE

The Authorized Version was a literal translation from the Hebrew that retained the idioms of the original. Read aloud, it would have sounded odd to its first public, but it gave us many now common phrases.

'Fall flat on his face'
'A man after his own heart'
'To pour out one's heart'
'The land of the living'
'From time to time'
'The skin of my teeth'
'To put words in his mouth'
'Like a lamb to the slaughter'
'Nothing new under the sun'
'The writing on the wall'
'The blind leading the blind'
'A fly in the ointment'

——

John Milton (1608–74)

——

> 'Let not England forget her precedence of teaching
> nations how to live.'

John Milton

Milton's father made a fortune as a notary and moneylender, and he gave his son an expensive education at St Paul's School, London, and Christ's College, Cambridge. The future poet would spend every day and night studying into the small hours. He blamed this exertion for his blindness in later life.

At Cambridge he was nicknamed 'The Lady' because of his feminine good looks and manner.

When Milton was 33, he took the teenage Mary Powell as his bride. She was so impressed with his erudition that not long afterwards she went on a visit to her family and refused to return. Mary was persuaded to rejoin him three years later and Milton took in her entire family of ten when they fell on hard times.

Milton campaigned for liberal values, including freedom of speech and the right to divorce on grounds of incompatibility. He also defended the execution of Charles I, which got him imprisoned briefly following the Restoration.

Paradise Lost (1667), Milton's version of the rebellion of Satan and the Fall of Man, is considered the greatest epic poem in the English language. It was written, he said, 'to justify the ways of God to men'.

―――

Jane Austen (1775–1817)

―――

Austen was a rector's daughter from Steventon in Hampshire, the seventh of eight children. She received a limited education and was tutored at home by her father.

She began writing when she was 12 years old and at 16 produced *The History of England*, a parody of Oliver Goldsmith's work of the same name. The subtitle read 'By a partial, prejudiced, & ignorant Historian... There will be very few Dates in this History.'

She never married. In around 1795, she flirted with Tom Lefroy, a family friend, but he was sent away to Ireland the following year. Lefroy's aunt later tried to set her up with the Reverend Samuel Blackall, who died before they could become engaged. In 1802 she accepted a proposal from a 21-year-old heir from Hampshire, Harris Bigg-Wither, but she changed her mind the next day. Her other love interests are unknown, as her sister Cassandra destroyed much of her private correspondence after her death.

The original title of *Pride and Prejudice* was *First Impressions*. *Northanger Abbey* was at first titled *Susan*. Austen's first published novel, *Sense and Sensibility*, was originally *Elinor and Marianne*.

During Austen's lifetime, her name did not appear on the title pages of her books, which instead read 'By a lady'.

The Prince Regent admired her works so much that he kept a complete set in each of his residences and asked her to dedicate a book to him. Though she disapproved of the prince's playboy lifestyle, she indulged him against her better judgement with her novel *Emma*.

She died from what is now thought to have been Addison's disease (the hormonal disorder suffered by John F. Kennedy that causes weight loss and fatigue) and was buried in Winchester Cathedral. Her memorial stone mentions nothing about her writing.

AUSTEN'S NOVELS

Sense and Sensibility (1811)
Pride and Prejudice (1813)
Mansfield Park (1814)
Emma (1816)
Northanger Abbey (1817)
Persuasion (1817)

The last two works were published posthumously.

The Brontë Sisters

The Brontës were the daughters of an Irish curate and his Cornish wife. Patrick Brunty had changed his name to Brontë upon taking a place at St John's College, Cambridge, and later became a published author himself. His daughters grew up in Haworth Rectory on the Yorkshire Moors. Two elder sisters – Maria and Elizabeth – died young.

Their brother Patrick Branwell Brontë showed early promise but sank into alcoholism and opium addiction. According to Charlotte's biographer, Elizabeth Gaskell, he at least earned 'the undesirable distinction of having his company recommended by the landlord of the Black Bull to any chance traveller who might happen to feel solitary or dull over his liquor'.

The girls began writing when they were very young – their first efforts were miniature tomes designed for their brother's set of toy soldiers. The desolate landscape around the Rectory left them to construct imaginary worlds for one another as children. In 1846 they jointly published a book of verse under pseudonyms: *Poems by Currer, Ellis and Acton Bell*. The work sold two copies.

Anne (1820–49), the youngest of the sisters, wrote two novels under the pen name 'Acton Bell'. *Agnes Grey* (1847) and *The Tenant of Wildfell Hall* (1848) were published before her death from consumption.

Emily (1818–48), under the name 'Ellis Bell', wrote only one novel: *Wuthering Heights*. This great classic, regarded as the finest work of any of the sisters, was published to poor reviews in 1847.

Charlotte (1816–55), aka 'Currer Bell', was the most successful during their lifetime. *Jane Eyre: An Autobiography* was published within eight weeks of being submitted in 1847 and became a bestseller.

In July 1848, Anne and Charlotte travelled to London and revealed their identities to Charlotte's publisher George Smith after his rival Thomas Cautley Newby attempted to capitalize on Currer Bell's fame by publishing Anne's second novel under the same moniker.

Patrick, Emily and Anne died of consumption within nine months of one another between 1848 and 1849.

Charlotte rejected a proposal of marriage from her father's curate, Arthur Bell Nichols, but her father was so angry that such a poor man should ask for the hand of his illustrious daughter that she later felt sorry for the man and relented in 1854. The marriage was happy but brief; Charlotte died while pregnant the following year.

Alfred Lord Tennyson (1809–92)

Tennyson was the son of an alcoholic Lincolnshire rector. He enjoyed swift success as a poet after leaving Cambridge University without a degree.

He succeeded William Wordsworth as Poet Laureate in 1850. After Tennyson died in 1892, the office was left vacant for four years as a mark of respect for his excellence in the role.

The final draft of The Charge of the Light Brigade was toned down to make the poem less critical of the Brigade's commanders. (The first stanza originally contained the line 'For up came an order which/ Someone had blunder'd.') A recording made by Thomas Edison in 1890 of Tennyson reading the poem survives to this day.

FAMOUS WORKS

Mariana (1830)
The Kraken (1830)
The Lady of Shalott (two versions, 1833 and 1842)
The Lotos-Eaters (1842)
Morte d'Arthur (1842)
Ulysses (1842)

In Memoriam (1850)
The Charge of the Light Brigade (1855)
Idylls of the King (1842–85)

___

Charles Dickens (1812–70)

___

Dickens was born in Portsmouth, the son of a clerk in the Navy pay office. Mr Micawber in *David Copperfield* was based on this spendthrift father who almost bankrupted the family on several occasions.

When his father ended up in a debtors' prison, the 12-year-old Charles was taken out of school and sent to work for three years in a boot-polish factory. This encounter with working-class life was to provide material for writing, including the name of the character Fagin.

Dickens was a skilled hypnotist and used hypnosis (or mesmerism as it was then called) to cure a woman of facial tics caused by anxiety.

In 1865, Dickens survived a train wreck at Staplehurst in which ten people died and fifty were injured. His carriage was left hanging off a bridge while others fell into the ravine below. The writer helped the casualties and felt calm immediately afterwards, but he later suffered a variety of post-traumatic stress disorder and was unable to travel on express trains again due to his nerves.

Dickens suffered episodes of insomnia during which he would spend the nights walking the streets of London. To stand any chance of falling asleep he had to lie exactly in the centre of the mattress, preferably facing north. He thought out *A Christmas Carol* during a 20-mile march and finished the tale in six weeks. The work made him both laugh and cry.

Dickens's first stories were published under the pen name 'Boz', a corruption of Moses – his favourite character in *The Vicar of Wakefield* by Oliver Goldsmith.

At times adaptations of his work were performed in twenty London theatres simultaneously.

He died with the novel *Edwin Drood* unfinished and was buried in Westminster Abbey.

DICKENS ON THE FRENCH REVOLUTION

The opening of *A Tale of Two Cities*: 'It was the best of times, it was the worst of times, it was the age of wisdom, it was the age of foolishness, it was the epoch of belief, it was the epoch of incredulity, it was the season of Light, it was the season of Darkness, it was the spring of hope, it was the winter of despair, we had everything before us, we had nothing before us, we were all going direct to Heaven, we were all going direct the other way.'

DICKENS'S MAJOR WORKS

Sketches by Boz (1836)
Pickwick Papers (1836–7)
Oliver Twist (1837–9)
Nicholas Nickleby (1838–9)
The Old Curiosity Shop (1840–41)
Barnaby Rudge (1841)
Martin Chuzzlewit (1843–4)
A Christmas Carol (1843)
Dombey and Son (1846–8)
David Copperfield (1849–50)
Bleak House (1852–3)
Hard Times (1854)

Little Dorrit (1855–7)
A Tale of Two Cities (1859)
Great Expectations (1860–61)
Our Mutual Friend (1864–5)
The Mystery of Edwin Drood (1870)

Anthony Trollope (1815–82)

Trollope first created fictional worlds as a form of escapism while he was a boy at Harrow and Winchester public schools, where he was friendless and regularly thrashed.

He failed to win a scholarship to university and joined the Post Office as a clerk, but he worked his way up to become Surveyor General and introduced the iconic red pillar box. He left in 1867 to stand for Parliament as a Liberal candidate, and took up writing full time when he failed.

Trollope wrote forty-seven novels, including:

THE BARSETSHIRE CHRONICLES

The Warden (1855)
Barchester Towers (1857)
Doctor Thorne (1858)
Framley Parsonage (1861)
The Small House at Allington (1864)
The Last Chronicle of Barset (1867)

THE PALLISER NOVELS

Can You Forgive Her? (1864)

Phineas Finn (1869)
The Eustace Diamonds (1873)
Phineas Redux (1874)
The Prime Minister (1876)
The Duke's Children (1879)

George Eliot (1819–80)

LIFE AND LOVES

George Eliot was the pen name of Mary Ann Evans, which she took in order to be seen as a man and thus considered a 'serious' author. She published only one book under her real name – a translation of Ludwig Feuerbach's *Essence of Christianity* (1854).

When she was 60 she married her friend John Cross, a man over twenty years her junior. During their honeymoon in Venice, Cross 'fell' from a balcony in what was thought to be a suicide attempt.

Several times in her life she suffered cruel remarks about her appearance, yet men often found her attractive. She inspired her lover Herbert Spencer to write essays on ugliness, while Henry James was moved to write, 'She is magnificently ugly – deliciously hideous... Now in this vast ugliness resides a most powerful beauty which, in a very few minutes steals forth and charms the mind, so that you end as I ended, in falling in love with her. Yes behold me in love with this great horse-faced bluestocking.'

Spencer made an exception for her novels when he banned all other fiction from the London Library.

ELIOT'S MAJOR NOVELS

Adam Bede (1859)
The Mill on the Floss (1860)
Silas Marner (1861)
Felix Holt, the Radical (1866)
Middlemarch (1871–2)
The Legend of Jubal (1874)
Daniel Deronda (1876)

***

Thomas Hardy (1840–1928)

***

Hardy was the son of a Dorset stonemason. His mother taught him to read before he went to school.

He worked as an architect before he achieved literary success. He destroyed the manuscript of his first novel, *The Poor Man and the Lady*, completed in 1868, when it failed to attract a publisher. Only fragments of the work survive today.

His novels were set largely in Wessex, a fictional county based on Dorset and its neighbours. His finest works, written from the mid 1870s onwards, were criticized as immoral and he swore never to write another novel after *Jude the Obscure* was published in 1895. Thenceforth he devoted himself to poetry.

Hardy's first wife, Emma, died in 1912, but two years later, when he was aged 74, he married Florence Dugdale, a woman forty years his junior.

His ashes were interred in Poets' Corner in Westminster Abbey, but his heart was buried at Stinsford Church, outside Dorchester.

Hardy divided his fiction into three categories:

'NOVELS OF CHARACTER AND ENVIRONMENT'

Under the Greenwood Tree (1872)
Far from the Madding Crowd (1874)
The Return of the Native (1878)
The Mayor of Casterbridge (1886)
The Woodlanders (1887)
Wessex Tales (1888)
Tess of the d'Urbervilles (1891)
Life's Little Ironies (1894)
Jude the Obscure (1895)

'ROMANCES AND FANTASIES'

A Pair of Blue Eyes (1873)
The Trumpet-Major (1880)
Two on a Tower (1882)
A Group of Noble Dames (1891)
The Well-Beloved (1897) (first published as a serial from 1892)

'NOVELS OF INGENUITY'

Desperate Remedies (1871)
The Hand of Ethelberta (1876)
A Laodicean (1881)

Rudyard Kipling (1865–1936)

Kipling was born in Bombay, the son of a scholar and museum curator, but he was taken to England when he was 6 years old and spent five years in a hated foster home. His life became worse at the

United Services College in Devon, a minor public school where he was treated brutally and where his eyesight deteriorated. However, he grew fond of the school's values, and its mix of cruelty and nobility are remembered warmly in his 1899 book, Stalky & Co.

He fell in love with Flo Garrard, a fellow boarder at his foster home, but she did not return his affections and declined to keep in touch with him after he went back to India in 1882, where he worked as a journalist for seven years. On his return to England, Kipling bumped into Flo walking along the Embankment and pursued her to Paris (where she was to become a painter), but she rejected him again. It transpired that she was a lesbian, and the experience was written up as his first novel, The Light That Failed.

His story The Man Who Would Be King was based on the life of an American – the mercenary Josiah Harlan, a lapsed Quaker and Freemason from Pennsylvania who made himself a tribal prince in Afghanistan.

In 1907 he became the first Englishman to win the Nobel Prize for Literature. At 41, he was, and still is, the youngest ever recipient. He refused a knighthood, the Order of Merit and the post of Poet Laureate.

An Australian fan once sent Kipling a dollar and a request for his autograph, adding that he understood that the great writer charged a dollar per word. Kipling sent a single word in reply: 'Thanks'.

In the years before and after the First World War, Kipling lived in France so that he could indulge his passion for driving automobiles on the country's smoother roads and take breaks at its superior motorway cafés.

Lines from his poem If are displayed above the players' entrance to Wimbledon's Centre Court.

Kipling lost his only son John at the Battle of Loos in France in

1915. He was later asked to write an epitaph for the nation's war dead, but the authorities declined to use the following part of his contribution: 'Had our fathers not lied to us, so many of us would not be here.'

He was buried in Poets' Corner in Westminster Abbey.

Kipling has suffered unjustly at the hands of political correctness and been wrongly vilified as a racist, even though his most famous line is 'You are a better man than I, Gunga Din', while the 'lesser breeds' he referred to were Kaiser Wilhelm's Germans, who disgraced the imperialist mission with their brutality in Africa and China. He also warned against allowing the Boers to establish a system of apartheid in South Africa. The first line of *The Ballad of East and West* reads, 'Oh, East is East, and West is West and never the twain shall meet.' However, it continues, 'But there is neither East nor West, Border, nor Breed, nor Birth/When two strong men stand face to face, though they come from the ends of the Earth!' The charge of fascism is even more indefensible considering how Kipling railed against the appeasement of Adolf Hitler in his dying days.

KIPLING'S MOST FAMOUS WORKS

The Phantom Rickshaw (1888)
The Light That Failed (1891)
Barrack Room Ballads (1892 and 1896)
The Jungle Book (1894)
The Second Jungle Book (1895)
Captains Courageous (1896)
Stalky & Co. (1899)
Kim (1901)
Just So Stories (1902)
Puck of Pook's Hill (1906)

Evelyn Waugh (1903–66)

Waugh was the son of a Hampstead publisher. He won a scholarship to read history at Oxford University, but he left without taking his degree rather than accept the third-class honours he was due having spent his college years drinking, socializing and experimenting with same sex partners. He later converted to Catholicism and hetero-sexuality.

While working as a teacher in 1925, he tried to commit suicide by swimming out to sea, but he turned back after he was stung by a jellyfish. Two years later he was sacked for making improper advances to the school matron.

The aristocrats in Brideshead Revisited were based on Waugh's Oxford contemporary, Hughie Lygon and his eccentric family. Lygon was the son of the Seventh Earl of Beauchamp and the 'real' Brideshead was his family's pile, Madresfield Court, which boasted 4,000 acres (1619 hectares) and its own railway station.

William Boot, the anti-hero of Scoop, was based on the Daily Telegraph's now veteran correspondent William Deedes, with whom he covered the war in Abyssinia in the 1930s.

Waugh served in the commandos during the Second World War. When the war was over, he would make his children watch as he ate their banana rations with cream and sugar. He explained, 'I despise all my seven children equally.'

WAUGH'S NOVELS
Decline and Fall (1928)
Vile Bodies (1930)

Black Mischief (1932)

A Handful of Dust (1934)

Scoop (1938)

Put Out More Flags (1942)

Brideshead Revisited (1945)

The Loved One (1947)

Helena (1950)

Love Among the Ruins: A Romance of the Near Future (1953)

The Ordeal of Gilbert Pinfold (1957)

Men at Arms (1952)

Officers and Gentlemen (1955)

Unconditional Surrender (1961)

The final three books make up the 'Sword of Honour' trilogy.

George Orwell (1903–50)

'To look at the places where his wisdom has been
invoked recently is to wonder if there is anyone,
excepting Stalinists, who would not think better of an
opinion knowing it to be one that Orwell endorsed.'

Catherine Bennett in the *Guardian*, 13 April 2006

Orwell occupies a unique place in modern English letters as a deeply
political man who has become a hero for both the left and the right.
He was born in Bengal, India, and his real name was Eric Arthur
Blair. He took his pen name from the River Orwell in East Anglia.

He won a scholarship to Eton College, where he was taught by

Aldous Huxley. He decided not to go on to university in order to join the Indian Imperial Police. His experiences as a civil servant in Burma turned him against colonialism.

Orwell disliked pacifists, explaining, 'Those who "abjure" violence can only do so because others are committing violence on their behalf', and lamenting, 'If only every vegetarian, teetotaller and creeping Jesus [could be] sent home to Welwyn Garden City to do his yoga exercises quietly!' In 1945, in *Notes on Nationalism*, he wrote, 'Pacifist propaganda usually boils down to saying that one side is as bad as the other, but if one looks closely at the writing... they do not as a rule condemn violence as such, but only violence used in defence of the western countries.'

He volunteered to fight for the socialists during the Spanish Civil War, where he was affiliated with the POUM workers' organization. Their mistreatment by the Stalinists opened his eyes to the evils of communism. In the Second World War he was declared physically unfit to fight due to wounds sustained whilst fighting in Spain.

Frederic Warburg published *Animal Farm*, Orwell's satire on the USSR, to the opposition of his wife and his sales manager, who both refused to believe that the Soviet Union was not a socialist Utopia. At the time, it was considered outrageous to criticize England's wartime ally, but western opinion soon changed as the Cold War got under way. The animated adaptation of the novel produced in 1954 was financed by the CIA.

He died from tuberculosis when he was 46.

ORWELL ON ENGLISHNESS

'The English share an unconscious patriotism and an inability to think logically.'

'Nearly every Englishman of working-class origin considers it effeminate to pronounce a foreign word correctly.'

'The horse plough will give way to the tractor... but England will still be England.'

'[The goose-step] is not used [here] because the people in the street would laugh.'

'The most stirring battle-poem in English is about a brigade of cavalry which charged in the wrong direction.'

'The outstanding quality of the English is their habit of not killing one another.'

'A family with the wrong members in control – that, perhaps, is as near as one can come to describing England in a phrase.'

ORWELL'S MAJOR WORKS

Down and Out in Paris and London (1933)
Burmese Days (1934)
A Clergyman's Daughter (1935)
Keep the Aspidistra Flying (1936)
The Road to Wigan Pier (1937)
Homage to Catalonia (1938)
Coming up for Air (1939)
The Lion and the Unicorn (1941)
Animal Farm (1945)
Nineteen Eighty-Four (1949)

The Bloomsbury Group

The Bloomsbury Group was a circle of English intellectuals and artists who met in the London district of Bloomsbury from 1907 to around 1930. It grew out of the 'Apostles', who had been members of a secretive, elitist discussion group at Cambridge University.

PROMINENT MEMBERS

Clive Bell (1881–1964) – art critic
Leonard Woolf (1880–1969) – activist
Virginia Woolf (1882–1941) – novelist
Bertrand Russell (1872–1970) – philosopher
Roger Fry (1866–1934) – artist
E. M. Forster (1879–1970) – novelist
Lytton Strachey (1880–1932) – biographer
John Maynard Keynes (1883–1946) – economist
Aldous Huxley (1894–1963) – novelist
T. S. Eliot (1888–1965) – poet
Desmond MacCarthy (1877–1952) – journalist
Arthur Waley (1889–1966) – sinologist
Robert Trevelyan (1872–1951) – poet

English Murder Mystery Writers
And their detectives

R. Austin Freeman (1862–1943)	Dr Thorndyke
G. K. Chesterton (1887–1936)	Father Brown
Agatha Christie (1890–1976)	Hercule Poirot, Miss Marple
Dorothy L. Sayers (1893–1957)	Lord Peter Wimsey
Anthony Berkeley (1893–1971)	Roger Sheringham
Margery Allingham (1904–66)	Albert Campion
Christianna Brand (1907–88)	Inspector Cockrill
John Creasey (1908–73)	Inspector Gideon, Inspector West, Sexton Blake
Julian Symons (1912–94)	Inspector Bland, Inspector Crambo
Ellis Peters (1913–95)	Brother Cadfael
Edmund Crispin (1921–78)	Gervase Fen
P. D. James (1920–)	Commander Dalgleish, Cordelia Gray
H. R. F. Keating (1926–)	Inspector Ghote
Colin Dexter (1930–)	Inspector Morse
Ruth Rendell (1930–)	Inspector Wexford

The 'Perfect' English Murder

'From a *News of the World* reader's point of view', as expressed by George Orwell in *The Decline of the English Murder* (1930):

'The murderer should be a little man of the professional class – a dentist or a solicitor, say – living an intensely respectable life somewhere in the suburbs, and preferably in a semi-detached house, which will allow the neighbours to hear suspicious sounds through the wall. He should be either chairman of the local Conservative Party branch, or a leading Nonconformist and strong Temperance advocate. He should go astray through cherishing a guilty passion for his secretary or the wife of a rival professional man, and should only bring himself to the point of murder after long and terrible wrestles with his conscience. Having decided on murder, he should plan it all with the utmost cunning, and only slip up over some tiny unforeseeable detail. The means chosen should, of course, be poison. In the last analysis he should commit murder because this seems to him less disgraceful, and less damaging to his career, than being detected in adultery.'

The 'Angry Young Men'

The name was given to the loose collection of young novelists, poets and playwrights who railed against life in post-war England in the 1950s, often through the medium of working-class social realism. The press picked up on the term after the Royal Court Theatre's publicist described John Osborne as 'an angry young man'.

THE ANGRIES AND THEIR SIGNATURE WORKS

Kingsley Amis	*Lucky Jim* (1954)
John Braine	*Room at the Top* (1957)

William Cooper	*Scenes from Provincial Life* (1950)
Bernard Kops	*The Hamlet of Stepney Green* (1956)
Philip Larkin	*The Less Deceived* (1955)
John Osborne	*Look Back in Anger* (1956)
Harold Pinter	*The Birthday Party* (1957)
Alan Sillitoe	*Saturday Night and Sunday Morning* (1958)
John Wain	*Hurry on Down* (1953)
Arnold Wesker	*Chicken Soup with Barley* (1958)
Colin Wilson	*The Outsider* (1956)

Philip Larkin (1922–85)

Larkin was the son of the city treasurer of Coventry, a man who admired Hitler and kept a statuette of the dictator on his mantelpiece. The poet's childhood in Coventry was by turns dull and miserable, yet he deliberately spent the rest of his life in places that were no less bleak, save for his time at St John's College Oxford, where he became friends with Kingsley Amis.

Larkin worked as a librarian at universities in Leicester and Belfast, followed by thirty years in Hull, where he died while still working. He took his inspiration from railways, dingy shops and waiting rooms. 'Deprivation is to me what daffodils are to Wordsworth,' he said.

He wrote that 'Life is first boredom, then fear', and that he used to think that he hated people, but then he grew up and found that it was just children he hated.

He was offered the post of Poet Laureate following the death of John Betjeman in 1984, but he turned it down. He was much happier about being invited to dine at No. 10 Downing Street with Margaret Thatcher, whom he adored.

COLLECTIONS OF POEMS

The North Ship (1945)
The Less Deceived (1955)
The Whitsun Weddings (1964)
High Windows (1974)
Collected Poems (1988)

———

Great Philosophers
And their signature ideas

———

WILLIAM OF OCKHAM (C. 1288–1348)

A Franciscan friar who invented 'Ockham's Razor', the principle that the simplest working explanation of a phenomenon should be assumed to be the correct one.

FRANCIS BACON (1561–1626)

Founded the empirical method of science and philosophy that proceeds from observation and induction. As Lord Chancellor under James I he was famously corrupt. He died from a cold caught while stuffing a chicken with snow as an early experiment in refrigeration.

THOMAS HOBBES (1588–1679)

Argued that the justification for the State lay in its power to protect its citizens and its willingness to do so, without which civil society would revert to the 'State of Nature', in which life was 'solitary, poor, nasty, brutish and short'.

JOHN LOCKE (1632–1704)

Formulated the view of the human mind at birth as a *'tabula rasa'* – a so-called 'blank slate' upon which our experiences make impressions. He became Lord High Chancellor of England in 1672. His political writings concerning the consent of the governed inspired the US Constitution.

JEREMY BENTHAM (1748–1832)

The founder of utilitarianism, according to which actions and legislation are morally correct only if they lead to 'the greatest happiness of the greatest number'. Bentham defined 'happiness' in terms of pleasure. His embalmed body sits on display in a glass case in University College, London.

JOHN STUART MILL (1806–73)

Utilitarian philosopher and parliamentarian who argued for the intellectual pleasures of happiness over sensual pleasure and the doctrine that one only ever has a right to curtail the liberty of another individual out of self-protection. In 1867, he initiated the first parliamentary debate on women's suffrage.

BERTRAND RUSSELL (1872–1970)

Helped to found the Anglo-American school known as 'analytic philosophy', which seeks to remove misunderstandings and root out meaningless notions masquerading as profound truths. He was famously vigorous into old age and survived a plane crash when he was 76 by swimming to safety through the icy waters outside Trondheim, holding the attaché case containing his lecture notes.

BERNARD WILLIAMS (1929–2003)

Invented the notion of 'moral luck', wherein not just our health and wealth but also our moral character is subject to fortune. The question of whether an intention is good or bad is settled in part by factors beyond one's control rather than by its inherent nature. Williams sat on several government commissions to consider policies on drugs, gambling and prostitution.

The Metaphysical Poets

The Metaphysical Poets of the seventeenth century concentrated on stirring the intellect rather than the emotions. They sought to achieve this by eschewing florid imagery in favour of irony, argument and juxtaposing ideas to create paradoxes. The term 'metaphysical' was originally applied to them as an insult.

JOHN DONNE (1572–1631)

Donne, the Dean of St Paul's, was the most celebrated metaphysical poet. Much of Donne's work was set to music for the lute in his day and turned into popular songs.

A portrait of Donne that the poet commissioned as a gift to woo a woman was 'saved for the nation' in May 2006 after a public appeal helped to raise £1.4 million.

Donne's son, also called John, felt that the archive of his father's correspondence was too thin and added a stash of fake letters to pad it out. Scholars still dispute which items are genuine.

Famous Donne Lines

'Any man's death diminishes me, because I am involved in Mankind; And therefore never send to know for whom the bell tolls; It tolls for thee.'

'No man is an Island, entire of it self; every man is a piece of the Continent.'

'Death be not proud, though some have called thee Mighty and dreadful, for thou art not so.'

'Be thine own palace, or the world's thy gaol.'

'Licence my roving hands, and let them go, Before, behind, between, above, below.'

OTHER ENGLISH METAPHYSICAL POETS

George Herbert
Edward Herbert
Richard Crawshaw
Andrew Marvell
John Cleveland
Abraham Cowley
Richard Lovelace
Sir John Suckling
Thomas Traherne
Robert Southwell
Thomas Carew

The Romantic Poets

England's Romantic Poets were part of a wider European movement consisting in a revolt against Enlightenment science's objectification of men and women.

WILLIAM BLAKE (1757–1827)

Blake was a mystic who saw visions as a child, including angels in a tree at Peckham Rye, the prophet Ezekiel in a field and the face of God peering in through a window.

On a whim he once joined a mob and helped to storm London's Newgate Prison, releasing the prisoners and setting the building on fire.

He was a famously passionate believer in sexual equality and acceded to his wife's wishes when she refused to allow him to bring a concubine into their home.

His masterpiece was *The Marriage of Heaven and Hell* (1790–93).

WILLIAM WORDSWORTH (1770–1850)

As a child, Wordsworth learned to read from copies of the *Spectator* magazine. He wrote a series of poems about 'Lucy'; who she was, however, has remained a much-debated mystery, if indeed she represented a real person.

He accepted the post of Poet Laureate in 1843 on the promise that he would not have to perform any duties.

SAMUEL TAYLOR COLERIDGE (1772–1834)

Lyrical Ballads, the book of poetry he co-authored with Wordsworth in 1798, initiated the English Romantic movement.

Coleridge became an opium addict after taking the drug regularly to alleviate toothache and neuralgia. The words of *Kubla Khan* (1816) came to him in an opium pipe dream in 1797.

LORD BYRON (1788–1824)

Byron was born in a caul, which his family took as a portent of a special destiny. He suffered from a club foot that made him partially lame throughout his life.

He had a voracious sexual appetite for both men and women, explaining 'my heart always alights upon the nearest perch'. His several thousand conquests included his own half-sister, Augusta.

He died from a fever while fighting with the Greek patriots. His family's request for his burial in Westminster Abbey was refused.

Don Juan (1819–24), one of his most famous works, was incomplete at his death.

PERCY BYSSE SHELLEY (1792–1822)

Shelley married his first wife, Harriet Westbrook, when he was 19 and she was 16. His young bride would tolerate his vegetarianism and atheism, but baulked at his efforts to set up a *ménage à trois* in the marital home with a friend from university.

Harriet later drowned herself in the Serpentine in London's Hyde Park after Shelley ran away to Switzerland with two more 16-year-olds, Mary Godwin (Mary Shelley, author of *Frankenstein*) and her stepsister Jane.

Shelley himself drowned at sea shortly before his thirtieth birthday.

His most famous poem is *Ozymandias* (1818).

John Keats (1795–1821)

Keats was the son of a pub landlord in London's Finsbury.

His famous works include *Endymion: A Poetic Romance* (1817) and *Ode to a Nightingale* (1819).

He died of tuberculosis, the disease that had claimed his mother and brother.

The epitaph he chose for himself reads, 'Here lies one whose name was writ in water.'

P. G. Wodehouse (1881–1975)

Pelham Grenville Wodehouse wrote over a hundred books. The Jeeves series alone comprises eleven novels and thirty-five short stories.

He resembled his creation Bertie Wooster in several respects, ever cheerful and naïve. He bought a car with the proceeds from his early work and drove it into a hedge after taking a single lesson. He never drove again.

He spent much of his life in the United States and France, which was where he was living when he was captured by the Germans in 1940. He had remained at his seaside home not realizing that he was in danger – even when his pet parrot attacked a passing German officer. In the event, he got on well with his captors and was released a year later. Living in a hotel in Berlin he made a series of good-natured broadcasts on German radio that saw him accused of treachery in England. He explained, 'I never was interested in politics. I'm quite unable to work up any kind of belligerent feeling. Just as I'm about to feel belligerent about some country I meet a decent sort of chap. We go out together and lose any fighting thoughts or feelings.'

George Orwell remarked that it was 'nonsense to talk of "Fascist tendencies" in Wodehouse's books. There are no post-1918 tendencies at all.'

When Wodehouse was put forward for a knighthood in 1967, Sir Patrick Dean, the British Ambassador to the United States, objected that it would 'give currency to a Bertie Wooster image of the British character which we are doing our best to eradicate'.

Wodehouse took American citizenship in 1955 and was eventually awarded his knighthood at the age of 93.

THE JEEVES BOOKS

The Man with Two Left Feet (1917)
  (containing *Extricating Young Gussie*)
My Man Jeeves (1919)
The Inimitable Jeeves (1923)
Carry on, Jeeves (1925)
Very Good, Jeeves (1930)
Thank You, Jeeves (1934)
Right Ho, Jeeves (1934)
The Code of the Woosters (1938)
Joy in the Morning (1946)
The Mating Season (1949)
Ring for Jeeves (1953)
Jeeves and the Feudal Spirit (1954)
A Few Quick Ones (1959)
  (containing *Jeeves Makes an Omelette*)
Jeeves in the Offing (1960)
Stiff Upper Lip, Jeeves (1963)

Plum Pie (1966)
   (containing *Jeeves and the Greasy Bird*)
Much Obliged, Jeeves (1971)
Aunts Aren't Gentlemen (1974)

Children's Writers

BEATRIX POTTER (1866–1943)

Potter's wealthy parents never sent her to school. Her only playmates as a child were a variety of small animals that she tamed.

Until she was 30 she kept a secret diary written in a code that was not deciphered for eighty years.

She was unable to find a publisher for her stories and resorted to vanity publishing, illustrating the books herself and designing them in a size suitable for children to hold. *The Tale of Peter Rabbit* has sold over 40 million copies.

She invented merchandising and designed Peter Rabbit wallpaper and jigsaw puzzles.

Potter once wrote a letter of apology to a 6-year-old fan for the below par effort of *The Tale of Pigling Bland*, explaining that though she had been ill, 'the printers said all the little friends would be disappointed if I did not screw out my usual Christmas book. I'm afraid it is not very good this time but I have done my best and now I am well again I will hope to do better next year.' The letter fetched £8,200 at auction in March 2006.

Potter's Stories

The Tale of Peter Rabbit (1902)

The Tale of Squirrel Nutkin (1903)

The Tailor of Gloucester (1903)

The Tale of Benjamin Bunny (1904)

The Tale of Two Bad Mice (1904)

The Tale of Mrs. Tiggy-Winkle (1905)

The Tale of the Pie and the Patty-Pan (1905)

The Tale of Mr. Jeremy Fisher (1906)

The Story of A Fierce Bad Rabbit (1906)

The Story of Miss Moppet (1906)

The Tale of Tom Kitten (1907)

The Tale of Jemima Puddle-Duck (1908)

The Tale of Samuel Whiskers or, The Roly-Poly Pudding (1908)

The Tale of the Flopsy Bunnies (1909)

The Tale of Ginger and Pickles (1909)

The Tale of Mrs. Tittlemouse (1910)

The Tale of Timmy Tiptoes (1911)

The Tale of Mr. Tod (1912)

The Tale of Pigling Bland (1913)

Appley Dapply's Nursery Rhymes (1917)

The Tale of Johnny Town-Mouse (1918)

Cecily Parsley's Nursery Rhymes (1922)

The Tale of Little Pig Robinson (1930)

ARTHUR RANSOME (1884–1967)

Born in Leeds, the son of a history professor, Ransome travelled widely. A Russian speaker, he was sent by the *Manchester Guardian* to Russia, where he became a war correspondent on the Eastern Front during the Great War.

Ransome befriended Lenin and fell in love with Leon Trotsky's secretary (whom he later brought to the Lake District where his books were inspired). He witnessed the October Revolution of 1917 and was arrested and interrogated by Special Branch under suspicion of treason on his return to England. It was later found that Ransome spied on the Bolsheviks for MI6. However, he also wrote a newspaper article defending the suppression of democracy, the censorship of the press and the Reds' taste for summary execution.

The Swallows and Amazons Series
Swallows and Amazons (1930)
Swallowdale (1931)
Peter Duck (1932)
Winter Holiday (1933)
Coot Club (1934)
Pigeon Post (1936)
We Didn't Mean to Go to Sea (1937)
Secret Water (1939)
The Big Six (1940)
Missee Lee (1941)
The Picts and the Martyrs: Or Not Welcome At All (1943)
Great Northern (1947)
Coots in the North (unfinished, published in 1988)

ENID BLYTON (1897–1968)
Blyton's creations include the Famous Five, the Magic Faraway Tree, the Wishing Chair, Noddy, Malory Towers, St Clare's and the Secret Seven.

She wrote up to 10,000 words a day and completed over seven hundred books.

Her books have sold 400 million copies in forty languages.

In the 1950s, *Noddy in Toyland* was turned into a pantomime, and Blyton was accused of racism when she made the Gollywogs into the villains. She changed them to goblins, but by then the image had stuck. In 1960, Blyton's publisher, Macmillan, turned down *The Mystery that Never Was* on the grounds that it was 'xenophobic and absurd'. However, her books are still borrowed from libraries more than a million times each year to this day.

Blyton does not mention the phrase 'lashings of ginger beer' in any of her Famous Five books. The tomboy, Georgina, was based on Blyton herself.

The Famous Five Series
Five on a Treasure Island (1942)
Five Go Adventuring Again (1943)
Five Run Away Together (1944)
Five Go to Smuggler's Top (1945)
Five Go Off in a Caravan (1946)
Five on Kirrin Island Again (1947)
Five Go Off to Camp (1948)
Five Fall into Adventure (1949)
Five Get into Trouble (1950)
Five on a Hike Together (1951)
Five Have a Wonderful Time (1952)
Five Go Down to the Sea (1953)
Five Go to Mystery Moor (1954)
Five Have Plenty of Fun (1955)
Five on a Secret Trail (1956)
Five Go to Billycock Hill (1957)

Five Get into a Fix (1958)
Five on Finniston Farm (1960)
Five Go to Demon's Rocks (1961)
Five Have a Mystery to Solve (1962)
Five Are Together Again (1963)

8
STAGE AND SCREEN

Film Makers

SIR ALFRED HITCHCOCK (1899–1980)

Hitchcock was an engineering graduate from Leytonstone who found his way into films by designing sets and title cards.

He often told the story of how, once when he had misbehaved as a child, his father sent him to the police station with a note. The duty officer read the note and locked Hitchcock in one of the cells briefly. He had a lifelong mistrust of the police.

Hitchcock made several silent films and the first British 'talkie', *Blackmail* (1929).

He had a prodigious appetite. During one interview he ate an extra-thick steak followed by ice cream, and then ordered the same two dishes twice more.

He was fond of practical jokes and once dared a technician to spend a night by himself in a dark, silent studio. The technician was handcuffed to a camera and given a bottle of brandy laced with laxatives. Other pranks included holding a dinner party where all the food was dyed blue, borrowing money and returning it the next day as a sack of loose change and locking horses inside actors' dressing rooms.

He took American citizenship in 1956.

He cultivated his interest in murder cases by watching trials from the spectators' gallery at the Old Bailey.

He liked to cast blondes in leading roles, remarking that 'Blondes make the best victims. They're like virgin snow that shows up the bloody footprints.'

He agreed to break from type and direct *Waltzes from Vienna* (1933), a musical about Joseph Strauss, in order to finish his contract with British International Pictures. One day on set he shouted, 'I hate this stuff.' It is widely regarded as his worst film.

The film *Rope* (1948), his first colour feature, appears to have been shot in a single take, but Hitchcock actually used eight takes, hiding the cuts at moments when a dark object fills the entire screen.

A 'MacGuffin' was the term Hitchcock used to refer to an incidental plot device that helps to create suspense, such as the dog that blocks the stairway in *Strangers on a Train* or the secret information known by the man Cary Grant is mistaken for in *North by Northwest*.

He never won an Oscar for Best Director despite six nominations; for *Rebecca* (1940), *Suspicion* (1941), *Lifeboat* (1944), *Spellbound* (1945), *Rear Window* (1954), and *Psycho* (1960). In 1967 the Academy gave him the Irving G. Thalberg Memorial Award.

Hitchcock's Greatest Thrillers
Notorious (1946)
Dial M for Murder (1954)
Vertigo (1958)
North by Northwest (1959)
Psycho (1960)
The Birds (1963)

Hitchcock Cameos
And approximately when, and how many minutes from the start, they appear in the movie

Hitchcock liked appearing in his own films to entertain his fans with a game of 'spot the director'...

Family Plot (1976): In silhouette through the door of the Registrar of Births and Deaths, pointing his finger at a woman. 41 mins.

Frenzy (1972): In the centre of a crowd, wearing a bowler hat. He is the only one who does not applaud the speaker. 3 mins.

Topaz (1969): In a wheelchair in La Guardia airport, pushed by a nurse. He gets up from the chair, shakes hands with a man, and walks off. 28 mins.

Torn Curtain (1966): Sitting with a blonde-haired baby in the lobby of the Hotel d'Angleterre, with his back to the camera. 8 mins.

Marnie (1964): Entering a hotel corridor and looking at the camera after Tippi Hedren has passed by. 5 mins.

The Birds (1963): Leaving Davidson's pet shop with two white terriers as Tippi Hedren enters. 2 mins.

Psycho (1960): Seen wearing a cowboy hat through Janet Leigh's window. 4 mins.

North by Northwest (1959): Missing a bus during the opening credits.

Vertigo (1958): Walking in the street, carrying a horn case. 11 mins.

The Wrong Man (1956): Narrating the prologue (the only appearance in which he speaks).

The Man Who Knew Too Much (1956): Watching the acrobats in a Moroccan market place with his back to the camera. 25 mins.

The Trouble with Harry (1955): Walking past the limousine of an old man who is looking at paintings. 20 mins.

To Catch a Thief (1955): Sitting behind Cary Grant on a bus. 10 mins.

Rear Window (1954): Winding the clock in the songwriter's apartment. 30 mins.

Dial M for Murder (1954): On the class-reunion photo. 13 mins.

I Confess (1953): Seen from a distance, crossing the top of a staircase. 1 min.

Strangers on a Train (1951): Boarding a train with a double bass as Farley Granger gets off. 10 mins.

Stage Fright (1950): Turning to stare at Jane Wyman in her disguise as Marlene Dietrich's maid. 38 mins.

Under Capricorn (1949): In the town square during a parade, wearing a blue coat and brown hat, in the first five minutes. Ten minutes later, he is one of three men on the steps of Government House.

Rope (1948): Crossing a street in the opening credits and with his trademark silhoutte profile flashing on a neon sign seen through the apartment window. 55 mins.

Paradine Case (1947): Leaving the train at Cumberland Station, carrying a cello. 36 mins.

Notorious (1946): Drinking champagne at a party in Claude Rain's mansion. 1 hr.

Spellbound (1945): Leaving a crowded lift at the Empire Hotel, carrying a violin case and smoking a cigarette. 40 mins.

Lifeboat (1944): In full body profile in the 'before' and 'after' photos in the ad for a fat-reducing corset in William Bendix's newspaper. 25 mins.

Shadow of a Doubt (1943): Playing cards with his back to the camera on the train to Santa Rosa. 17 mins.

Saboteur (1942): At a news-stand in front of a drug store as the saboteur's car pulls up. 1 hr.

Suspicion (1941): Posting a letter at the village postbox. 45 mins.

Mr. and Mrs. Smith (1941): Halfway through, passing Robert Montgomery in front of his building. 41 mins.

Foreign Correspondent (1940): Reading a newspaper in the street as Joel McCrea leaves his hotel. 11 mins.

Rebecca (1938): Walking past the phone box as George Sanders calls Judith Anderson. 2 hrs 3 mins.

The Lady Vanishes (1938): Wearing a black coat and smoking a cigarette in Victoria Station. 1 hr 30 mins.

Young and Innocent (1937): Holding a camera, outside the courthouse. 15 mins.

The 39 Steps (1935): Throwing away some litter in front of a bus at a bus stop. 7 mins.

Murder! (1930): Walking with a woman past the boarding house where the murder was committed. 60 mins.

Blackmail (1929): Being pestered by a small boy as he reads a book on a tube train. 11 mins.

Easy Virtue (1927): Walking past a tennis court with a walking stick. 15 mins.

The Lodger (1926): At a newsroom desk with his back to the camera and then in a crowd, wearing a flat cap, watching an arrest. 3 mins and 1hr 32 mins.

He made a single television cameo, in *Alfred Hitchcock Presents: Dip in the Pool* (1958), where he appears on the cover of a magazine.

SIR DAVID LEAN (1908–91)

Lean's strict Quaker parents would not allow him to watch films, and he did not see one until he was 17. Two years later he got a job as a tea boy at Lime Grove Studios, against the wishes of his father who wanted him to become an accountant. He worked his way up from clapperboard boy to film editor before forming a partnership with Noël Coward that lasted throughout his first four feature films.

Brief Encounter (1945) was based on Noël Coward's play, *Still Life*. The film made Lean the first English director ever to be nominated for an Academy Award.

He became the first chairman of the British Academy of Film and Television Arts (BAFTA) in 1947.

The Bridge on the River Kwai (1957) won the 'triple' of Best Film, Best Director and Best Actor at the Oscars.

Lawrence of Arabia (1962) won seven Academy Awards, including Best Director and Best Picture. Albert Finney and Marlon Brando were offered the part of Lawrence before it was taken by Peter O'Toole.

Ryan's Daughter (1970), a romantic melodrama set in Ireland, received such a damning reception that Lean gave up directing for fourteen years. American critic Pauline Kael wrote, 'They don't have it in them to create Irish characters; there isn't a joke in it except maybe the idea that an Irish girl needs a half-dead Englishman to arouse her.'

'Colonel Bogey', the theme tune to *The Bridge on the River Kwai*, was played at Lean's memorial service at St Paul's Cathedral.

Lean's Oeuvre

In Which We Serve (1942)
This Happy Breed (1944)
Blithe Spirit (1945)
Brief Encounter (1945)
Great Expectations (1947)
Oliver Twist (1948)
The Passionate Friends (1949)
Madeleine (1950)
The Sound Barrier (1952)
Hobson's Choice (1953)
Summer Madness (1954)
The Bridge on the River Kwai (1957)
Lawrence of Arabia (1962)
Doctor Zhivago (1965)
Ryan's Daughter (1970)
A Passage to India (1984)

POWELL AND PRESSBURGER

The director Michael Powell (1905–90) and the writer Emeric Pressburger (1902–88), a Hungarian émigré who had fled the Nazis, produced nineteen feature films together between 1939 and 1972, mostly for their own company, The Archers, in the 1940s and 1950s.

The *Life and Death of Colonel Blimp* (1943) was a runaway success despite the efforts of Winston Churchill to have it banned as unpatriotic. The film tells the story of a dashing officer from the Boer War who in later life comes to personify English military amateurism with his insistence on fair play.

Michael Powell worked as a consultant to Francis Ford Coppola and Martin Scorsese towards the end of his life.

Filmography
The Spy in Black (1939)
Contraband/Blackout (1940)
49th Parallel (1941)
'…One of Our Aircraft Is Missing' (1942)
The Life and Death of Colonel Blimp (1943)
A Canterbury Tale (1944)
I Know Where I'm Going! (1945)
A Matter of Life and Death (1946)
Black Narcissus (1947)
The Red Shoes (1948)
The Small Back Room (1949)
Gone to Earth (1950)
The Elusive Pimpernel (1950)
The Tales of Hoffmann (1951)
Oh… Rosalinda!! (1955)
The Battle of the River Plate (1956)
Ill Met by Moonlight (1957)
They're a Weird Mob (1966)
The Boy Who Turned Yellow (1972)

James Bond

Bond's creator was Ian Fleming (1908–64), the son of a wealthy Conservative MP. His early career gave him a familiarity with the spy's milieu of casinos and diplomatic receptions, having worked as a foreign correspondent in Moscow, a stockbroker and a commander in naval intelligence.

Fleming wrote the Bond novels in his villa, 'Goldeneye', in Jamaica. He took the name of his character from a book he had lying around, *Birds of the West Indies*, by James Bond. The real Dr Bond was reportedly pleased with the association.

The first Bond was not Sean Connery but Barry Nelson, who starred in a CBS Climax Mystery Theater production of *Casino Royale* in 1954.

Fleming was so pleased with Sean Connery's performance in *Dr No* that he changed Bond into a Scotsman for the rest of the novels.

The Bond of the books is slightly different from the Bond of the films, with Timothy Dalton (a Welshman) being the most faithful to Fleming's novels in his violence and shamelessness on screen. According to the author, 'Bond is not a hero, nor is he depicted as being very likeable or admirable. He's not a bad man, but he is ruthless and self-indulgent. He enjoys the fight, but he also enjoys the prizes.'

'M' was Fleming's nickname for his domineering mother.

In *Goldfinger*, Shirley Eaton's character, Jill Masterson, dies of suffocation after her entire body is covered with gold paint. In real life it would not have been fatal.

007'S CURRICULUM VITAE

Bond attended Eton College, where he was expelled for an indiscretion with a maid. He then achieved a First Class degree in Oriental Languages from Cambridge University before reaching the rank of commander in Royal Naval Intelligence and joining MI6.

The Soviet Union awarded Bond the Order of Lenin in *The Spy Who Loved Me*.

Bond's family motto is 'The World is Not Enough' (*Orbis non sufficit*).

Before *Die Another Day*, the Hollywood James Bond had had sex on screen eighty-five times with sixty different women, twenty-one of whom died shortly afterwards. The locations included seven boats, a submarine, a gondola, a motorized iceberg, two cars, a steam bath and a space shuttle.

He was married only once, to the shortly-to-be-murdered Tracy de Vicenzo, daughter of the godfather of the Corsican mafia, in *On Her Majesty's Secret Service*.

In most Bond films, the hero enjoys liaisons with three different women. Condoms are never used and there are never any unfortunate consequences. In 1984, the Family Planning Association pointed out that if the secret agent were real, 'he would have fathered fifty illegitimate children and suffered from every sexual disease from herpes to terminal syphilis'. In response to the AIDS crisis, *The Living Daylights* featured Timothy Dalton bedding the same girl three times.

THE BOND FILMS AND THEIR STARS

Twenty Bond movies were filmed by the producer Albert 'Cubby' Broccoli and, since Cubby's death, by his successors Barbara Broccoli and Michael J. Wilson. *Casino Royale* starring David Niven and *Never Say Never Again*, in which Sean Connery wore a hairpiece, were the exceptions.

Dr No (1962)	Sean Connery
From Russia with Love (1963)	Sean Connery
Goldfinger (1964)	Sean Connery
Thunderball (1965)	Sean Connery
You Only Live Twice (1967)	Sean Connery
Casino Royale (1967)	David Niven
On Her Majesty's Secret Service (1969)	George Lazenby
Diamonds Are Forever (1971)	Sean Connery
Live and Let Die (1973)	Roger Moore
The Man with the Golden Gun (1975)	Roger Moore
The Spy Who Loved Me (1977)	Roger Moore
Moonraker (1979)	Roger Moore
For Your Eyes Only (1981)	Roger Moore
Never Say Never Again (1983)	Sean Connery
Octopussy (1983)	Roger Moore
A View to a Kill (1985)	Roger Moore
The Living Daylights (1987)	Timothy Dalton
Licence to Kill (1989)	Timothy Dalton
Goldeneye (1995)	Pierce Brosnan
Tomorrow Never Dies (1997)	Pierce Brosnan
The World Is Not Enough (1999)	Pierce Brosnan
Die Another Day (2002)	Pierce Brosnan
Casino Royale (2006)	Daniel Craig

Merchant Ivory

Merchant Ivory Productions is famous for its period dramas recreating Edwardian England and the Grand Tour, but none of the company's three key members are English. James Ivory, the director, is American, Ruth Prawer Jhabvala, the screenwriter, is a German Jew, and the late Ismail Merchant (d. 2005), the producer, was an Indian Muslim.

The company has been making films since 1963, since when they have made over forty films and won six Oscars. The *Guinness Book of Records* lists Merchant, Ivory and Prawer Jhabvala as cinema's longest- running partnership.

Their first features were produced with rupees from the frozen bank accounts of US distributors whose profits the Indian government had not allowed them to repatriate to the US.

Merchant delivered a political speech to ten thousand Muslims in Bombay soon after India's independence when he was just 9 years old. He was a talented chef who made curries for the cast and crew of his films, opened a restaurant and wrote cookery books as a sideline: *Ismail Merchant's Indian Cuisine* (1986), *Ismail Merchant's Passionate Meals* (1994) and *Ismail Merchant's Paris: filming and feasting in France* (1999).

Their three classic works of 'Englishness' are *The Remains of the Day* (1993), adapted from the novel by Kazuo Ishiguro, and *A Room with a View* (1985) and *Howard's End* (1991), adapted from novels by E. M. Forster. Before the first showing of his violent drama, *Pulp Fiction* (1994), Quentin Tarantino asked members of the audience who had enjoyed *The Remains of the Day* to raise their hands. Those who did so were asked to leave.

Quintessential Screen Englishmen and Women

Jenny Agutter (b. 1952)

Julie Andrews (b. 1935)

Richard Attenborough (b. 1923)

Dirk Bogarde (1921–99)

Helena Bonham Carter (b. 1966)

Michael Caine (b. 1933)

Noël Coward (1899–1973)

Charles Dance (b. 1946)

Hugh Grant (b. 1960)

Joyce Grenfell (1910–79)

Alec Guinness (1914–2000)

Trevor Howard (1913–88)

John Hurt (b. 1940)

Jeremy Irons (b. 1948)

Celia Johnson (1908–82)

James Mason (1909–84)

John Mills (1908–2005)

Roger Moore (b. 1927)

David Niven (1910–83)

Leslie Phillips (b. 1924)

Vanessa Redgrave (b. 1937)

Alan Rickman (b. 1946)

Diana Rigg (b. 1938)

Maggie Smith (b. 1934)

Terence Stamp (b. 1939)

Michael York (b. 1942)

Famous and Infamous 'English' Foreigners on Screen

YOU'D THINK THEY WERE ENGLISH

Pierce Brosnan	Irish	*Goldeneye* (1995) etc.
Johnny Depp	American	*The Libertine* (2004)
Mel Gibson	Australian	*Hamlet* (1990)
Richard E. Grant	b. Swaziland	*Withnail and I* (1987)
Christopher Guest*	American	*This is Spinal Tap* (1984)
Nicole Kidman	Australian	*The Others* (2001)
Michael McKean	American	*This is Spinal Tap* (1984)

Julianne Moore	American	*The End of the Affair* (1999)
Gwyneth Paltrow	American	*Sliding Doors* (1998)
Meryl Streep	American	*The French Lieutenant's Woman* (1981)
René Zelweger	American	*Bridget Jones' Diary* (2001)

SPOTTED A MILE AWAY

Marlon Brando	American	*Mutiny on the Bounty* (1963)
Don Cheadle	American	*Ocean's Eleven* (2001)
Sean Connery	Scottish	*Dr No* (1962) etc.
Kevin Costner	American	*Robin Hood: Prince of Thieves* (1991)
Kate Hudson	American	*The Four Feathers* (2002)
Natalie Portman	American	*V for Vendetta* (2006)
Keanu Reeves	American	*Bram Stoker's Dracula* (1992)
Dick Van Dyke	American	*Mary Poppins* (1964)
Denzel Washington	American	*For Queen and Country* (1988)

* Although Christopher Guest's mother was American and he grew up in New York, his father was England's Fourth Baron Haden-Guest.

———

Restoration Comedy

———

One of Charles II's first acts after the Restoration of 1660 was to reverse the Puritan ban on the dramatic arts. He established the King's Players and the Duke's Players and the revival of English theatre saw women take the stage for the first time. The period also created the first celebrity performers. In an age of wits and rakes, it was a theatre that reflected its audience. This was largely composed of the aristocracy and their hangers-on, who wanted to see court intrigue and sexual adventure writ larger than life.

The era came to a close at the turn of the century when the licentious court of Charles II was replaced by the austerity of William and Mary.

NOTABLE COMEDIES

Love in a Tub (1664) – George Etherege
The Forced Marriage (1670) – Aphra Behn★
The Rehearsal (1671) – George Villiers
Marriage-a-la-Mode (1672) – John Dryden
The Country Wife (1675) – William Wycherley
The Man of Mode (1676) – George Etherege
The Plain-Dealer (1676) – William Wycherley
The Mistress (1687) – Charles Sedley
The Wives' Excuse (1691) – Thomas Southerne
Love for Love (1695) – William Congreve
The Provok'd Wife (1697) – John Vanbrugh
The Way of the World (1700) – William Congreve

APHRA BEHN (1640–89)

Behn was the first female English playwright. She became a spy in Belgium during the Dutch War of 1665–7 and adopted the pseudonym 'Astrea'. After the king neglected to pay her wages, she found herself in a debtors' prison and took to writing for her living.

Music Hall

'Let me know where you're working tomorrow night –
and I'll come and see YOU.'

The final words of John Osborne's Archie Rice to
his audience in *The Entertainer* (1957)

The first music hall was Morton's Canterbury Hall in London, built by Charles Morton in 1852. Similar venues proliferated due to the laws of the day, which prohibited drinking and smoking in theatres but not in the music halls attached to pubs. Performances consisted of variety acts designed to appeal to the working classes, from acrobats and singers to stand-up comedians. The format lasted into the early twentieth century, when many halls were converted into cinemas and variety moved to larger 'palace' theatres.

ENGLISH MUSIC HALL STARS

Albert Chevalier (1861–1923)
Gracie Fields (1898–1979)
George Leybourne (1842–84)
Lillie Langtry (1853–1929)
Dan Leno (1860–1904)
Vesta Tilley (1864–1952)

Ealing Comedies

Ealing Studios was founded in 1931 and made over 150 feature films in the 1930s, 1940s and 1950s before it became part of the BBC.

The great Ealing comedies told stories of the 'little people' battling against the authorities.

THE D'ASCOYNES

Alec Guinness played eight different members of the D'Ascoyne family in *Kind Hearts and Coronets* (1949), the tale of Dennis Price's commoner murdering his way to the top of a dynasty by the following means:

Ascoyne D'Ascoyne: Unties his punt and sends him over a weir.
Henry D'Ascoyne: Replaces the paraffin in his darkroom lamp with petrol.
The Reverend Lord Henry D'Ascoyne: Poisons his port.
Lady Agatha D'Ascoyne: Shoots down her balloon with a bow and arrow over Berkeley Square as she scatters suffragette pamphlets.
Admiral Lord Horatio D'Ascoyne: Not murdered – goes down with his ship after an accident.
General Lord Rufus D'Ascoyne: Puts explosives in a jar of caviar.
Ethelred D'Ascoyne, Eighth Duke of Chalfont: Catches him in a man-trap and shoots him with his own shotgun.
Lord Ascoyne D'Ascoyne: Not murdered – suffers a stroke and dies of shock on succeeding to the dukedom.

Guinness received £6,000 for his role in *The Lavender Hill Mob*. He received over £150 million for his part in *Star Wars* after negotiating a 2 per cent royalty in lieu of his fee.

Classic Comedies

Hue and Cry (1947)

Whisky Galore! (1948)

Passport to Pimlico (1949)

Kind Hearts and Coronets (1949)

The Lavender Hill Mob (1951)

The Man in the White Suit (1951)

The Titfield Thunderbolt (1953)

The Ladykillers (1955)

'Carry On' Films

'Kenny (Williams) and me would be together, while Joan (Sims) would be elsewhere discussing the price of meat at Tesco. Kenny said she was terribly suburban. Bernie (Bresslaw) would be off somewhere doing the Guardian crossword, while Sid would delve into his pockets and bring out a pack of cards and a big cigar. Hattie was the mother figure. She would take in the waifs and strays. She was sexy too, Hattie. Charlie Hawtrey would go off and sit on his chair and get out his Woodbines. He felt it was all beneath him and only really liked two people – Kenny and me.'

Barbara Windsor on life between takes,
The Sun, 13 February 2006

Between 1958 and 1978, thirty films were produced at Pinewood Studios that brought saucy seaside postcards to life and for a while made the double entendre synonymous with English humour. According to the most regular cast member, Kenneth Williams, the Carry On films represented 'a culture that's cruder than the Tudors'.

Sid James conducted an off-set love affair with the Carry On team's sex symbol Barbara Windsor, but he couldn't get on with her best friend, Williams. He remarked, 'Kenneth doesn't love men. He loves himself and other men are the next best thing.'

Windsor is 4 feet 10 inches tall. She won the inaugural Rear of the Year award in 1976. She reportedly still gets whistles from building sites at the age of 68. Her husband is twenty-six years her junior.

Carry On Cleo recycled the costumes from Elizabeth Taylor and Richard Burton's *Cleopatra*.

Carry On Up the Khyber was filmed in Snowdonia. Princess Margaret visited the set during the filming and reportedly stormed off in a rage after watching a scene in which Sid James addresses a letter to Queen Victoria, 'Dear Vicky...'

Cast regular Peter Butterworth met Talbot Rothwell, the co-writer of many of the films, in a POW camp during the Second World War. He sang in a revue where the booing covered the noise of prisoners digging an escape tunnel.

In *Carry On Doctor*, Jim Dale broke his arm in the scene where he careers through the hospital corridors on a trolley.

Bernard Bresslaw's pop single, 'Mad, Passionate Love', reached No. 6 in the charts before he began his Carry On career.

Kenneth Williams was once attempting to cash a cheque when the star-struck bank clerk began to explain at length how she loved his films and couldn't wait to tell her family that she had met him. When he reminded her about the cheque, she asked him if he had any proof of identity. In 1988, Williams committed suicide with an overdose of barbiturates. The last entry in his journal read, 'Oh – what's the bloody point?'

Two planned films were abandoned. *Carry On Smoking* was set in a fire station, but the producers feared that it might appear in bad taste should there be a fire-related tragedy close to the release date. *Carry On Dallas* was shelved for fear of legal action from the makers of the American soap opera.

THE REVIVAL

The format was revived in 1992 with *Carry On Columbus*. The new cast included Alexei Sayle, Rik Mayall and Julian Clary, but it was a critical and box-office disaster. Some say that society's increasing openness towards sex made the double entendre redundant, while others blame political correctness for the death of the Carry On series. More likely explanations are the poor scripts of the later efforts – Barbara Windsor refused a role in *Carry On Columbus* after she read it – and the deaths of several lead members of the cast.

A new film, *Carry On London*, has been mooted.

THE FILMS

Carry On Sergeant (1958)
Carry On Nurse (1959)
Carry On Teacher (1959)
Carry On Constable (1959)
Carry On Regardless (1961)
Carry On Cruising (1962)
Carry On Cabby (1963)
Carry On Jack (1963)
Carry On Spying (1964)

Carry On Cleo (1964)
Carry On Cowboy (1965)
Carry On Screaming! (1966)
Carry On Don't Lose your Head (1966)
Carry On Follow that Camel (1967)
Carry On Doctor (1967)
Carry On Up the Khyber (1968)
Carry On Camping (1969)
Carry On Again Doctor (1969)
Carry On Up the Jungle (1970)
Carry On Loving (1970)
Carry On Henry (1971)
Carry On at your Convenience (1971)
Carry On Matron (1972)
Carry On Abroad (1972)
Carry On Girls (1973)
Carry On Dick (1974)
Carry On Behind (1975)
Carry On England (1976)
That's Carry On (1978)
Carry On Emmannuelle (1978)
Carry On Columbus (1992)

CAST STALWARTS
Ranked by their appearances

Kenneth Williams (26 films)
Joan Sims (24)
Charles Hawtrey (23)
Sid James (19)
Kenneth Connor (17)

Peter Butterworth (16)

Bernard Bresslaw (14)

Hattie Jacques (14)

Jim Dale (11)

Peter Gilmore (11)

Barbara Windsor (10)*

Patsy Rowlands (9)

Jack Douglas (8)

Julian Holloway (8)

Valerie Leon (7)

Terry Scott (7)

Leslie Phillips (4)

Bernard Cribbins (4)

Frankie Howerd (2)

* Includes presenting *That's Carry On.*

Monty Python

The Pythons – John Cleese, Terry Gilliam, Eric Idle, Terry Jones, Michael Palin and Graham Chapman (d. 1989) – made four feature films and forty-five episodes of *Monty Python's Flying Circus* between 1969 and 1983.

John Cleese and Graham Chapman wrote as a pair, as did Terry Jones and Michael Palin, while Eric Idle worked alone. They would then meet together with Terry Gilliam who would help decide what was funny and what was not, and design the animations for the links between sketches.

After Graham Chapman had revealed that he was gay, the group received a letter from a concerned Christian woman who had heard that one of their number, though she did not know who, was homosexual. She enclosed prayers and readings from the Bible that would help to save his soul. Eric Idle wrote back and told her not to worry, as they had discovered who it was and killed him. John Cleese subsequently left the programme before its final series.

Terry Jones is Welsh and Terry Gilliam is American.

THE LIFE OF BRIAN

EMI withdrew their $2 million funding for *The Life of Brian* (1979) after they were horrified at the script, but former Beatle George Harrison stepped in to save the production. Blasphemy protests saw it banned in several American states, and it was not shown on domestic television until 1993. The film's main characters belong to The People's Front of Judea. Their rivals are:

The Judean People's Front
The Judean Popular People's Front
The Popular Front of Judea (one member)

FAMOUS SKETCHES

The Four Yorkshiremen
The Dead Parrot
The Ministry of Silly Walks
The Cheese Shop
The Lumberjack Song
Spam
The Spanish Inquisition

Nudge Nudge
Upper Class Twit of the Year
The Philosophers' Football Match: Germany vs Greece

Cambridge Footlights Alumni

The Cambridge University Footlights Dramatic Club began performing dramas, farces and burlesques in 1883. Since the 1960s it has launched the careers of dozens of comedians, satirists and comedy actors.

Famous former members include:

Clive Anderson	Graeme Garden	Lucy Montgomery
Alexander Armstrong	Nick Hancock	Neil Mullarkey
	Tony Hendra	Jimmy Mulville
David Baddiel	Jack Hulbert	Bill Oddie
Sacha Baron Cohen	Eric Idle	Sue Perkins
Eleanor Bron*	Clive James	Steve Punt
Tim Brooke-Taylor	Simon Jones	Jan Ravens
Graham Chapman	Hugh Laurie	Griff Rhys Jones
John Cleese	Jonathan Lynn	Tony Slattery
Peter Cook	Rory McGrath	Emma Thompson
Jimmy Edwards	Ben Miller	Sandi Toksvig
David Frost	Jonathan Miller	Robert Webb
Stephen Fry	David Mitchell	

* Bron became the first female member in 1959.

The Archers

The Archers, 'an everyday story of country folk', is set in the fictional village of Ambridge in 'Borsetshire', somewhere in the Midlands. The programme is recorded in Birmingham.

Norman Painting has played the character of Phil Archer since the first episode in 1950. He has also written scripts for the show. His first, involving the death of Phil's wife Grace in a fire, was aired as a 'spoiler' on the opening day of ITV in 1955.

The programme attracts around half a million listeners every week.

Storylines have included drugs, problem gambling, homosexuality, rape and political issues. In 2003, David Archer shot a badger for infecting his cattle with bovine tuberculosis, while in August 2002 Liberal Democrat MP Norman Baker wrote to the *Guardian* complaining that 'Anyone listening to *The Archers* over the last two months could be forgiven for thinking the programme has been sponsored by the Countryside Alliance.'

The Archers Anarchists Club, founded in 1995, is dedicated to maintaining that the show is not a soap opera but a fly-on-the-wall documentary featuring real people.

Great Sitcom Writers

John Sullivan (b. 1946)*: *Only Fools and Horses, Citizen Smith, Dear John*
David Renwick (b. 1951): *One Foot in the Grave*

John Cleese (b. 1939)†: *Fawlty Towers*

Dick Clement (b. 1937) and **Ian La Frenais** (b. 1937): *The Likely Lads, Whatever Happened to the Likely Lads?, Porridge, Auf Wiedersehen, Pet*

David Croft (b.1922) and **Jimmy Perry** (b. 1923): *Dad's Army, It Ain't Half Hot Mum, Hi-De-Hi!*

Jeremy Lloyd (b. 1932): *Are You Being Served?* (co-written with David Croft)

Ben Elton (b. 1959): *The Young Ones* (co-written with Rik Mayall and Lise Meyer), *Blackadder, Blackadder II, Blackadder the Third, Blackadder Goes Forth* (all co-written with New Zealand-born Richard Curtis)

Ray Galton (b. 1935): *Steptoe and Son, Hancock's Half-Hour* (with Alan Simpson)

David Nobbs (b. 1935): *The Fall and Rise of Reginald Perrin*

Jennifer Saunders (b. 1958): *Absolutely Fabulous*

Ricky Gervais (b. 1961) and **Stephen Merchant** (b. 1974): *The Office, Extras*

* Sullivan also wrote the theme tune for *Only Fools and Horses*.

† With his then wife, Connie Booth, the American actress who played Polly the maid.

―――

Great Shakespearian Actors

―――

Richard Burbage (1567–1619)*
Edmund Kean (1787–1833)
Henry Irving (1838–1905)†
John Gielgud (1904–2000)
Laurence Olivier (1907–89)

Paul Scofield (b. 1922)
Judi Dench (b. 1934)‡
Derek Jacobi (b. 1938)
Ian McKellen (b. 1939)
Kenneth Branagh (b. 1960)

* Burbage was the first actor to play Shakespeare's Richard III, Romeo,
Henry V, Hamlet, Macbeth, Othello and King Lear.
† Irving was the first actor to receive a knighthood.
‡ Dench won the Best Supporting Actress Oscar for her role as Elizabeth I
in *Shakespeare in Love* (1998) even though she was only on screen for eight
minutes.

Oliver Postgate's Children's Programmes

Oliver Postgate founded Smallfilms with the artist and animator
Peter Firmin in 1958. Together they made several of the most popular
children's programmes of the 1960s and 1970s.

When not making programmes Postgate has carried on the family
tradition of political activism, campaigning for nuclear disarmament
and against the war in Iraq. His grandfather was the Labour Party
founder George Lansbury and his mother once impersonated Emily
Pankhurst to save the Suffragette leader from prison. Postgate was
jailed as a conscientious objector during the Second World War.

In 1999, Postgate's *Bagpuss* was voted the most popular children's
programme of all time in a BBC poll. Only thirteen episodes were
ever made. The character 'Professor Yaffle' was based on the philosopher Bertrand Russell.

A NASA scientist once called *The Clangers* 'A doomed attempt to bring a dose of realism into science fiction'.

SMALLFILMS'S TELEVISION OUTPUT

Ivor the Engine (1958–63, 1975–7)
The Saga of Noggin the Nog (1959–65, 1979–80)
Pingwings (1960–65)
The Dogwatch (1962)
The Sea of Neptune and the Mermaid Pearls (1963–5)
The Pogles and Pogles Wood (1964–8)
The Clangers (1968–71)
Bagpuss (1973–4)
What-a-Mess (1980)
Tottie, the Story of a Doll's House (1980)
Pinny's House (1986)

9
MUSIC

'Opera in English is, in the main, just about as sensible as baseball in Italian.'

H. L. Mencken

Nine National Anthems

1. 'Jerusalem': lyrics by William Blake, music by Hubert Parry
2. 'There'll Always be an England': lyrics by Hugh Charles, music by Ross Parker and Harry Par-Davies
3. 'I Vow to Thee, My Country': lyrics by Cecil Spring-Rice, music by Gustav Holst
4. 'Nimrod': Edward Elgar
5. 'The Roast Beef of Olde England': lyrics by Henry Fielding, music by Richard Leveridge
6. 'Hearts of Oak': lyrics by David Garrick, music by William Boyce
7. 'The White Cliffs of Dover': lyrics by Nat Burton, music by Walter Kent
8. 'Swing Low, Sweet Chariot': Wallace Willis
9. 'The English': lyrics by Michael Flanders, music by Donald Swann

Classical Composers

JOHN DOWLAND (1563–1626)

The greatest English lutenist and composer of his day was never favoured at the Elizabethan court despite an international reputation. He blamed this on his conversion to Catholicism in 1580.

Dowland did not take the indifference of his countrymen well and wrote a piece he called 'Semper Dowland, semper dolens' ('Always Dowland, always doleful').

Around six hundred of his 'ayres' for the lute survive today, including:

'Flow my Teares'
'Awake, Sweet Love'
'Come Again, Sweet Love'
'Fine Knacks for Ladies'
'Flow not so fast, ye Fountains'
'In Darkness let me Dwell'
'Sweet, Stay Awhile'
'Weep ye no more, sad Fountains'
'Welcome, Black Night'

HENRY PURCELL (1659–95)

Purcell was England's greatest Baroque composer and is known as the 'English Orpheus'. He sang in the Chapel Royal Choir as a boy and worked as an organ tuner at Westminster Abbey when his voice broke.

He became court composer for Charles II's string orchestra in 1677 and was appointed Keeper of the King's Instruments six years later. He managed to retain these posts throughout the reigns of James II and William III and Mary.

His only full opera, *Dido and Aeneas* (1689), was England's first. It tells the story from Virgil's *Aeneid* of the love between the Queen of Carthage, Dido, and the shipwrecked Trojan, Aeneas. There were no public performances of the opera in London during Purcell's lifetime.

He was buried in Westminster Abbey, where his epitaph reads, 'Here lyes Henry Purcell Esq., who left this life and is gone to that blessed place where only his harmony can be exceeded.' The inscription on the tombstone of the composer John Blow, his tutor at the Chapel Royal, reads, 'Master to the famous Henry Purcell'.

The title theme to Stanley Kubrick's *A Clockwork Orange* (1971) was taken from the march Purcell composed for the funeral of Queen Mary in 1695.

Purcell's Semi-Operas
Dioclesian (1690)
King Arthur (1691)
The Fairy Queen (1692)
The Tempest (1695)
The Indian Queen (1695)*

* Completed after his death by his brother, Daniel.

SIR EDWARD ELGAR (1857–1934)
Elgar was the son of a Worcester piano tuner and taught himself music with the instruments and manuscripts in his father's shop.

He composed some of his earliest pieces while he was bandmaster for Powick Lunatic Asylum, which had its own orchestra. Elgar himself suffered from depression and sometimes contemplated suicide.

The Enigma Variations, first performed in 1899, were so named because they formed the counter-melody to an unheard theme. According to Elgar, the tune in question was well known, but he refused to identify it. No one has ever solved the mystery, but popular candidates include the British national anthem, 'God Save the King', 'Auld Lang Syne', Mozart's Prague Symphony and the 'never, never, never' section of 'Rule Britannia'. Elgar once said that 'English music is white – it evades everything.'

Thirteen of the Enigma Variations represent Elgar's friends, while the fourteenth is a self-portrait. Variation Nine, 'Nimrod', has become the theme tune of the Battle of Britain, but it was written to capture the noble character of a German – Elgar's best friend, Augustus Jaeger.

The Dream of Gerontius, his greatest work, is the story of a soul on the Day of Judgment. It was bungled by the orchestra on its first performance in Birmingham in 1900 and was appreciated in Elgar's homeland only after it won acclaim in Germany for its Wagnerian composition.

There are six *Pomp and Circumstance Marches*. Number One was performed for the first time in 1901 and is the tune to which 'Land of Hope and Glory' is sung on the Last Night of the Proms. It is often played at universities in the United States at graduation ceremonies.

GUSTAV HOLST (1874–1934)

Holst was born Gustavus von Holst to Swedish parents in Cheltenham, but he changed his name during the First World War to make it sound less Germanic.

He did not fight in the war because he was declared unfit for active service. From childhood he suffered from poor eyesight and a weak chest, and severe neuritis in his right hand meant that he was forced to give up the piano in his teens.

After he failed to win a scholarship to any of London's music colleges, he worked as an organist and choirmaster in the Cotswolds. There he composed an operetta in the fashion of Arthur Sullivan which impressed his father so much that he decided to pay for his son to go to the Royal College of Music.

His first opera, *The Revoke* (1895), has never received a public performance.

In 1895, Holst developed a passion for Hindu mysticism. He learned Sanskrit to help him set hymns from the *Rig Veda* to music.

He spent seven years working on the opera *Sita*, based on the *Ramayana*, but it was never performed in his lifetime.

The Planets was inspired by Holst's love for astrology, which he called his 'pet vice'. The names for the movements were taken from the subtitles of chapters in *What is a Horoscope?*, by Alan Leo.

Holst was a non-smoking, teetotal vegetarian.

The Planets Suite

1. Mars, the Bringer of War
2. Venus, the Bringer of Peace
3. Mercury, the Winged Messenger
4. Jupiter, the Bringer of Jollity
5. Saturn, the Bringer of Old Age
6. Uranus, the Magician
7. Neptune, the Mystic

He declined to write a movement for the planet Pluto after it was discovered in 1930.

BENJAMIN BRITTEN (1913–76)

Britten was born on 22 November, the day of the patron saint of music, St Cecilia.

From the age of 5, he would get up early so that he could compose music before going to school.

During the 1930s, Britten collaborated with the poet W. H. Auden on documentaries such as *Night Mail* and *Coal Face* for the film unit of the General Post Office.

His greatest work, the *War Requiem*, was written for the opening of the new Coventry Cathedral in 1962. Although it was based on Wilfred Owen's poetry, it provoked criticism, as Britten had been a conscientious objector during the Second World War. Igor Stravinsky argued that the piece was overrated and complained that in saying so he had been made to feel 'as if one had failed to stand up for "God Save the Queen"'.

He wrote the *Sinfonia da Requiem* to mark the 2,600th year of Japan's Mikado dynasty in 1940, a year before that country entered the war.

He was able to compose thirty pages of full score in a single day.

Britten was the first composer ever to receive a life peerage.

Britten's Operas

Peter Grimes (1945)
Young Person's Guide to the Opera (1946)
The Rape of Lucretia (1946)
Albert Herring (1947)
The Beggar's Opera (1948)
Let's Make an Opera! (1949)
Billy Budd (1951)
Gloriana (1953)
The Turn of the Screw (1954)
Noye's Fludde (1958)
A Midsummer Night's Dream (1960)
Owen Wingrave (1970)
Death in Venice (1973)

OTHER ENGLISH COMPOSERS

And their famous pieces

Thomas Tallis (1510–85): Masses, anthems
William Byrd (1543–1623): Masses, psalms, anthems
Thomas Arne (1710–78): 'Rule, Britannia', 'Where the Bee Sucks', 'Rise, Glory, Rise'

William Boyce (1711–79): 'Hearts of Oak', Symphonies, Trio Sonatas

Hubert Parry (1848–1918): 'Jerusalem', *King Saul, Blest Pair of Sirens*, 'I was Glad'

Frederick Delius (1862–1934): 'Over the Hills and Far Away', Dance Rhapsodies, *On Hearing the First Cuckoo in Spring*

Ralph Vaughan Williams (1872–1958): *Fantasia on a Theme by Thomas Tallis, London Symphony, The Lark Ascending*

William Walton (1902–83): Symphony No. 2, Viola Concerto, *Belshazzar's Feast*

Michael Tippett (1905–98): *A Child of our Time, The Midsummer Marriage, King Priam*

John Tavener (b. 1944): *The Whale, The Protecting Veil*, 'Song for Athene'*

*Sung at the funeral of Diana, Princess of Wales, in 1997.

Musical Theatre

GILBERT AND SULLIVAN (1836–1911 AND 1842–1900)

Sir W. S. Gilbert wrote the librettos and Sir Arthur Sullivan composed the music for their Victorian comic operas.

Their works were known as the 'Savoy Operas' because the Savoy Theatre was built to stage them. When it was opened in 1881 it was the world's first building to be lit entirely by electric lights.

In 1890, the pair quarrelled when Gilbert accused Richard D'Oyly Carte, the theatre's impresario, of swindling them out of £500 for a new carpet. Sullivan sided with D'Oyly Carte and also criticized

Gilbert for his repetitive plots. The partnership was never the same again. They composed only two more operas, neither of which was a success.

Sullivan also composed over sixty hymns, including 'Onward Christian Soldiers'.

Gilbert died from a heart attack after rescuing a woman from drowning in a lake.

The Savoy Operas

Thespis (1871)
Trial by Jury (1875)
The Sorcerer (1877)
HMS Pinafore (1878)
The Pirates of Penzance (1879)
Patience (1881)
Iolanthe (1882)
Princess Ida (1884)
The Mikado (1885)
Ruddigore (1887)
The Yeomen of the Guard (1888)
The Gondoliers (1889)
Utopia Limited (1893)
The Grand Duke (1896)

SIR ANDREW LLOYD WEBBER (B. 1948)

Lloyd Webber began playing the violin at the age of 3 and had written nine musicals by the time he left the Royal Academy of Music. He was only 19 when he had his first success, working with the lyricist Tim Rice to create *Joseph and the Amazing Technicolor Dreamcoat*.

Cats has been translated into ten languages and performed in over twenty countries. It is based on Lloyd Webber's favourite poems as a child, *Old Possum's Book of Practical Cats* by T. S. Eliot. Between 1981 and 2001 at the New London Theatre in Drury Lane, *Cats* became the longest-running musical of all time, with 8,949 performances.

Lloyd Webber bought London's Palace Theatre in Charing Cross Road in 1983 and now owns seven London theatres, including the Theatre Royal Drury Lane and the London Palladium.

In 1983, he wrote the music for a party political broadcast on behalf of the Conservative Party.

Shows

The Likes of Us (1965)*
Joseph and the Amazing Technicolor Dreamcoat (1968)
Jesus Christ Superstar (1970)
Jeeves (1975)
Evita (1978)
Tell Me on a Sunday (1980)
Cats (1981)
Song and Dance (1982)
Starlight Express (1984)
The Phantom of the Opera (1986)
Aspects of Love (1989)
Sunset Boulevard (1993)
Whistle Down the Wind (1996)
The Beautiful Game (2000)
The Woman in White (2004)

* The first and last performance of *The Likes of Us* was at Lloyd Webber's Sydmonton Festival in July 2005, when Stephen Fry described it as the musical that 'failed to launch the careers of Tim Rice and Andrew Lloyd Webber forty years ago'.

Film Scores

JOHN BARRY (B. 1933)

Barry was born in York as John Barry Prendergast. He learned to arrange jazz music while completing his National Service and went on to become England's greatest composer of film scores.

James Bond Themes
Dr No (1962)*
From Russia with Love (1963)
Goldfinger (1964)
Thunderball (1965)
You Only Live Twice (1967)
On Her Majesty's Secret Service (1969)
Diamonds Are Forever (1971)
The Man with the Golden Gun (1974)
Moonraker (1979)
Octopussy (1983)
A View to a Kill (1985)
The Living Daylights (1987)

* Uncredited. The original theme was written by Monty Norman, with Barry composing additional material.

Other Major Scores
Zulu (1964)
King Rat (1965)
The Ipcress File (1965)
Born Free (1966)*†

The Lion in Winter (1968)*

Midnight Cowboy (1969)

Walkabout (1971)

Mary, Queen of Scots (1971)

Robin and Marian (1976)

The Deep (1977)

Hanover Street (1979)

The Black Hole (1979)

Raise the Titanic (1981)

The Cotton Club (1984)

Jagged Edge (1985)

Out of Africa (1985)*

Dances with Wolves (1990)*

Chaplin (1992)

Indecent Proposal (1993)

* Academy Award for Best Music, Original Score.

† Academy Award for Best Music, Original Song.

Popular Music

NOËL COWARD (1899–1973)

> 'There are probably greater painters than Noël, greater
> novelists than Noël, greater librettists, greater
> composers of music, greater singers, greater dancers,
> greater comedians, greater tragedians, greater stage
> producers, greater film directors, greater cabaret
> artists, greater TV stars. If there are, they are fourteen

different people. Only one man combined all fourteen different labels – The Master.'

Lord Louis Mountbatten at Coward's
seventieth birthday party, 1969

Coward was England's greatest artistic all-rounder, but he grew up in a relatively poor middle-class family in Teddington, Middlesex and had little formal education. He began performing at the age of 7, and his mother turned their home into a boarding-house to support her son's dreams.

Coward made his name writing, producing, directing and starring in *The Vortex* (1924), a tale of adultery and cocaine abuse among the upper classes. He went on to write the great plays *Private Lives* (1930), *Cavalcade* (1931), *Design for Living* (1933), *Blithe Spirit* (1941) and the short *Still Life* which was filmed as *Brief Encounter* (1946).

Despite his thirty-year relationship with the actor Graham Payne, he never publicly acknowledged that he was gay, explaining, 'There is still a woman in Paddington Square who wants to marry me, and I don't want to disappoint her.'

He lived much of his life as a tax exile in Jamaica, next door to the James Bond author Ian Fleming whom he disliked. Fleming offered him the part of the villain in *Dr No*.

His Most Famous Songs
'Mad Dogs and Englishmen'
'Mad About the Boy'
'Don't Put Your Daughter on the Stage, Mrs Worthington'
'Don't Let's Be Beastly to the Germans'
'Could You Please Oblige Us With a Bren Gun?'
'London Pride'

'There's Always Something Fishy About the French'
'I'll See You Again'
'Some Day I'll Find You'
'Poor Little Rich Girl'
'Marvellous Party'

GEORGE FORMBY (1904–61)

He was born George Hoy Booth, the eldest of seven children, in Wigan, Lancashire. Formby was his father's stage name in the music halls. He became an apprentice jockey when he was 7 years old and turned professional at 10.

Formby played the banjulele, a cross between the Hawaiian ukulele and the American banjo. He took the instrument on stage for the first time for a bet.

He never learned to read or write more than a few words, but in the 1930s he was earning an estimated £100,000 a year. In 1941, he signed a contract with Columbia Pictures worth £500,000.

He smoked forty Woodbine cigarettes a day from the age of 12. His favourite food was beef-dripping on toast.

In 1946, Formby was expelled from South Africa for playing to black audiences.

Over a hundred thousand mourners turned out for his funeral. At his peak he was domestic cinema's top-drawing star for six years running, as well as a favourite among the royal family.

His Most Famous Songs
'The Window Cleaner'
'Fanlight Fanny'
'Riding in the T.T. Races'
'Leaning on a Lamp Post'

'With My Little Stick of Blackpool Rock'
'With My Little Ukulele in My Hand'
'Auntie Maggie's Remedy'

NOTABLE ENGLISH FOLK ARTISTS
And some of their famous albums

The Copper Family: *Come Write Me Down* (1952)
Sam Larner: *Now Is the Time for Fishing* (1961)
The Watersons: *Frost and Fire* (1965)
Fairport Convention: *Liege and Lief* (1969)
Shirley Collins: *Anthems in Eden* (1969)
Nick Drake: *Five Leaves Left* (1969)
Pentangle: *Cruel Sister* (1970)
Sandy Denny: *The North Star Grassman and the Ravens* (1971)
Steeleye Span: *Please to See the King* (1971)
Ashley Hutchings: *Morris On* (1971)
Eliza Carthy: *Red Rice* (1998)
June Tabor: *An Echo of Hooves* (2003)
Kate Rusby: *Underneath the Stars* (2003)

THE BEATLES

> 'We don't like their sound, and guitar music is on the way out.'

> Decca Records executive rejecting the Beatles in 1962

The band were named The Quarrymen, Johnny and The Moondogs, The Silver Beats and The Silver Beetles before they settled on The Beatles. The name was taken from a line in the movie *The Wild Ones*, where Lee Marvin rides into town with Marlon Brando's old motorcycle gang and asks him, 'Where ya been, Johnny? We've been missing you. All the Beetles been missing you.' Paul McCartney once added that they chose 'Beatles' because they liked the name of Buddy Holly's band, The Crickets. The 'ee' was changed to 'ea' to allude to the word 'beat'.

More cover versions (over three thousand) of 'Yesterday' by Paul McCartney have been recorded than of any other song. McCartney's working lyrics at first were 'Scrambled eggs, Oh, baby how I love your legs.' The tune came to him in a dream, and for several weeks he was convinced that he must have plagiarized someone else's work unconsciously.

Brian Wilson of The Beach Boys suffered a mental breakdown after hearing 'Strawberry Fields Forever' on the radio and realizing that this was the music he had been striving to create. The song referred to the Strawberry Field children's home where John Lennon had played as a child. The institution is set to close down in 2007.

John Lennon originally wrote 'Come Together', the first track on the *Abbey Road* album, for LSD guru Timothy Leary's campaign to become governor of California in 1969.

The Beatles's Seventeen No. 1 Singles
And their weeks at the top of the UK charts, compiled by
Record Retailer *magazine*

'From Me to You'	2 May 1963	7
'She Loves You'	12 September 1963	6
'I Want to Hold Your Hand'	12 December 1963	5
'Can't Buy Me Love'	2 April 1964	3
'A Hard Day's Night'	23 July 1964	3
'I Feel Fine'	10 December 1964	5
'Ticket to Ride'	22 April 1965	3

'Help!'	5 August 1965	3
'Day Tripper'/	16 December 1965	5
'We Can Work It Out'		
'Paperback Writer'	23 June 1966	2
'Eleanor Rigby'/	18 August 1966	4
'Yellow Submarine'		
'All You Need Is Love'	19 July 1967	3
'Hello Goodbye'	6 December 1967	7
'Lady Madonna'	27 March 1968	2
'Hey Jude'	11 September 1968	2
'Get Back'	23 April 1969	6
'Ballad of John and Yoko'	11 June 1969	3

The Beatles were the second English group to go to No. 1 in the United States, with 'I Want to Hold Your Hand'. The first was The Tornados, with 'Telstar' in 1962.

HEAVY METAL

Heavy Metal was developed in the early 1970s by three English rock bands: Black Sabbath, Deep Purple and Led Zeppelin. They elaborated on the distorted electric guitar sounds of Jimi Hendrix and variously added thunderous drumbeats, screaming vocals and morbid lyrics. Although the term 'heavy metal' has antecedents, Hendrix's manager, Chas Chandler, claimed that it came from a gig review that described Hendrix's music as 'like the sound of heavy metal falling from the sky'.

In 1980, Led Zeppelin's drummer John Bonham choked to death on his own vomit after an all-day drinking session. He is widely considered to have been the greatest rock drummer of all time.

Metal's heyday in the 1980s was led by Iron Maiden. The band's lead singer, Bruce Dickinson, is a former public schoolboy, history graduate, published novelist, qualified airline pilot and once represented Great Britain at the European Fencing Championships. Tour commitments meant that he was unable to join the Olympic team.

Iron Maiden's zombie mascot Eddie the Head, who appears in a range of scenarios on their album covers, was created by the artist Derek Riggs. He based the character on an American head that he saw dangling from a Vietnamese tank on a news programme.

When the 'mockumentary' film Spinal Tap was released in 1984, the parody of the English heavy metal subculture was so painfully accurate that many fans refused to believe that the lead actors were American.

Subliminal Messages

When Led Zeppelin's 'Stairway to Heaven' is played backwards, the words 'my sweet Satan' can allegedly be heard. However, the band have denied that this is anything but a freak coincidence. Their lead singer, Robert Plant, complained, 'To me it's very sad, because "Stairway To Heaven" was written with every best intention, and as far as reversing tapes and putting messages on the end, that's not my idea of making music.'

In 1990, the band Judas Priest were taken to court in Nevada after two of their teenage fans committed suicide. The families alleged that one of their songs contained a subliminal message to 'Do it'. The case was dismissed after the band members showed that words could be read into any number of songs played backwards. They added that if they had wanted to insert a subliminal message it would have been 'Buy more of our records'.

When Ozzy Osbourne, Black Sabbath's front man, was accused of encouraging Satanism, he responded, 'I can't even conjure myself out of bed in the morning, let alone conjure up the Devil.'

Classic English Metal Albums

Led Zeppelin II, Led Zeppelin (1969)
Deep Purple in Rock, Deep Purple (1970)
Black Sabbath, Black Sabbath (1970)
Paranoid, Black Sabbath (1971)
Long Live Rock and Roll, Rainbow (1978)
Ace of Spades, Mötorhead (1980)
British Steel, Judas Priest (1980)
No Sleep 'Til Hammersmith, Mötorhead (1981)
Blizzard of Oz, Ozzy Osbourne (1981)
The Number of the Beast, Iron Maiden (1982)
Screaming for Vengeance, Judas Priest (1982)
Pyromania, Def Leppard (1983)
Piece of Mind, Iron Maiden (1983)
Powerslave, Iron Maiden (1984)
Hysteria, Def Leppard (1987)

PUNK ROCK

> 'When the chips were down, we always failed to come through.'
>
> Johnny Rotten

Punk rock was invented in New York in the early 1970s and brought to London by former art student Malcolm McLaren, where it became associated with anarchism and working-class idealism as 'The Sound of the Suburbs'.

The first English punk single was 'New Rose' by The Damned, from Croydon, released in October 1976.

The luminous mohican hairdos and outrageous clothing of punk stereotype only ever belonged to a small subset of King's Road punks inspired by McLaren and the designer Vivienne Westwood. Punk's youth fan-base in the suburbs spurned such overt anti-fashion as a pose. They made do with little more than drainpipe trousers, PVC miniskirts and tin badges of their favourite bands.

In April 2006, Asian mobile-phone salesman Harraj Mann was arrested on board a flight leaving Durham on suspicion of terrorism. A taxi driver had alerted police after his passenger began singing along to 'London Calling' by The Clash during his journey to Tees Valley Airport. He was particularly worried by the line, 'London calling from the faraway towns, now war is declared and battle come down'. In June 2004, Bristol resident Mike Devine was questioned by Special Branch officers after he had sent text messages of the lyrics from The Clash's song 'Tommy Gun', which includes the words 'gun' and 'jet airliner'.

The Sex Pistols

Malcolm McLaren became manager of The Strand in 1975, which he renamed The Sex Pistols and made Johnny Rotten their lead singer. The *Daily Mirror* ran the headline, 'The Filth and the Fury!' on 2 December 1976 after the band appeared on Bill Grundy's teatime television show. At the end of the interview, Grundy said, 'Go on, you've got another five seconds. Say something outrageous.' Guitarist Steve Jones's response included the f-word. However, this was not the first use of the word on television – a distinction earned by theatre critic Kenneth Tynan in 1965.

'God Save the Queen' was released during the week of the Queen's

Silver Jubilee in 1977. When the band performed a loud rendition of the song on a boat outside the House of Commons, the police boarded the vessel and arrested McLaren. The fracas was recorded by his film crew and used for publicity purposes.

Sid Vicious was killed by an overdose of heroin given to him by his mother, Anne Beverley. She explained that she had taken lengths to procure an extremely pure sample and her son died 'because I tried to help him'.

The Twelve Best English Punk Monikers
Rat Scabies – drums, The Damned
Steve Ignorant – vocals, Crass*
Poly Styrene – vocals, X-Ray Spex
Billy Bostik – drums, Sham 69
Johnny Goodfornothing – guitar, Sham 69
Joy DeVivre – keyboards, Crass
Lora Logic – saxophone, X-Ray Spex
Captain Sensible – vocals/guitar, The Damned
Roman Jugg – keyboards, The Damned
Garrie Dreadful – drums, The Damned
Cosey Fanni Tutti – guitar, Throbbing Gristle
Vic Vomit – bass guitar, The Killermeters

*Steve Ignorant changed his name to 'Stephen Intelligent' when he joined Current 93.

STOCK, AITKEN AND WATERMAN
The Hit Factory
Songwriters and producers Mike Stock, Matt Aitken and Pete Waterman dominated pop in the 1980s and early 1990s, with 101 UK Top 40 hits.

They had their first No. 1 single in 1985 when they produced 'You Spin Me Round' by Dead or Alive, but they soon saw the money to be made in writing lightweight 'bubblegum' pop performed by young, attractive artists aimed primarily at a young or pre-teen audience. They were so successful that they were christened 'The Hit Factory', while for their many critics their initials came to stand for 'Stop Aitken and Waterman'.

In 1987, the trio helped to launch the singing career of *Neighbours* actress Kylie Minogue, which heralded a chart invasion by former soap stars. They were unfamiliar with *Neighbours* at the time and when Minogue first arrived at their London offices, the planned meeting had slipped their minds. They quickly wrote 'I Should Be So Lucky' while she waited outside.

Artists Who Have Performed Songs Written or Produced by the Hit Factory

Rick Astley, Bananarama, Thereza Bazar, Big Fun, Gayle & Gillian Blakeney, Boy Krazy, Laura Branigan, Brilliant, Brother Beyond, Errol Brown, O'Chi Brown, Canton, Suzette Charles, The Cool Notes, E. G. Daily, The Danse Society, Michael Davidson, Nancy Davis, Dead or Alive, Hazell Dean, Delage, Divine, Jason Donovan, Dolly Dots, Erik, Georgie Fame, Phil Fearon, Samantha Fox, Fresh, Girl Talk, Lonnie Gordon, Debbie Harry, Haywoode, Carol Hitchcock, Austin Howard, I'm Talking, La Toya Jackson, Judas Priest, Kakko, Mel & Kim, Jeb Million, Kylie Minogue, Mint Julips, Nick Straker Band, Pat & Mick, Andy Paul, Pepsi & Shirley, Michael Prince, Princess, Reynolds Girls, Cliff Richard, Rin Tin Tin, Roland Rat, Romi & Jazz, Sabrina Salerno, Sequal, Tracy Shaw, Sigue Sigue Sputnik, Sinitta, Slamm, Mandy Smith, Sonia, Splash, Edwin Starr, Donna Summer, Sybil, Taco, The Three Degrees, The Twins, Paul

Varney, Steve Walsh, Precious Wilson, Worlds Apart, WWF
Superstars, Yell!

NB List does not include remixes.

No. 1 Singles in the UK Charts

'You Spin Me Round (Like a Record)'	Dead or Alive	1/12/1984
'Respectable'	Mel & Kim	7/3/1987
'Let it be'	Ferry Aid	4/4/1987
'Never Gonna Give You Up'	Rick Astley	8/8/1987
'I Should Be So Lucky'	Kylie Minogue	23/1/1988
'Especially for You'	Kylie & Jason	10/12/1988
'Too Many Broken Hearts'	Jason Donovan	4/3/1989
'Hand on Your Heart'	Kylie Minogue	6/5/1989
'Ferry 'cross the Mersey'	Various	20/5/1989
'Sealed With a Kiss'	Jason Donovan	10/6/1989
'You'll Never Stop Me Loving You'	Sonia	24/6/1989
'Do They Know it's Christmas?'	Band Aid 2	23/12/1989
'Tears on My Pillow'	Kylie Minogue	20/1/1990

EUROVISION SONG CONTEST WINNERS

1967	Sandie Shaw	'Puppet on a String'
1969	Lulu	'Boom Bang-A-Bang'
1976	Brotherhood of Man	'Save Your Kisses for Me' *
1981	Buck's Fizz	'Making Your Mind Up'†
1997	Katrina and the Waves	'Love Shine a Light'‡

* One of the foursome was Welsh.
† One of their number was Irish.
‡ Katrina herself was American.

10

ART AND ARCHITECTURE

'The English public, as a mass, takes no interest in a work of art until it is told that the work in question is immoral.'

Oscar Wilde

Painters and Engravers

WILLIAM HOGARTH (1697–1764)

Hogarth was the first internationally famous English artist. He was also the first English-born artist to receive a knighthood.

He began by sketching London street life as a child, but later taught himself the skill of memorizing every detail of a scene so that he could later commit it to canvas.

Hogarth 'wasted' his early years as a copper engraver before he turned to a painting career when he was 30 years old.

He campaigned for copyright legislation to protect his livelihood, and in 1735 Parliament passed the Hogarth Act.

A Rake's Progress (1733–5)

Hogarth's great narrative series of paintings charts the downfall, in eight steps, of an heir to a large fortune:

1. 'Funeral preparation'
2. 'Opulence'
3. 'Orgy'
4. 'Arrest'
5. 'Marriage'
6. 'Gambling den'
7. 'Prison'
8. 'Bedlam'

Other Notable Works

A Harlot's Progress (six scenes, 1731)
Marriage à la mode (six scenes, 1743–5)
The Gate of Calais (The Roast Beef of Old England) (1749)

Beer Street (1751)
Gin Lane (1751)

JOSHUA REYNOLDS (1723–92)

Reynolds, the pre-eminent portrait painter of his age, is credited with making art a respectable profession in England. While in Rome studying the Renaissance masters he caught an ear infection that exacerbated his hereditary deafness and left him with profound hearing loss. In one self-portrait he squints at the viewer with a hand cupped to his ear. Reynolds helped to organize London's first exhibitions of the work of living artists and became the founding president of the Royal Academy in 1768. He brought the techniques of the Old Masters to bear on English portraiture and encouraged an academic approach to painting.

Reynolds's *Omai* was sold at Sotheby's for £10.3 million in 2001.

Notable Works
Augustus, 1st Viscount Keppel (1753)
Samuel Johnson (1772–8)
Edmund Burke (1774)
Omai (1776)
The Family of the Duke of Marlborough (1777)
The Duchess of Devonshire and Her Daughter (1786)

THOMAS GAINSBOROUGH (1727–88)

At the age of 13, Gainsborough produced a landscape drawing that convinced his father to let him move to London to pursue a career as a painter.

He was unable to earn a subsistence income from landscapes and lived off his wife's annuity until he moved to Bath in 1759, after which he found sufficient portrait commissions to pay his debts, though it was work he affected to despise. Painters like Gainsborough and Joshua Reynolds received up to £90,000 in today's money for ancestor portraits. These works would generally lose 90 per cent of their value a generation later when no one wanted to buy a picture of other people's ancestors.

Modern critics judge that he underestimated himself when he said of his rival, Sir Joshua Reynolds, 'Damn him, how various he is.' Gainsborough is now considered the most original painter of his day in contrast to the classically derivative Reynolds. Like the author Charles Dickens, Gainsborough was timeless by virtue of being contemporary.

Notable Works
Portrait of Mrs Graham (1777)
Painter's Daughters Chasing a Butterfly (c. 1758)
The Morning Walk (1785)
The Cottage Girl with a Bowl of Milk (1786)

JAMES GILLRAY (1756–1815)

Gillray was born in London, the son of a Scottish soldier recuperating in Chelsea's Royal Hospital after the loss of an arm. He started as a portrait painter but gained fame for his political caricatures. The Tory Prime Minister George Canning was rumoured to have granted Gillray a pension of £200 a year for his attacks on the Whigs. He said that '[the Whigs] are poor, they do not buy my prints and I must draw on the purses of the larger parties'. He went insane in 1807 and once tried to commit suicide by throwing himself out of a window.

Gillray's Satirical Targets

A Voluptuary under the Horrors of Digestion – the Prince Regent

Farmer George and his Wife – George III

The Plum Pudding in Danger – William Pitt and Napoleon

MONSTROUS CRAWS, at a New Coalition Feast – The King, Queen and
the Prince Regent

*Fashionable Contrasts, or, the Duchess's little shoe yielding to the magnitude
of the Duke's foot* – The Duke and Duchess of York

The Bridal Night – The French Revolution

The Friend of the People – Charles Fox

Man Trying to Fit a Woman into a French Corset – Tom Paine

J. M. W. TURNER (1775–1851)

England's greatest romantic painter, known as 'The Painter of
Light', was the son of a London barber who sold the boy's drawings
to his customers. After Turner's mother was later committed to a
mental asylum, his father lived with him as his studio assistant.

His greatest works presage the age of the Impressionists in explor-
ing the effect of light. He seemed sometimes to paint only the light,
leading the critic William Hazlitt to accuse him of painting 'pictures
of nothing'.

Turner's Venetian landscape *Giudecca, La Donna della Salute and San
Giorgio* (1841) was sold at Christie's in New York for £20.5 million in
2006.

Turner produced *Burning of the Houses of Lords and Commons* (1835)
after he witnessed the fire that destroyed much of the Palace of
Westminster.

In his later years he lived as a recluse in Chelsea, where he was
known to the locals as 'Puggy' or 'Admiral Booth'.

When he died, he left his large fortune to a charity for what he called 'decayed artists'. He left three hundred paintings and twenty thousand watercolours and drawings to the nation.

Notable Works

Dortrecht: The Dort Packet Boat from Rotterdam Becalmed (1818)
The Battle of Trafalgar, as Seen from the Mizen Starboard Shrouds of the Victory (1806)
The Fighting Temeraire Tugged to Her Last Berth to Be Broken up (1838)
Fishing Boats with Hucksters Bargaining for Fish (1842)
Rain, Steam and Speed – The Great Western Railway (1844)

JOHN CONSTABLE (1776–1837)

Constable was the son of a wealthy Suffolk mill owner. He did no more than sketch as a child and did not begin his training in art until he entered the Royal Academy at the age of 23.

Upon leaving the Royal Academy Schools he turned down an offer of a job as an art teacher at a military college. He let his younger brother take over the family business and embarked on a decade of relative poverty as a landscape painter. His work won prizes in France in the early 1820s, but he enjoyed little success at home. He refused to emigrate, explaining, 'I would rather be a poor man in England than a rich man abroad.' He would sell only twenty paintings in England during his lifetime and had to wait until he was 52 before he was made a Royal Academician.

Constable's The Lock fetched £10.9 million at Sotheby's in 1990.

Today, the valley of the River Stour where he painted several of his finest works is known as 'Constable Country'.

Notable Works

Dedham Vale: Morning (1811)
View on the Stour (1819)

The Haywain (1821)
Salisbury Cathedral (1823)
The Cornfield (1826)
Salisbury Cathedral from the Meadows (1829)

FRANCIS BACON (1909–92)

Bacon is considered second only to Pablo Picasso among the twentieth century's greatest painters. He was born in Dublin, a distant descendant of his philosopher namesake.

He had only eighteen months of schooling and no formal training as an artist.

Bacon was sent to work with a group of rugged horse trainers when his father realized that he was gay, hoping that they would 'make a man out of him'. To Bacon's delight, they turned out to be homosexuals. His father also had him horsewhipped by a groom, a pleasure that he often sought out in later life.

He lived much of his life between his studios and the pubs and drinking clubs of Soho, particularly the Colony Room, where he drank only champagne and held court surrounded by hangers-on. Before a night on the town, Bacon would colour his hair with Kiwi shoe polish and brush his teeth with Vim floor cleaner.

He had a vaunted capacity for alcohol, and when he was invited to appear on the *South Bank Show*, he took Melvyn Bragg out for a drink beforehand and deliberately got him drunk so that he would have an 'edge' in their interview.

Bacon destroyed many of his early works. Once he noticed one of his paintings that he had omitted to burn as he walked past a gallery window. He wrote out a cheque for several thousand pounds on the spot and stomped the piece into shreds on the pavement outside.

His greatest inspirations were the violent scenes in Eisenstein's

Battleship Potemkin (1925) and a medical textbook containing colour plates of mouth diseases that he found in a secondhand bookshop in Paris in 1935. When he was later introduced to Prime Minister Margaret Thatcher as 'the greatest living English artist', she asked him, 'Aren't you the man who paints those awful pictures?' 'Yes,' he replied with pride.

Notable Works
Three Studies for Figures at the Base of a Crucifixion (1944)
Painting (1946) (The 'butcher's shop' picture)
Study after Velázquez's Portrait of Pope Innocent X (1953)
Man with Dog (1953)
Crucifixion (1965)
Triptych May–June (1973)

The Pre-Raphaelite Brotherhood

The Pre-Raphaelites were a society formed by three students in 1848 in protest against what they judged to be the dull and stifling values of the Royal Academy. They turned from the tradition of historical painting to the religiously inspired art that preceded the High Renaissance. The Pre-Raphaelites broke up in 1853.

THE BROTHERHOOD
Dante Gabriel Rossetti (1828–82) – Founder member
William Holman Hunt (1827–1910) – Founder member
John Everett Millais (1829–96) – Founder member
James Collinson

F. G. Stephens
Thomas Woolner
William Michael Rossetti
William Dyce – Supporter
Ford Madox Brown – Supporter

The Arts and Crafts Movement

In 1859, William Morris (1834–96) married Jane Burden, one of the most painted Pre-Raphaelite beauties, and moved into the architect Philip Webb's Red House at Bexley. Morris was unable to find suitable furniture to match their new home and despaired at the products of the new industrial manufacturing methods.

In 1861, Morris founded a firm of interior decorators to produce handcrafted furniture, wallpaper, metalwork and other items designed by some of the foremost artists of the day. Under the influence of the critic John Ruskin (1819–1900), they believed that mass production and advertising were destroying the souls of modern man and that a revival of medieval craftsmanship would help restore society's moral and spiritual health.

Morris's Associates
Edward Burne-Jones (1833–98) – Painter
Ford Madox Brown (1821–93) – Painter
Dante Gabriel Rossetti (1828–82) – Painter
Philip Webb – Architect
Charles Faulkner – Mathematician
Peter Paul Marshall – Surveyor

Sculptors

HENRY MOORE (1898–1996)

Moore was the son of a Yorkshire coal miner. He was gassed in the First World War but survived to study sculpture at the Royal Academy.

His monumental bronze and marble abstract figures were influenced by the African and pre-Columbian sculptures in the British Museum.

BARBARA HEPWORTH (1903–75)

Hepworth's early abstract works created the illusion that they had been weathered by the elements rather than carved. Her later work was notable for the exploration of the object's interior and hollow spaces. She burned to death in a fire at her home in St Ives.

ELISABETH FRINK (1930–93)

Her most famous works were bronzes of birds of prey, dogs, horses and male nudes, of which she said, 'I have focused on the male because to me he is a subtle combination of sensuality and strength with vulnerability.'

ANTHONY CARO (B. 1924)

Regarded as the most influential living English sculptor for his abstract works in welded steel.

ANTHONY GORMLEY (B. 1950)

The nation's most popular living sculptor is famous for *The Angel of the North* (1998), near Gateshead. This is England's largest sculpture. Made of steel, it is 65 feet (20 metres) high with a 169-foot (52-metre) wingspan. Other famous works include *Field* (1991), consisting of 35,000 terracotta figurines, and *Quantum Cloud* (1999), a 30-foot-tall diffuse steel sculpture of the artist's body .

RACHEL WHITEREAD (B. 1963)

Whiteread is the revolutionary sculptor of the space that surrounds objects. Her most famous work was *House* (1993), a concrete cast of the interior of a nineteenth-century terraced house in London's East End. Tower Hamlets Council bulldozed the piece after a few months in the face of a public campaign for its preservation. *House* won her both the Turner Prize and the K Foundation Prize for worst British artist.

Architects

INIGO JONES (1573–1652)

England's finest Renaissance architect was the self-taught son of a cloth-maker. His first job at the court of James I was costume designer for royal masques. He became the king's architect in 1615 and brought designs home from his travels in Italy to study ruins.

Notable Works
The Queen's House, Greenwich, London (part of the National Maritime Museum)

Banqueting House, Whitehall, London
The original Covent Garden
Marlborough House Chapel
St Paul's (destroyed in the Great Fire of London)
Lincoln's Inn Fields

SIR CHRISTOPHER WREN (1632–1723)

Wren is considered the greatest English architect, with fifty-three London churches to his name, including the current St Paul's Cathedral, completed in 1711.

He was a founder of the Royal Society in 1660, having devoted his early career to mathematics, astronomy, meteorology and physiology. He was appointed Professor of Astronomy at Oxford University in 1661. The following year he designed the Sheldonian Theatre.

He submitted several designs for St Paul's to Charles II, and when his favourite was not chosen, he slipped its main features into the plans without informing the authorities until after they had been built. Wren and Robert Hooke conducted scientific experiments concerning pendulums and gravity inside the half-finished structure.

Notable Works
St Paul's
Tom Tower at Christ Church, Oxford
Trinity College Library, Cambridge
The Royal Hospital, Chelsea
Hampton Court Palace (redevelopment)
Kensington Palace (redevelopment)
The Royal Observatory, Greenwich
St Clement Danes, Strand, London
St Mary-le-Bow, Cheapside, London

Temple Bar, London
The Custom House, London

NICHOLAS HAWKSMOOR (1661–1736)

Hawksmoor was a pupil of Sir Christopher Wren and helped him to build St Paul's. He also worked with Sir John Vanbrugh on Castle Howard and Blenheim Palace. He is thought to be responsible for the more elaborate features of the latter.

In 1711 Hawksmoor was commissioned to help build fifty new churches in London and Westminster.

Notable Works
Westminster Abbey, London (West Towers)
All Soul's College, Oxford (Hall and Library)
The Clarendon Building, Oxford
St Anne's, Limehouse, London
St George-in-the-East, Stepney, London
Christ Church, Spitalfields, London
St Mary's, Woolnoth, London

SIR JOHN VANBRUGH (1664–1726)

Vanbrugh designed England's finest contribution to baroque architecture, Blenheim Palace, completed for the Duke of Marlborough in 1716. He was dismissed by the duke's wife after a dispute over spiralling costs.

He was also one of the most celebrated Restoration Comedy writers.

Notable Works
Blenheim Palace, Oxfordshire
Castle Howard, Yorkshire

Kimbolton Castle, Huntingdon
Kings Weston, Bristol
Eastbury, Dorset
Seaton Delaval, Northumberland
Grimsthorpe Castle, Lincolnshire

THOMAS ARCHER (1668–1743)

Archer was thought to be the pre-eminent English baroque architect in his day. His designs were based on the classical styles he studied in Italy during the Grand Tour.

Notable Works
Birmingham Cathedral
St Paul's, Deptford
Church of St John, Westminster
Chatsworth House, Derbyshire

LANCELOT 'CAPABILITY' BROWN (1715–83)

England's greatest landscape architect was the son of a Northumberland farm labourer.

He favoured the rolling lawns and clumps of trees of the Romantic Naturalist style and gained his nickname from the way he would describe the already beautiful gardens of his clients as having 'capabilities'. The satirist Richard Cambridge remarked that he hoped to die before Brown so that he could 'see heaven before it was "improved".'

Notable Gardens
Althorp House, Northampton
Blenheim Palace, Oxfordshire
Bowood House, Wiltshire

Burghley House, Stamford
Chatsworth, Derbyshire
Clandon Park, Guildford
Cliveden, Buckinghamshire
Harewoood House, Leeds
Kew Gardens, Richmond (part designed)
Longleat, Wiltshire
Milton Abbey, Dorset
Petworth House, West Sussex
Scampston Hall, Yorkshire
Warwick Castle, Warwickshire

JOHN NASH (1752–1835)

Celebrated for his country-house designs, Nash was employed by the Prince Regent, later George IV, between 1811 and 1825 to plan the new Regent's Park and its surrounding terraces in London.

Notable Works
Buckingham Palace (redevelopment)
Marble Arch
Regent Street
The Royal Mews
Cumberland Terrace
Trafalgar Square
The Royal Pavilion, Brighton (rebuilding)

SIR CHARLES BARRY (1795–1860)

Barry built London's first Italian Renaissance-style palace – the Travellers Club, completed in 1832. He also built the Reform Club, completed in 1841.

He straddled the Anglo-Italian and Gothic periods of nineteenth-century English architecture. In 1836, he won the competition to rebuild the Palace of Westminster after the fire of 1834. He devoted the rest of his life to the project.

His work was continued by three of his sons. John Wolfe-Barry designed Tower Bridge, Charles Barry rebuilt Burlington House in Piccadilly and Edward Barry completed the Palace of Westminster and Halifax Town Hall.

Notable Works
The Athenaeum, Manchester (Manchester City Art Gallery)
Cliveden, Buckinghamshire
Bridgewater House, London
The Treasury Building, Whitehall, London
The Royal College of Surgeons, London
Bowood, Wiltshire (redevelopment)
Duncombe Park, North Yorkshire (redevelopment)
Dunrobin Castle, Sutherland, Scotland (redevelopment)
Eynsham Hall, Oxfordshire (redevelopment)
Gawthorpe Hall, Lancashire (redevelopment)
Harewood House, West Yorkshire (redevelopment)
Highclere Castle, Hampshire (rebuilding)
Kiddington Hall, Oxfordshire
King Edward's School, Birmingham
Kingston Lacy House, Dorset (redevelopment)
Parliament Square, Westminster, London
The Reform Club, London
St Peter's, Brighton
The Travellers Club, London

Augustus W. Pugin (1812–52)

Pugin was the son of a French aristocrat who had fled from the Revolution. He began designing furniture for Windsor Castle in his teens before setting up his own architectural practice. He argued that the quality of a society was commensurate with its architecture and instigated a revival of 'authentic' Gothic design for churches as part of a Roman Catholic revival. Pugin contrasted his buildings with the shoddy Gothic structures, reinforced with iron, erected in the early years of the nineteenth century.

He worked with Charles Barry on the interior of the new Palace of Westminster.

Pugin worked himself to a nervous breakdown while preparing the Medieval Court for the Great Exhibition in 1851. He retreated to a mental asylum.

Notable Works
St Chad's Cathedral, Birmingham
St George's Cathedral, Southwark
St Giles' Church, Cheadle
Alton Castle
Scarisbrick Hall, Lancashire (redevelopment)
St Mary's College, Birmingham

Edwin Lutyens (1869–1944)

Lutyens formed a partnership with the landscape gardener Gertrude Jekyll, and their combined styles defined the post-Victorian English Country House style.

He became Chief Architect of New Delhi in 1912.

Notable Works
The Cenotaph, Whitehall, London

The Viceroy's House, New Delhi
The British Embassy, Washington DC
The Midland Bank, Poultry, London

―――

Modern Architects
And some of their notable works...

―――

RICHARD ROGERS (B. 1933)

Centre Pompidou, Paris
Lloyd's Building, London
Millennium Dome, London
The Welsh Assembly Building

NORMAN FOSTER (B. 1935)

'The Gherkin', 30 St Mary Axe, London
Hearst Tower (New York City)
Millennium Bridge in London
London City Hall
McLaren Technology Centre, Woking
Reichstag redevelopment in Berlin
The Great Court, British Museum, London
The Sage, Gateshead

NICHOLAS GRIMSHAW (B. 1939)

Bibliothèque Nationale de France, Paris
International Terminal at Waterloo Station, London
Lord's Cricket Ground Grandstand, London

Bath Spa, Bath
The Eden Project, Cornwall
Berlin Stock Exchange

11
FOOD AND DRINK

'You can't trust people who cook as badly as that. After
Finland, it's the country with the worst food.'

Jacques Chirac

'England has forty-two religions and only two sauces.'

Voltaire

'To eat well in England, you should have breakfast
three times a day.'

Somerset Maugham

English Cuisine

England's reputation for poor food can be blamed on the rapid urbanization that followed the Industrial Revolution. Food transport did not keep pace with the growing towns and cities, whose populations were cut off from the source of many ingredients and learned to live on tinned food and root vegetables. Overcooking food was a rational response to the threat of infection, and by the time refrigeration became widespread enough to make it unnecessary, the English palate had become used to bland, sub-standard fare. Wartime rationing did not help either. However, in rushing to admit the inferiority of their cuisine, the English have also downplayed the classic dishes that have survived or been reinvented.

Regional Dishes

BLACK PUDDING

The traditional recipe for an English black pudding involves onions, pork fat, oatmeal and pig's blood.

Ramsbottom in Greater Manchester hosts the annual World Black Pudding Throwing Championships. Each competitor throws three standard six-ounce black puddings at a stack of Yorkshire puddings on a 20-foot plinth. Locals claim that the contest is based on an incident during the Wars of the Roses when groups of men ran out of ammunition and threw food at each other.

The Lancashire town of Bury gets through so much of the dish that a 2002 article in the *British Medical Journal* warned that its presence in the bowels of local residents interfered with testing for colorectal cancer.

CORNISH PASTY

Cornwall's traditional pasty contains beef, potato, onion and swede or turnip, although for others few ingredients are ruled out. According to an old Cornish saying, the Devil takes care to stay on the Devon side of the River Tamar in case he ends up diced and cooked inside a pasty.

'Pasty' is an old English word for a pie baked without a dish.

It is considered bad luck for fishermen to take a pasty out to sea with them.

Tin miners would take them to work with a meat filling in one end and a fruit filling in the other so that they could eat a two-course lunch – and, by using the pastry edging as a 'handle' which was later thrown away, they were able to eat without contaminating the food with the mineral dust on their hands.

CUMBERLAND SAUSAGE

The coiled sausage was originally made in Cumbria from Cumberland pigs, a breed that became extinct in the 1960s. Modern replacements include Gloucestershire Old Spot and Large Black.

Cumberland sausage is still distinctive for its coarse texture and length uncoiled – sometimes over a foot (25cm).

JELLIED EELS

The traditional Cockney recipe consists of eels caught in the Thames Estuary, boiled in herbs and vinegar and served in their own jelly, with mashed potato, peas and 'liquor' – a thin parsley sauce.

The popularity of the dish has declined, but East London still boasts around eighty eel, pie and mash shops. The oldest establishment is M. Manze, opened in Tower Bridge Road in 1902.

LANCASHIRE HOT POT

Until the nineteenth century, before it became a stew, hot pot was a soup. It was cooked slowly in an earthenware pot by cotton mill workers who would leave it in the oven so that it would be ready when they returned home in the evening.

Today's hot pots are made with lamb, carrots and onions and a layer of sliced potatoes on the top, but they used to contain oysters in the days when these were cheap.

The novelist Anthony Burgess frequently referred to hot pot in his writing and claimed that he was 'sometimes mentally and physically ill for Lancashire food – lobscouse, hot pot and so on – and I have to have these things'.

LINCOLNSHIRE SAUSAGE

A course-cut pork sausage flavoured with sage.

In 2004, Lincolnshire local newspaper *The Echo* found that Walls' Lincolnshire Sausages were made in Manchester, Morrisons' in Yorkshire and Tesco's in East Yorkshire, Suffolk and Kent. Four out of five people preferred the genuine local article in a blind tasting.

MELTON MOWBRAY PORK PIE

Melton Mowbray's pork industry sprang from its cheese-making. The whey created as a by-product of Stilton made excellent pig feed.

The town's oldest bakery, Dickinson & Morris, has been making the pies since 1851.

Authentic pies do not contain cured meat. The filling is grey rather than pink and encased in a pork jelly inside the pastry.

YORKSHIRE PUDDING

The dish was originally cooked underneath a spit roast, so that meat juices would drip into the pudding tin. The result would be eaten as a starter, or might constitute the entire meal for the children of the house.

The Yorkshire pudding and meat dish known as Toad in the Hole was created in the early eighteenth century as a use for leftovers – not always the sausages with which it is usually made today. No convincing explanation has been put forward for the origin of the name. In Norfolk, Toad in the Hole is called Pudding-pye-doll.

Michelin-starred Restaurants (2006)

THREE MICHELIN STARS

The Fat Duck, Bray, Berkshire
Restaurant Gordon Ramsay, Chelsea, London
The Waterside Inn, Bray, Berkshire

TWO MICHELIN STARS

The Capital Hotel, Knightsbridge, London
Le Gavroche, Mayfair, London
Pied à Terre, Bloomsbury, London
The Square, Mayfair, London
Le Champignon Sauvage, Cheltenham, Gloucestershire

Gidleigh Park, Chagford, Devon
Hibiscus, Ludlow, Shropshire

ONE MICHELIN STAR – LONDON
1 Lombard Street, City of London
Amaya, Belgravia
Assagi, Notting Hill
Aubergine, Chelsea
Chez Bruce, Wandsworth
Club Gascon, West Smithfield
L'Escargot, Soho
Foliage, Mandarin Oriental Hyde Park Hotel, Knightsbridge
The Glasshouse, Kew Village
Gordon Ramsay at Claridge's, Mayfair
The Greenhouse, Mayfair
Hakkasan, Bloomsbury
The Ledbury, Notting Hill
Locanda Locatelli, Marylebone
Maze, London Marriott Hotel, Grosvenor Square, Mayfair
Menu and Grill, Connaught Hotel, Mayfair
Mirabelle, Curzon Street, Mayfair
Nahm, Halkin Hotel, Chelsea
Nobu, Metropolitan Hotel, Mayfair
Nobu Berkeley, Mayfair
Orrery, Marylebone
Pétrus, Berkeley Hotel, Knightsbridge
Rasoi Vineet Bhatia, Chelsea
Rhodes Twenty Four, Tower 42, City of London
Richard Corrigan at Lindsay House, Soho

River Café, Hammersmith
Roussillon, Pimlico
The Savoy Grill, Savoy Hotel, The Strand
Sketch (The Lecture Room), Mayfair
Tamarind, Mayfair
Tom Aikens, Chelsea
Umu, Mayfair
Yauatcha, Soho
Zafferano, Knightsbridge

ONE MICHELIN STAR – REST OF ENGLAND
North Street, Winchcombe, Gloucestershire
36 on the Quay, Emsworth, Hampshire
Arkle, Chester Grosvenor Hotel, Chester, Cheshire
Bath Priory Hotel and Restaurant, Bath, Somerset
Bohemia, St Helier, Jersey
Box Tree, Ilkley, West Yorkshire
Burlington Restaurant, Devonshire Arms, Bolton Abbey, Yorkshire
The Castle Hotel, Taunton, Somerset
Chapter One, Farnborough, Kent
Drake's, Ripley, Surrey
Drakes on the Pond, Abinger Hammer, Surrey
The Elephant, Torquay, Devon
L'Enclume, Grange-over-Sands, Cumbria
Fischer's, Baslow Hall, Derbyshire
The George, Yarmouth, Isle of Wight
Gilpin Lodge, Windermere, Cumbria
The Goose, Britwell Salome, Oxfordshire
Gravetye Manor, East Grinstead, Surrey
The Greyhound, Stockbridge, Hampshire

Hambleton Hall, Oakham, Rutland

The Hand and Flowers, Marlow, Buckinghamshire

The Hare, Hungerford, Berkshire

Harry's Place, Grantham, Lincolnshire

Holbeck Ghyll Country House Hotel, Windermere, Cumbria

Horn of Plenty, Tavistock, Devon

Jessica's, Birmingham

JSW, Petersfield, Hampshire

Juniper, Altrincham, Greater Manchester

The Longridge Restaurant, Longridge, Lancashire

Lucknam Park Country House Hotel, Colerne, Wiltshire

Mallory Court Country House Hotel, Leamington Spa, Warwickshire

The Masons Arms, South Molton, Devon

The Moody Goose at the Old Priory, Midsomer Norton, Somerset

Morston Hall, Blakeney, Norfolk

Mr Underhill's at Dinham Weir, Ludlow, Shropshire

The New Angel, Dartmouth, Devon

Northcote Manor, Blackburn, Lancashire

Ockenden Manor, Cuckfield, West Sussex

Old Vicarage, Ridgeway, near Sheffield, South Yorkshire

The Olive Branch, Clipsham, Rutland

Orestone Manor, Torquay, Devon

L'Ortolan, Shinfield, near Reading, Berkshire

Le Poussin at Whitley Ridge, Brockenhurst, Hampshire

Pool Court at 42, Leeds, West Yorkshire

Read's, Faversham, Kent

Restaurant Sat Bains, Nottingham

Ripley's, Padstow, Cornwall

Sharrow Bay Country House Hotel, Ullswater, Cumbria

Simpsons, Birmingham

Stagg Inn, Kington, Herefordshire
The Star Inn, Harome, Helmsley, North Yorkshire
St Ervan Manor, Padstow, Cornwall
The Trouble House Inn, Tetbury, Gloucestershire
The Vineyard at Stockcross, Newbury, Berkshire
Waldo's, Cliveden, Taplow, Berkshire
The West House, Biddenden, Kent
Whatley Manor, Malmesbury, Wiltshire
Winteringham Fields, Winteringham, North Lincolnshire
Yorke Arms, Pateley Bridge, North Yorkshire

―――

Fruits and Vegetables and their Dates of Introduction

―――

Native	Blackberry, Blackcurrant, Blueberry, Broad Beans, Crab Apple, Raspberry, Redcurrant, Samphire
Roman period	Apple, Apricot, Artichoke, Cabbage, Damson, Purple Carrot, Cherry, Cucumber, Garlic, Grapes, Leek, Onion, Parsnip, Peach, Pear, Peas, Plum, Shallots, Turnip
Twelfth century	Spinach
Thirteenth century	Chicory
Fouteenth century	Cauliflower, Lettuce, Radish
Fifteenth century	Beetroot, Swede
Sixteenth century	Asparagus, Gooseberry, Green Beans, Parsnip, Potato (1563),* Rhubarb, Salsify, Tomato (c. 1570)†

Seventeenth century	Orange Carrot,‡ Celery, Fennel, Kale, Strawberry, Swiss Chard
Eighteenth century	Broccoli, Celeriac, Greengage
Nineteenth century	Brussels Sprouts, Marrow, Watercress

* John Hawkins brought the potato to England twenty years before it was reintroduced by Sir Walter Ralegh.

† The English originally believed that tomatoes were poisonous and first began eating them in small amounts as an aphrodisiac after the French practice.

‡ Orange carrots were a mutation from Holland, where they were grown patriotically.

NB Some dates are disputed by historians, as many vegetables made an appearance in England before they were cultivated here, others had to be reintroduced, while certain less well-known varieties were indigenous. For example, a variety of wild cabbage grew in the British Isles before the Roman period.

Sandwiches

ORIGIN

The modern sandwich – using slices of bread as opposed to whole pieces or small loaves such as matzohs – was invented by John Montagu (1718–92), the Fourth Earl of Sandwich. Montagu was a gambling addict and asked for meat to be brought to him between two slices of bread so that he could eat without getting grease on his playing cards. The first sandwich was a salt-beef toastie.

ENGLAND'S MOST POPULAR FILLINGS

1. Chicken (30 per cent of all sales)
2. Cheese
3. Ham
4. Egg
5. Tuna
6. Prawn
7. Bacon
8. 'Breakfast'
9. Salmon
10. Beef

Source: British Sandwich Association 2006

Earliest Foreign Restaurants

Chinese:	Maxim's	1908	Soho, London
French:	Universal Symposium	1851	Kensington, London
Greek:	The White Tower	1939	Percy Street, London
Indian:	Hindostanee Coffee House	1809	George Street, London
Italian:	Salvo Jure	1859	Brushfield Street, London
Japanese:	The Ajimura	1972	Shelton Street, London
Spanish:	The Spanish Club	1920	Cavendish Square, London
Thai:	The Bangkok	1967	Bute Street, London

Tea

EARLY HISTORY

Tea was brought to England by East India Company traders in 1644 and was first sold to the general public from Thomas Garway's London coffee house in Exchange Alley in 1657. This was an age in which no new foodstuff was ever sold without outlandish claims concerning its medicinal properties, and Garway's tea was promised to extend longevity and increase the libido.

However, it still did not become widely popular among the wealthy classes until it was drunk in vast quantities at the court of Charles II by his Portuguese wife Catherine of Braganza. The drink then took the country by storm, leading to a drop in the consumption of alcohol and, with it, a fall in the Crown's tax revenues. The pot of tea became such a social hub that in 1675 Charles attempted to forbid its sale from private houses as a move to hamper seditious meetings. The resulting outcry forced him to reverse his proclamation in under a week.

Charles II's reign also saw the advent of tea gardens, where the leisured classes could stroll and enjoy a drink and a game of bowls while listening to open-air orchestras. The practice of tipping was born from coin boxes marked 'To Insure Prompt Service', which was essential if the tea was not to go cold on its long journey from the kitchens.

MODERN HISTORY

Earl Grey tea was named after Prime Minister Charles Grey, who put an end to the East India Company's monopoly on tea importing in

1858. Two tea companies – Twinings and Jacksons of Piccadilly – both claim to have invented the original recipe. The Seville orange and lemon added later to make Lady Grey were said to dampen the increased sexual urges that tea was thought to bring on.

Englishman Richard Blechynden invented iced tea at the World's Fair in St Louis, Missouri, in 1904.

During the First World War, the German U-Boat blockade led to a severe shortage of the national drink. This would never be allowed to happen again, and during the Second World War tea stockpiles were spread across five hundred locations to minimize the risk of loss in an air raid.

No fewer than 137 million cups of tea are drunk every day in England.

TEA SHOPS

John Cadbury, founder of the Cadbury Chocolate Company, originally ran a tea shop, while Henry Charles Harrod was a tea wholesaler before he founded his famous department store.

The custom of High Tea served in the afternoon was begun in the early nineteenth century by Anna, Seventh Duchess of Bedford, who would invite guests for tea and cakes at 5 p.m.

In the mid eighteenth century tea duty reached 119 per cent, creating a lucrative trade for smugglers from Holland and Scandinavia. Quality suffered as unscrupulous suppliers 'cut' their product with sloe leaves, liquorice or the collected and dried dregs from used teapots. William Pitt the Younger saved the English cuppa with the 1784 Commutation Act that reduced the duty to 12.5 per cent. The following year, the Food and Drug Act instigated harsh penalties for those who dared to mix the national drink with impurities.

In 1864, the manageress of the Aerated Bread Company's shop at

London Bridge persuaded her bosses to let her sell cups of tea to customers, thereby establishing England's first tea shop. Her success led to a chain of ABC establishments across the country. The first Lyons tea shop opened in 1894, and the Lyons brand soon became a staple of the English high street. At the chain's high point there were 250 outlets, including seven in Oxford Street. However, only three were corner houses.

Roast Beef

The night before the Battle of Agincourt in Shakespeare's *Henry V*, the French Constable quivers at the prospect of facing the English with their 'great meals of beef and iron and steel, they will eat like wolves and fight like devils'.

However, beef did not become a national dish until the eighteenth century, when huge roasts were thought manly and patriotic in comparison with the dainty meals eaten by the hated French enemy. The notion was reprised in the *Daily Telegraph* when France limped out of the 2002 World Cup, having failed to score a single goal. The correspondent blamed four years without imported beef after the BSE scare for enfeebling the French players.

In 1735, the theatre impresario John Rich founded the Sublime Society of Beefsteaks, a dining club dedicated to fine grills and claret that spawned many imitators.

Under James I, the Yeomen of the Guard were given special rations of beef and acquired the name 'Beefeaters'.

ENGLISH CATTLE BREEDS

British White	North Devon
English Longhorn	Polled Hereford
Gloucester	Shorthorn
Hereford	South Devon
Jersey	Sussex
Lincoln Red	

Fish and Chips

'We stood between the Government and grave
discontent in congested districts and, more than any
other trade in the country, between the very poorest of
our population and famine and revolt.'

Statement from the Northern Counties Confederation
of Fish Friers after the First World War

ORIGINS

According to Professor Panikos Panayi of Leicester's De Montfort University, the dish is a combination of the French invention of chipped potatoes and the Jewish tradition of deep-frying fish.

Fried fish shops were common in the nineteenth century, when they were often a public nuisance, with many operating out of a room in shared lodgings.

Fish was not sold with chips as a fast-food meal until John Lees set up a wooden hut in Mossley in Lancashire in 1863 and Joseph Malin had opened a shop in Cleveland Street in London in 1860.

The world's first recorded fast-food delivery service was started in 1936 when a member of the Keighley Fish Friers thought of riding around the newly built estates on the outskirts of the town on a motorbike and selling his meals from his sidecar.

Harry Ramsden opened his first fish shop in Bradford after the First World War. It stayed open every day of the year, including Christmas. He once asked a critic, 'Don't you get bloody fed up with turkey?' The chain now has 170 branches.

Fish and chips was so important that it was one of the few foods not to be rationed during the Second World War.

The EC once ordered the National Federation of Fish Fryers to rename fishcakes 'fried fish fillet potato sandwiches'.

The story that the New Labour politician Peter Mandelson once pointed at the mushy peas in a Hartlepool fish and chip shop and said, 'I'll have some of that guacamole', was fabricated by journalists.

On the Plate

The fish is usually haddock or hake in the north of England and cod in the south. While the south uses cooking oil for frying, Yorkshire and other parts of the north use beef dripping. Northern dishes are generally thought far superior, if less healthy, while London itself has only a handful of fish and chip shops worth visiting.

The most generous portions of chips are served in the West Midlands. Birmingham holds the record.

The average portion of fish and chips contains 870 calories, half of them in the form of fat.

Newspaper was phased out as a wrapping in the 1980s after it was discovered that printers' ink could release trace quantities of cyanide.

Cheeses

The English consume only half as much cheese per person as the French, Germans, Italians and Greeks. This is chiefly because cheese features in the Continental breakfast. Goat's milk was favoured historically, but since the Middle Ages cow's milk has replaced it.

CHEDDAR

'Cheddar' is a verb meaning to dice the curd so that the whey can be drained off. Cheddar is ready to eat after three months but can be aged for up to two years or more inside muslin.

Henry II bought 10,240lbs (4,645 kg) of Cheddar in 1170, having declared it the best cheese in the kingdom.

During the reign of Charles I, Cheddar was so popular that the entire supply was made to order for the king's court.

Cheese once had to be made within 30 miles (48 km) of Wells Cathedral to be called Cheddar. Today, the original West Country Farmhouse Cheddar must be produced in Devon, Dorset, Somerset or Cornwall.

Captain Scott took 3,500lbs (1,588 kg) of Cheddar with him on his expedition to the Antarctic in 1901.

CHESHIRE

Made from cow's milk, it matures in two to six months and comes in white, red and blue varieties, the red being coloured with the vegetable dye annatto.

It is England's oldest cheese and appears in the Domesday Book.

The local church once believed that cheese-making on a Sunday was a grievous sin that contributed to the divine punishment of the 1865 cattle plague.

DOUBLE GLOUCESTER

Every year for several centuries, a cheese-rolling race has been held on Cooper's Hill in Gloucestershire. On the last weekend in May, participants chase a specially made 7lb (3 kg) cheese down a 200-yard (183 metre) slope with a two in one gradient. Broken bones and other injuries are common.

The less popular Single Gloucester is made mainly from skimmed milk.

It was originally made from the milk of Old Gloucester cattle, of which very few specimens survive.

STILTON

Stilton was first sold in the eighteenth century from the Bell Inn in the village of Stilton to coach passengers on the Great North Road. However, it was never made in the village and came from Melton Mowbray.

It can only be produced in Nottinghamshire, Derbyshire and Leicestershire. Only six dairies are licensed to produce it.

The blue veins are created by adding blue mould spores and piercing the cheese with stainless steel needles.

RED LEICESTER

Red is the only variety of Leicester cheese. It originally acquired its tint from carrot or beetroot juice, but today annatto is used.

WENSLEYDALE

Brought to England by Cistercian monks who came over with William the Conqueror.

T. S. Eliot called it 'The Mozart of cheeses'.

It is eaten young, matured for only three weeks.

Wensleydale almost fell out of production in the 1990s until its role in the Wallace and Gromit animated films turned it into a supermarket bestseller.

LANCASHIRE

Arguably the best of all cheeses for making cheese on toast. Its old name was Leigh Toaster after the town of Leigh near Manchester.

Lancashire was the cheese the marooned pirate Ben Gunn dreamed of in Robert Louis Stevenson's *Treasure Island*.

The British Cheese Board recommends eating it with ruby port, sauvignon blanc or Coca Cola.

Condiments and Sauces

The paucity of recipes and refinement in English cuisine has prompted some of the best condiments and relishes in the world. Jars of Marmite and bottles of salad cream are often highly prized in ex-pat communities.

WORCESTERSHIRE SAUCE

When the former Governor of Bengal, Lord Marcus Sandys, returned to his Worcester home in the early nineteenth century, he wanted to reproduce a sauce that he had tasted on his travels. In 1835 he asked

John Lea and William Perrin, the owners of a chemist shop, to make up the recipe. However, the result was unpalatable and the barrel containing the mixture was left in a cellar. Several months later they decided to taste it again before they threw it out and found that it had matured and become delicious. The two men bought the rights to the recipe from Lord Sandys and launched Lea and Perrin's Sauce in 1838.

SALAD CREAM

Developed for the English market by Heinz in 1925.

During the Second World War, it was widely used to spice up bland rationed food.

Despite its low-rent image, Marco Pierre White described salad cream as 'one of the greatest culinary inventions of the twentieth century'.

HP SAUCE

The sauce was launched by the Midland Vinegar Company in 1903 after the recipe was acquired for £150 from F. G. Garton, a Nottingham shopkeeper, to settle a debt.

Garton had given his invention its name after hearing that a bottle had been seen in a restaurant at the Houses of Parliament.

MARMITE

The Marmite Food Company was established in Burton upon Trent in 1902, but it was a German chemist, Justus Liebig, who first learned that the yeast by-product of the brewing industry could be turned into a vegetarian spread.

Marmite did not take off for several years and only started to become popular after the health benefits of vitamin B were discovered in 1912. It was included in army rations during the world wars.

The name comes from the French word for the stockpot featured on the label.

BRANSTON PICKLE

The sweet pickle was first produced by Crosse & Blackwell in the Staffordshire village of Branston in 1922.

Rumours of a shortage following a fire at the firm's factory in 2004 led to jars selling for up to £25 each on the internet auction site eBay.

COLMAN'S MUSTARD

Invented in Norwich by Jeremiah Colman in 1814. It was made at Stoke Mill, now a Colman's-themed restaurant.

Colman's heirs pioneered employee welfare schemes by funding healthcare and education for their staff.

BIRD'S CUSTARD

Birmingham pharmacist Alfred Bird invented custard powder in 1837. Bird's wife was unable to eat ordinary custard as she was allergic to eggs, so her husband formulated an alternative. After it met with the approval of his dinner guests, he went into full-scale production. Bird also invented baking powder so that he could make yeast-free bread for his wife.

BISTO GRAVY

Bisto powder was invented in 1908 by Messrs Roberts & Patterson after their wives asked them to find an easier way to make gravy.

It was so named because it Browns, Seasons and Thickens in One.

The 'Bisto Kids' were created by cartoonist Wilf Owen and became cult figures in the 1920s and 1930s.

MINT SAUCE

Mint sauce was used by the Romans, but it has always been far more popular in England than in any of the Imperium's other former provinces. The French react with horror when they see an Englishman add a dollop to roast lamb.

Apples

England produces the best apples in the world, which is largely thanks to Henry VIII and his fruiterer Richard Harris, who collected the finest varieties from around the globe and planted orchards at Teynham in Kent.

The National Fruit Collection at Brogdale Horticultural Trust in Faversham houses the world's largest collection of apple trees, with 2,040 varieties.

It has become increasingly difficult to find home-grown apples in the shops in recent years. Two-thirds of the apples we eat are now imported and two-thirds of the country's apple orchards have disappeared since 1970.

The two most famous English apples are Bramley and Cox's.

BRAMLEY

In around 1809 Mary Ann Brailsford, a young girl from Southwell, Nottinghamshire, grew the first Bramley tree in her garden from a pip. The tree is still alive and producing fruit today. A butcher named Matthew Bramley later bought the property and allowed cuttings from the tree to be sold on condition that the fruit was named after him.

Unlike other varieties, the Bramley's low sugar and high malic acid content allows its flavour to survive the cooking process, and 95 per cent of all cooking apples sold are Bramleys.

COX'S ORANGE PIPPIN

England's finest dessert apple was bred in 1825 in Colnbrook, Berkshire, by Richard Cox, a brewer from Bermondsey.

The Orange Pippin now accounts for half the country's output of dessert apples. It is available from September to April and is at its best around Christmas time.

The variety is difficult to grow and tends to be susceptible to disease.

OTHER NOTABLE VARIETIES

Adams Pearmain: A dryer, blushed apple with an elongated shape, it was popular with the Victorians.

Ashmead's Kernel: A small, lumpy russet that tastes similar to a pear.

Charles Ross: A cross between a Cox's Orange Pippin and a cooking apple.

Discovery: An early season apple ready in August, it is pale green with red patches and dates from the 1940s.

Early Windsor: Similar to a Cox, but crunchier and sweeter.

Egremont Russet: First recorded in 1872, this brown, rough-skinned apple has dry flesh with a nutty flavour.

Lord Lambourne: An acidic and fragrant fruit in shops between September and November.

Worcester Pearmain: A rosy apple with a strawberry flavour.

The Quaker Chocolatiers

England's most famous confectioners were Quaker families. Due to their non-conformist religious beliefs they could not enter the universities – which were associated with the Church of England. This meant they could not go into the professions, while their pacifism ruled out careers in the army. However, there were no restrictions on a life in business, and the Quakers' involvement in the temperance movement led them to manufacture and promote drinking chocolate and cocoa as alternatives to alcohol. As employers, they were concerned with social justice and better working conditions.

CADBURY'S OF BIRMINGHAM

Cadbury Ltd was set up by John Cadbury in Birmingham in 1824. The firm started life as a grocer's shop and became a drinking-chocolate and cocoa manufacturer.

The Bournville factory and village was created 4 miles (6.4 km) south of Birmingham in 1878 so that working-class employees could enjoy living and working in a pastoral setting.

Cadbury's pioneered holidays, introducing the half-day working day on Saturdays and closing the factory on bank holidays.

Cadbury's Dairy Milk was introduced in the early 1900s. Fruit & Nut was invented in 1928 and Whole Nut in 1933.

The company merged with Schweppes in 1969.

ROWNTREES OF YORK

Joseph Rowntree joined his brother at the company in 1869 and transformed it from a small business with thirty employees to a concern employing four thousand by the end of the century. He gave half his estate to create three Rowntree Trusts to 'seek out the underlying causes of weakness or evil'. In 1999, readers of the *York Evening Press* voted him York's 'Man of the Millennium'.

The company makes Aero, Kit Kat, Black Magic, Quality Street, Smarties, Fruit Pastilles, Fruit Gums and Polo Mints.

Rowntree was taken over by Nestlé in 1988.

TERRY'S OF YORK

The factory set up by Joseph Terry in Clementhorpe in 1886 went on to create the Chocolate Orange, which is flavoured with real orange oil. Before that came the now forgotten Chocolate Apple. A Chocolate Lemon also made a brief appearance.

FRY'S OF BRISTOL

Joseph Fry began making chocolate in the 1750s, and the business grew into J. S. Fry & Sons, which launched the first mass-produced chocolate bar in 1847. Fry's Chocolate Cream, which to this day remains a vegan recipe, was invented in 1866 and Fry's Turkish Delight in 1914.

English Winemaking

'The English have a miraculous power of turning wine into water.'

Oscar Wilde

THE ROMAN PERIOD

The Romans had brought winemaking to the British Isles, but the art was largely lost due to the Saxon and Viking invasions until it was reintroduced by French abbots after the Norman Conquest. Vinticulture was then able to flourish for around three centuries due to an auspicious shift in England's climate.

THE MIDDLE AGES

The Domesday Book of 1085–6 listed forty-six vineyards, twelve of which were owned by monastic orders and the rest by noblemen. By the fifteenth century the number had grown to 139. Production was concentrated in Somerset, Gloucestershire, Herefordshire and Worcestershire and along the south-east coast.

Wine was first imported from Bordeaux in the mid twelfth century during the reign of Henry II, and within two hundred years improvements in transport and preserving techniques gave French wine the edge over home-grown vintages.

In the fourteenth century, the onset of wetter, colder summers coincided with the Black Death, which left a shortage of manpower that contributed to a long-term decline in winemaking. The Dissolution of the Monasteries in 1536 dealt a further blow to a sickly industry.

THE INVENTION OF CHAMPAGNE

Champagne was invented in England thirty-five years before Dom Perignon first made it in France. In 1662, Christopher Merrett presented a paper to the Royal Society describing a process whereby coopers added large quantities of sugar and molasses to create a 'gay, brisk and sparkling' wine. In more recent years, winemakers have used clones of the French Pinot Noir, Pinot Meunier and Chardonnay grapes to make English champagne. The chalk and clay soils of much of southern England are similar to those of the Champagne region of France. English vineyards have twice won the trophy for Best Sparkling Wine in the World: Nyetimber Vineyard of West Sussex in 1998 and Ridgeview Wine Estate of East Sussex in 2005.

THE RETURN OF WINEMAKING

After a revival in the 1980s and 1990s, there are now more than three hundred vineyards in England. Most are in the south, but the most northerly commercial operation is Leventhorpe Vineyard, near Leeds.

Prime Minister Tony Blair served English reds at a European Union summit in 2005 to a mixed reception. Afterwards, Italian Prime Minister Silvio Berlusconi sent his Swedish counterpart, Goran Persson, twenty-four bottles of Italian wine, saying they would help him recover from the experience.

London Gin

Distillers began to experiment with juniper berries in the 1560s, though during this period spirits, or aqua vitae, were produced mainly for medicinal purposes. In 1585, the Earl of Leicester's men brought back gin from their military service in Holland, where it was administered to the troops as 'Dutch courage'.

After the Glorious Revolution, William of Orange raised tariffs on brandy imported from Catholic winemaking countries and encouraged the local production of gin in its place.

Gin was so cheap that by the 1720s London was in the grip of 'gin fever', with a quarter of its houses used for the production or sale of the spirit. William Hogarth's engraving *Gin Lane* depicts a gin shop with a sign reading, 'Drunk for a penny, Dead drunk for twopence, Clean straw for Nothing'. The government's attempt to curb public drunkenness with the Gin Act of 1736 led to rioting in the streets. Distilling went underground, while its products were passed off as medicine.

The smoother, less sweet spirit known as London Dry Gin was developed in the mid nineteenth century.

Gin and tonic was invented as a way to mask the bitter taste of the quinine dissolved in tonic water that was drunk in India and the tropics to treat malaria.

'English Rose' Cocktail Recipe

¾ oz apricot brandy
1 ½ oz gin
¾ oz dry vermouth
1 tsp grenadine syrup
¼ tsp lemon juice
1 cherry

Rub rim of cocktail glass with lemon juice and dip rim of glass in powdered sugar. Shake all ingredients (except cherry) with ice and strain into sugar-rimmed glass. Top with the cherry and serve.

Pimm's No 1 Cup

Pimm's was invented by James Pimm, landlord of London's Oyster Bar in 1823. He mixed a cocktail of gin, liqueurs and fruit extracts to complement his patrons' food.

The No. 1 Cup was the size of the tankard the drink was served in.

Pimm concocted two more cups: No. 2, based on whisky, and No. 3, based on brandy. The company later added Nos. 4, 5 and 6, made with rum, rye and vodka respectively.

Eighty thousand half-pints of Pimm's and lemonade were sold at Wimbledon in 2005.

Cider and Perry

HISTORY

The art of making cider was brought to England by the Normans, who introduced new apple varieties for the purpose.

Workers in medieval monastic orchards and farm labourers in the eighteenth century received part of their wages in cider. At three to four pints a day on average, this amounted to around a fifth of their income. A clause was added to the Truck Act of 1887 to put a stop to the practice.

In the 1640s, Lord Scudamore, who bred the classic English cider apple, the Redstreak, made the first sparkling cider by bottling it in newly developed tough glass before it had finished fermenting.

In 1626, Francis Bacon noted the power of cider and perry to cure scurvy. In 1747, the naval surgeon James Lind conducted a trial aboard HMS *Salisbury* that showed that when citrus fruit was unavailable, cider drunk in sufficient quantities was the next best thing.

THE CIDER RIOTS

In 1763, the Prime Minister, Lord Bute, introduced a tax of four shillings a hogshead on cider and perry to help pay debts incurred during the Seven Years War. Rioting ensued and his effigy was burnt in market squares across the country. Bute's measure gave Excise men the right to enter homes for inspection without a warrant and was opposed by William Pitt with the phrase 'An Englishman's home is his castle'. Bute was forced to resign soon afterwards and the tax was reduced. The grateful Somerset landowner Sir William Pynsent left Pitt his estate, on which Capability Brown built a monument now known as the Cider Monument.

THE CIDER MP

C. W. Radcliffe Cooke, the MP for Hereford, is credited with saving England's cider and perry industries in the late nineteenth century by campaigning for expansion and conducting a crusade against government plans to tax the drinks. He was so obsessive that he became known as the 'Member for Cider'.

English Beer

ALE

'Ale' was the term originally given in England to mead adulterated with malted grain to differentiate it from pure honey mead. Eventually, the honey was eschewed entirely.

Adding hops to ale to make beer was banned for a period under Henry VIII, as he believed that it spoiled the flavour.

Ale was traditionally brewed by women, or alewives, since it was a low-status profession. Poor-performing ales or small measures resulted in the alewife being ducked, a practice that continued in places such as Chelmsford until the turn of the nineteenth century.

In 975, King Edgar tried to control public drunkenness by decreeing that the standard alehouse serving of a four-pint tankard, or 'pottle', be subdivided into eight measures by means of pegs set inside the vessel. No one was to drink more than a single measure at a time. However, the act of setting a 'reasonable' level of intake only incited the red-blooded Englishman to surpass it and to 'take his fellows down a peg or two' by out-drinking them.

Ale was first taxed in 1188, when Henry II levied the Saladin Tithe to fund the crusades.

England's oldest brewery is Shepherd Neame Ltd of Faversham, Kent, which opened in 1698.

After D-Day during the Second World War, Spitfires occasionally carried English beer over to France in either kegs under their wings or in their spare fuel tanks as a treat for the troops.

STOUT

Stout was invented in the 1730s in London, where it was originally called 'porter' due to its popularity among the porters in the city's markets.

IPA

India Pale Ale (IPA) was the first beer to be made specifically for export. Its higher alcohol and hop content prevented it from spoiling on the long, warm sea voyage to India in the days of the Raj.

Domestic sales of pale ale took off in the mid nineteenth century after glass replaced pewter tankards and people could see the consistency of what they were drinking.

CAMRA

The Campaign for Real Ale (CAMRA) was founded in St Albans in 1971 to promote cask-conditioned beer. This is a more flavourful drink that has not been pasteurized or filtered and undergoes secondary fermentation in the cask from which it is served.

Pubs

'When you have lost your inns, drown your empty selves, for you will have lost the last of England!'

Hilaire Belloc

THE OLDEST PUB

Ye Olde Fighting Cocks in St Albans is England's oldest pub. It dates to 795, though it was converted to a dovecote in the Middle Ages before being rebuilt in 1485. The cockfighting pit is now a bar. Another contender is Ye Olde Trip to Jerusalem in Nottingham. Part of its premises was once Nottingham Castle's malt house, cut from the rock of the castle, and dates from 1189. The pub acquired its name because Richard the Lionheart gathered knights at the castle before his journey to Jerusalem to fight in the Third Crusade.

The Highest Pub

The highest inn in England is the Tan Hill Inn (1,742 feet) (531 metres), north of Keld, Yorkshire, located on the route of the Pennine Way long-distance path.

The Smallest Pub

The Nutshell in Bury St Edmunds, Suffolk, measures 15 feet by 7 feet 6 inches (4.6 metres by 2.3 metres).

History of Pubs

Pub signs derive from the Roman practice of advertising the profession of a building's occupants in a carved terracotta relief with, for example, a goat representing a dairy. England's earliest pub names can therefore be said to be the Bush or the Vine after the motif used to designate a drinking house.

Since the Middle Ages it has been the job of the 'ale-conner' to test the quality of a pub's beer by donning a pair of leather breeches and sitting in a puddle of its best bitter poured on to any flat surface in the establishment while he enjoys a drink. When he has finished, he gets up and examines the trousers for stickiness, which gives an indication of the beer's alcohol content. Four ale-conners are still chosen annually by London's liverymen.

Pub licensing laws were brought in during the First World War. In 1915 David Lloyd George complained, 'We are fighting Germany, Austria and drink; and, as far as I can see, the greatest of these three deadly foes is drink.' The government also banned 'treating' – buying a round.

Pub Names

The most common pub names are The Red Lion and The Crown, with roughly equal numbers.

Heraldry

Red Lion: The first Red Lions referred to the badge of John of Gaunt, Duke of Lancaster and son of Edward III, but many more were created at the instigation of James I to popularize his rule under the sign of the Scottish lion rampant.

Rose and Crown: A name that became popular in response to the creep of Red Lions. It showed loyalty both to the Scottish king of England and to the English nation represented by the rose.

Blue Lion: A symbol of Denmark thought to have been used in honour of James I's queen, Anne of Denmark.

Golden Lion: The badge of Henry I.

White Lion: The badge of Edward IV.

White Hart: The badge of Richard II, which all London inns were compelled to display during his reign on pain of forfeiting their ale.

White Horse: The House of Hanover's emblem.

Rising Sun: The badge of Edward III.

Marquis of Granby: Named after the benevolent eighteenth-century military leader who would sometimes set up old soldiers in the pub business.

Cross Keys: The arms of the Archbishop of York, though they also denote the bishops of Winchester, St Asaph, Gloucester, Exeter and Peterborough along with St Peter.

Bear and Ragged Staff: The Earl of Warwick's emblem.

Royal Oak: Recalls the oak tree used as a hiding place by Charles II after his defeat at the Battle of Worcester in 1651.

Phraseology

Some pub names derive from corruptions and adaptations of common phrases:

Pig and Whistle: A corruption of pig and wassail, referring to the cup of spiced ale known as a 'wassail bowl' and either the pegs once used to mark drinking measures or an earthenware vessel called a 'piggin'.

Bag O'Nails: Said to be a corruption of 'Bacchanals', though it could also simply refer to an ironmonger's sign.

Goat and Compasses: Widely believed to be a corruption of 'God encompasseth us'.

Salutation: From the Annunciation, in which the Archangel Gabriel informed Mary that she was to bear the Son of God.

Elephant and Castle: A seventeenth-century pub at Newington Butts was supposedly named after a corruption of the Infanta de Castile, otherwise known as Eleanor of Castile, wife of Edward I. A more likely theory is that the name comes from the merchants who used to drink there – an elephant with an ornamental carriage or 'castle' on its back was the logo of the ivory-trading Cutlers' Company.

Entertainments

Other pub names referred to popular amusements and other activities that took place inside or on their grounds:

Bear: A celebration of bear baiting.

Dog and Duck: Although many such signs today feature a happy-looking duck, the name originally signified that a sport lethal to the creatures could be played at the establishment. A duck with clipped wings would be put to water and a dog sent in to catch it.

Blue Posts: There are four pubs in London's Soho bearing this name, which refers to the blue posts that were once used to mark the boundaries of a hunting ground.

Chequers: From the coat of arms of the Fitzwarren family, who licensed alehouses in the fifteenth century, but also from the 'exchequer board' that some medieval innkeepers used to advertise their other role as moneylenders.

Nag's Head: Denoted a pub where a riding horse could be hired.

Cock and Bottle: The 'cock' in the name refers to the tap through which draught ale and beer is dispensed rather than to a bird.

12

SYMBOLS AND INSTITUTIONS

Saint George

LIFE AND MARTYRDOM

George was born in Cappadocia in Turkey and never set foot in England.

He was a Roman officer martyred at Lydda in Palestine (now Lod in Israel) around AD 300 during the Emperor Diocletian's persecution of the Christians. He was thrown into jail for defending the emperor's victims, tortured and finally beheaded when he refused to renounce his faith.

The Church of St George in Rome supposedly possesses his preserved head.

MYTHOLOGY

Miracles associated with the saint include raising the dead, destroying entire armies instantly, surviving repeated dismemberment, immolation and burial, causing timber to burst into flames, and milk instead of blood flowing from his severed head.

However, he was described by Pope Gelasius as one of the saints 'whose names are rightly reverenced among us, but whose actions are known only to God'.

THE DRAGON

Diocletian is thought to be the origin of George's association with the dragon. The tyrant was sometimes referred to as a 'Dragon' and in the Middle Ages he was allegorized as a giant serpent slain by the saint. There is a less likely story that St George rescued a Libyan king's daughter from the beast, which he defeated and then dragged into the town of Silene, using the princess's girdle, before beheading it. He refused the king's offer of a reward and rode off on his white charger. According to a further theory, George's battle was a christianization of the Greek legend of Perseus, who rescued Andromeda from a sea monster near Lydda.

THE CRUSADES

He became associated with the crusades when his ghostly form was said to have aided the Frankish knights at the Battle of Antioch in 1098.

In c. 1348 Edward III founded the Order of the Garter and made George its patron. This was the first step towards making him the patron saint of England. The process was completed when Henry V's army won the Battle of Agincourt in 1415.

St George's arms of the red cross on a white background became part of English military uniform in the fourteenth century. Large orders were made for pennants in the 1340s at the time of the Battle of Crécy, and Richard II subsequently ordered his troops invading Scotland in 1385 to wear the sign on their chests and backs. The flag was used as an ensign on ships as early as 1284, when it was incorporated into the seal of Lyme Regis. In 2005, Neil Prendergast was fined £30 by Oldham police for sticking a Cross of St George over the EU banner on his car's licence plate.

THE PATRON SAINT

St George's Day has been 23 April ever since the national Synod of Oxford of 1222.

St George is also a patron saint of Aragon, Catalonia, Georgia, Lithuania, Palestine, Portugal, Greece, Moscow, Beirut, Czechoslovakia, Istanbul, Genoa, Venice and Germany.

He is patron saint of soldiers, archers, cavalry and chivalry, farmers and field workers, riders, saddlers, boy scouts and victims of leprosy, plague, scrofula and syphilis.

———

Ten Nicknames for the English

———

Limey – USA (from the Royal Navy's use of lime juice to prevent scurvy)

Pommy – Australia (from 'immigrant' and 'pomegranate' – for their sunburn)

Rosbif – France (from the favourite English dish)

Goddam – France (from the favourite oath of English soldiers during the Hundred Years War)

Gwailo – Hong Kong (Cantonese for 'ghost-person')

Rooinek – Afrikaans ('red neck')

Soutpiel– Afrikaans ('salt dick' – from 'one leg in England, one in South Africa...')

Sassenach – Scotland (from the Gaelic '*Sassunoch*' for 'southerner')

SELF-IMPOSED

Tommy Atkins – the archetypal infantryman

Jack Tar – the archetypal English sailor

The Red Pillar Box

The Royal Mail pillar box was designed by the novelist Anthony Trollope. The first was installed in 1853 at Botchergate in Carlisle. The oldest surviving box stands at Barnes Cross, Bishop's Caundle in Dorset, and dates from the same year.

Early Victorian boxes were green. Red became the standard colour in the later nineteenth century after it was introduced in 1874 for better visibility.

Each box bears the monogram of the reigning monarch. Most of those erected during Edward VIII's brief reign had their doors bearing his insignia replaced.

The Red Telephone Box

'The Englishman's telephone box is his castle. Like the London taxi, it can be entered by a gentleman in a top hat. It protects the user's privacy, keeps him warm and is large enough for a small cocktail party.'

Letter protesting the replacement of England's bright red phone boxes, *International Herald Tribune*, 30 August 1985

The classic red telephone box was designed by the architect Sir Giles Gilbert Scott in 1924 in response to a design competition. Gilbert Scott was an architect who also designed Waterloo Bridge, Battersea

Power Station and Liverpool's Anglican cathedral. He wanted the boxes to be painted silver, but the Post Office decided on red. The roof of the box was inspired by the dome Sir John Soane designed in 1815 for his family tomb in St Pancras Old Church Gardens in London.

They were erected in almost every English town to mark the Silver Jubilee of George V in 1935.

The box was replaced by the KX100 model in 1996. With only one sheet of toughened glass on each side of the kiosk, it was less easy to vandalize. Its successors did away with the door, rendering mistreatment difficult and hearing one's conversation over the noise of traffic near impossible.

The Nottinghamshire village of Kirsall claims to have the best-kept telephone box in the world. Locals place fresh flowers in the box and decorate it with lights at Christmas time.

The Routemaster Bus

ADVENT

The first hop-on hop-off precursor to the Routemaster, the 'RT', was designed by London Transport's chief engineer of buses, Albert Durrent, in 1939 to replace trams and trolleybuses. Durrent worked in tank research during the Second World War and brought military technologies to bear on future models. Colin Curtis's design for the 64-seat 'RM' Routemaster, constructed with an all-aluminium body, was introduced in 1956. Its new features included independent front suspension, power steering and a fully automatic gearbox.

A lengthened version called the 'RML' became the standard type from 1965 until the Routemaster was phased out in 2005. It could carry seventy-two passengers – the same capacity as a modern double-decker despite weighing two tons less.

A Routemaster was driven in the Cliff Richard film *Summer Holiday*. However, contrary to popular belief, they were not used in the comedy series *On the Buses*.

THE END OF THE ROUTEMASTER

In 1967, Transport Secretary Barbara Castle decided to give subsidies to companies building rear-engined buses. The front-engined Routemaster was unable to compete and the last vehicle was built in 1968. Designed to last around twenty years, refurbished examples were still in service almost forty years later.

As the oldest buses required ever more maintenance and parts became harder to source, it was inevitable that the Routemaster would have to be scrapped at some point, but many Londoners feel that its end was premature. After Mayor Ken Livingstone backtracked on an earlier promise to save the bus, Transport for London cited various reasons beyond economics and, some would say, sense. One was safety: on average, three people died each year from falling off the open platform. Though most of the victims were adults, this was regarded as too high a toll for an increasingly risk-averse society. The crucial issue in the Routemasters' demise was to be their lack of disabled access, yet few Londoners have ever seen a disabled person use the supposedly wheelchair-friendly but road-hogging 'bendy buses' that replaced them. Cynics argue that a sudden halt in early complaints about the new vehicles followed the realization that by embarking at the rear or middle doors of the bus one did not have to pay the fare.

The last normal service was the 159 from Marble Arch to Streatham, which arrived at the depot just after 2 p.m. on 9 December 2005. It took ten minutes to turn through the gates due to the throng of cheering supporters. Disabled protesters reportedly countered with howls and boos.

RELICS

Sixteen buses still run for the benefit of tourists on two short Heritage Routes – the No. 9, running between the Royal Albert Hall and the Aldwych, and the No. 15, between Trafalgar Square and Tower Hill. Standard fares apply.

Old Routemasters are available for sale and can be driven on a regular driving licence so long as they carry no more than eight passengers. Buyers have included Natalie Appleton and Sir Andrew Lloyd Webber. One bus is used as an estate agent's office in London's Camden Town.

Eurosceptics were furious in 1998 when a Routemaster was repainted blue and yellow and driven around Europe to publicize the European Single Currency.

A successor model called the 'Q Master' has failed to attract investment, as manufacturers prefer vehicles not designed with just one city in mind.

Oldest Universities

1. Oxford — 1249
2. Cambridge — 1284
3. University of Manchester Institute of Science and Technology (UMIST) — 1824
4. Durham — 1832
5. London — 1836
6. Manchester — 1851
7. Newcastle — 1852
8. Birmingham — 1900
9. Liverpool — 1903
10. Leeds — 1904

OLDEST OXBRIDGE COLLEGES

1. University, Oxford — 1249
2. Balliol, Oxford — 1263
3. Merton, Oxford — 1264
4. St Edmund Hall, Oxford — 1278*
5. Peterhouse, Cambridge — 1284
6. Exeter, Oxford — 1314
7. Oriel, Oxford — c. 1326
8. Clare, Cambridge — c. 1326
9. Queen's, Oxford — 1340
10. Pembroke, Cambridge — 1347

* NB St Edmund Hall was founded as a hall for students rather than as a true college.

The English Oak

England's oldest is the Bowthorpe Oak in Bourne, Lincolnshire, and is around a thousand years old. In 1768 the hollow interior was fitted with seats and a door.

England's largest 'maiden' oak is Majesty in Fredville, Kent, with a girth of 40 feet (12.06 metres). (There are six larger short-trunk pollards, including the Bowthorpe Oak.)

King Arthur's Round Table was said to have been made from a single slice of oak.

Oak trees were so important to the shipbuilding industry that Elizabeth I passed a law to protect them. If the Armada had landed in 1588, the Spanish planned to burn the Forest of Dean.

Over 5,500 oaks were used to construct Nelson's flagship, HMS *Victory*.

John Bull

Bull was the archetypal stout, prosperous and well-meaning (albeit slow-witted) Englishman in John Arbuthnot's satire, *Law is a Bottomless Pit* (1712), reprinted as *The History of John Bull* later that year. Bull had a Dutch friend, Nicholas Frog, with whom he opposed their common enemy, the Frenchman Louis Baboon.

Arbuthnot was a Scotsman, and he gave Bull a poor Scottish sister, Jenny.

In the nineteenth century, *Punch* cartoonists gave Bull a Union Jack waistcoat and a pet bulldog.

The 'Social Calendar'

CRUFTS (MARCH)

In 2006 the world's largest dog show involved 24,640 dogs from 178 different breeds from thirty-two different countries.

It was established in 1891 by Charles Cruft, a travelling salesman, and has been held at Birmingham's NEC since 1991.

There are over 6 million dogs in England. The most popular breed is the Labrador retriever.

Crufts entrants are judged in seven groups: Gundog, Hound, Pastoral, Terrier, Toy, Utility and Working.

Cocker Spaniel has been the most successful breed, with seven 'Best in Show' wins.

'Scruffts' is held in November for cross-bred dogs in four categories: Prettiest Bitch, Most Handsome Dog, Golden Oldie and Child's Best Friend.

THE OXFORD AND CAMBRIDGE BOAT RACE (APRIL)

The first event on the Thames was held in 1829 and the four-mile (6.4 km) race between Putney and Mortlake became annual in 1856. The loser traditionally challenges the winner to a rematch the following year.

The contest attracts around 250,000 spectators.

The first woman to participate was Sue Brown, the Oxford cox, in 1981.

Scores to 2006 are: Cambridge 78 wins, Oxford 73 wins. There was a dead heat in 1877 when, according to legend, the judge at the finish line, 'Honest' John Phelps, was asleep under a bush when the crews raced past.

Each crew member trains for two hours for every stroke in the race, of which around six hundred are needed to complete the course.

GLYNDEBOURNE OPERA FESTIVAL (MAY)

John Christie established the festival in 1934, complaining that opera was at that time 'almost non-existent' in England. Christie was inspired to expand his amateur productions on the estate after he and his wife Audrey, a professional singer, spent their honeymoon at the Salzburg and Bayreuth festivals.

The vaunted Fritz Busch and Carl Ebert from Germany became conductor and producer respectively after they fled Nazism.

There were no star performers in the early days, but both male and female singers were expected to be good-looking.

Over 85,000 people attend the festival each year. Evening dress is customary at performances.

CHELSEA FLOWER SHOW (MAY)

The world's largest and most renowned horticultural festival is held for four days every May in the grounds of the Royal Hospital, Chelsea. The 'Royal Horticultural Society's Great Spring Show' was first held in 1862 in the society's garden in Kensington, London (now the site of the Science Museum and Imperial College). In 1888, the garden closed and the event was moved to Temple Gardens on the north embankment of the Thames. The show took up its current 11-acre (4.5 hectare) home in 1913 and has run every year since, save for closures in 1917 and 1918 during the Great War, and again during the Second World War, when the land was used for an anti-aircraft position.

Over the week, the public and exhibitors get through 6,500 bottles of champagne, 18,000 glasses of Pimm's, 5,000 lobsters, 110,000 cups of tea and coffee and 28,000 sandwiches. Exhibitors come from all over the world, but room is still given to the work of English amateur gardeners.

In 2002 one of the exhibitors was Prince Charles, who created what he called the 'Healing Garden'. He won a silver medal, and repeated the feat in 2003.

ROYAL ACADEMY SUMMER EXHIBITION (JUNE–AUGUST)

The world's largest open submission contemporary art exhibition show-cases work from both famous and unknown artists. It has been held annually since 1769, the year after the Royal Academy's foundation.

After the 1780 exhibition, a public campaign forced the Academy to affix fig leaves to the genitalia of male nude sculptures.

Around 8,000 works are submitted each year, of which 1,000 or so are chosen.

Royal Academicians may exhibit up to six works. Other artists are limited to three.

ROYAL ASCOT (JUNE)

A race meeting was first organized at Ascot at the behest of Queen Anne in 1711. The inaugural event was Her Majesty's Plate, comprising three 4-mile (6.4 km) heats.

Ladies' Day is traditionally the third day of Royal Ascot, when the Gold Cup takes place. In the Royal Enclosure, men must wear morning dress while women are required to wear a hat. Strapless dresses and bare midriffs are strictly forbidden. Casual wear such as jeans, shorts and T-shirts are banned throughout the grandstands. However, on the Heath area on the opposite side of the course, anything goes apart from bare chests.

Divorcees were not allowed to enter the Royal Enclosure until 1955. Today, access to the area is limited to those who have attended in the past or who have been nominated by an existing badge-holder of four years' standing.

WIMBLEDON LAWN TENNIS CHAMPIONSHIPS (JUNE)

(See **Sports and Pastimes.**)

HENLEY ROYAL REGATTA (JUNE)

Henley Regatta has been held annually since 1839, when it was part of a public fair. It has since grown to become a five-day festival of rowing races.

The first royal patron was Prince Albert in 1851.

Races are conducted on a two-lane, head-to-head knockout format that attracts teams from over a dozen countries.

In the Stewards' Enclosure, women's skirts must not show the knees, while men must wear jackets and ties.

The American rower and future Olympic champion John Kelly Snr was barred from racing at Henley in 1920. The official reason was that he was a member of a boat club that had violated its amateur status, but many believed that it was really due to his lowly social status as a bricklayer. Kelly had the last laugh when his son John Jnr went on to win at Henley in 1947 and 1949, and he also became the grandfather of royalty – Prince Albert II of Monaco, the son of his daughter, Grace Kelly.

CARTIER INTERNATIONAL POLO DAY (JULY)

The day has featured in the Social Calendar since 1984, helped by the sponsor's lavish hospitality that every year attracts Hollywood celebrities and rock stars along with the highest echelons of England's upper classes.

Over 25,000 people gather to watch two polo matches at the Guards Polo Club in Windsor Great Park, Berkshire – England versus a foreign nation and a game involving a Prince of Wales side. Prince Harry has been his father's representative since 2004.

COWES WEEK (AUGUST)

Cowes Week is the world's longest-running yachting regatta, first held on the Solent in 1812, when seven vessels took part.

It is now an eight-day event with over a thousand entries in forty classes each year, involving around 8,500 yachtsmen and amateur sailors competing with Olympic champions.

Over 170,000 spectators watch the closing-day ceremonies. Locals refer to the tourists who watch the races as 'grockles' – originally the name of a cartoon dragon in the *Dandy* comic that a local swimming-pool attendant thought resembled an elderly regular visitor.

LAST NIGHT OF THE PROMS (SEPTEMBER)

The first 'promenade concerts' were organized in the Queen's Hall by Robert Newman in 1895, the name referring to the audience's licence to wander around the auditorium during the proceedings. An informal atmosphere was encouraged to make the events more inclusive than traditional performances.

The Proms now run from July to September each year, chiefly in the Royal Albert Hall, to where they were moved after the Queen's Hall was destroyed in an air raid in 1941.

The Last Night of the Proms is reserved for a night of patriotic celebration featuring 'Jerusalem', 'Land of Hope and Glory' and 'God Save the Queen', which the audience joins in singing.

13

SCIENCE AND TECHNOLOGY

Fifty English Inventions

Many inventions have been the work of several individuals working independently at roughly the same time. Often, the first inventor to have an idea is not given credit in the history books, either for political reasons or because he or she did not perfect their device. The innovations below are attributed on the basis of working prototypes or, failing that, working designs.

Lead pencil	1546	A source of pure graphite was discovered at Borrowdale in Cumbria, the only such deposit ever found. Graphite from other parts of the world had to be refined before it could be used, but Borrowdale's was ready to be cut into writing sticks straight from the mine. Export of the material was banned, and a satisfactory substitute was not developed for another hundred years.
Submarine	1573	William Bourne (not built – the first working craft was constructed in 1620 and tested in the Thames by Cornelius Van Drebbel, a Dutchman living in England)

Knitting machine	1589	Rev. William Lee
Flushing toilet	1596	John Harington (he also invented toilet humour with an instruction manual full of puns)
Railway tracks	1603	Huntingdon Beaumont
Slide rule	1632	William Oughtred
Syringe	1656	Christopher Wren (made from a quill)
Calculus	1665	Isaac Newton (invented at around the same time also by Gottfried Leibniz in Germany)
Lead crystal	1674	George Ravenscroft
Sparkling wine	1662	Christopher Merrett
Matches	1680	Robert Boyle (did not catch on immediately because his versions were highly dangerous)
Steam engine	1698	Thomas Savery (used to pump water out of mines)
Seed drill	1701	Jethro Tull (made from the pedals of a church organ)
Tuning fork	1711	John Shore
Diving bell	1717	Edmund Halley (first modern design)
Maritime clock	1740	John Harrison (for determining longitude)
Sandwich	1762	John Montagu, Fourth Earl of Sandwich
Spinning jenny	1764	James Hargreaves (named after his daughter, who gave him the idea by knocking over a spinning

		wheel that continued to turn)
Jigsaw puzzle	1767	John Spilsbury (the first puzzle was a map of the world)
Carbonated water	1767	Joseph Priestley (later moved to Pennsylvania when his home was burned down because of his support for the French Revolution)
Universal joint	1676	Robert Hooke
Pencil eraser	1770	Joseph Priestley
Steam locomotive	1804	Richard Trevithick (designed for roads)
Steam railway	1814	George Stephenson
Fire extinguisher	1816	George Manby
Electromagnet	1825	William Sturgeon
Lawnmower	1830	Edwin Budding
Dynamo	1831	Michael Faraday (first electric motor)
Difference engine	1822	Charles Babbage (the earliest mechanical computer)
Analytical engine	1823	Charles Babbage (first programmable computer)
Postage stamp	1837	Rowland Hill (Penny Black stamp launched in 1840)
Computer programme	1843	Ada Lovelace
Glider	1853	Sir George Cayley (his coachman performed the first manned heavier-than-air flight)
Plastic	1862	Alexander Parkes
Traffic lights	1868	J. P. Knight (erected at the

		junction of George and Bridge streets near the Houses of Parliament in London)
Moving pictures	1877	Eadweard Muybridge (lost his place in history to the Lumière brothers because he was a mentally ill murderer who used his invention to film naked American prostitutes)
Light bulb	1878	Joseph Swan (several months before Thomas Edison)
Steam turbine	1884	Charles Parsons (used on the *Titanic*)
Vacuum cleaner	1901	Hubert Booth (it was a large petrol-driven, horse-drawn machine that had to be parked outside the house)
Vacuum tube diode	1904	Sir John Fleming (founder of electronics)
Crossword puzzle	1913	Arthur Wynne (his first puzzle appeared in a New York newspaper)
Mass spectrometer	1919	Francis Aston
Jet engine	1930	Frank Whittle (his design was initially rejected by the Air Ministry)
Polythene	1933	Reginald Gibson and Eric Fawcett
Cat's-eyes	1934	Percy Shaw
Hovercraft	1955	Christopher Cockerell

Liquid Crystal Display (LCD)	1970	George Gray
Digital music player	1979	Kane Kramer (invented a device that could store five minutes of music, but his patents ran out several years before Apple developed the iPod)
World-Wide Web	1990	Tim Berners-Lee (invented URLs, HTML and first web browser)
Clockwork radio	1991	Trevor Bayliss

Twenty English Scientific Discoveries

Circulation of the blood	1628	William Harvey
Hooke's Law of Elasticity	1660	Robert Hooke
Red blood cells	1663	Robert Hooke
Binary stars	1664	Robert Hooke
Law of Universal Gravitation	1666	Isaac Newton
Laws of Motion	1687	Isaac Newton
Orbiting comets	1705	Edmund Halley
Hydrogen	1766	Henry Cavendish
Smallpox vaccine	1796	Edward Jenner
Atomic Theory	1805	John Dalton
Chemical electrolysis	1807	Humphrey Davy
Law of Conservation of Energy	1843	James Joule
Diamagnetism	1845	Michael Faraday
Planet Neptune	1846	John Couch Adams
Absolute zero temperature	1848	Lord Kelvin

Evolution by natural selection	1859	Charles Darwin
Electrons	1897	Joseph Thomson
Hormones	1903	William Bayliss and Ernest Starling
Neutrons	1932	James Chadwick
Structure of DNA	1953	Francis Crick (with James Watson, US)

Robert Hooke (1635–1703)

The 'English Leonardo' was born on the Isle of Wight. He survived smallpox as a boy, though it left his body terribly scarred and he grew up with a pronounced curvature of the spine. When he was 13, his clergyman father hanged himself.

Before becoming a scientist he trained first as a painter, but he was allergic to paint fumes.

Grace Hooke, the love of his life, was unfortunately also his niece.

He coined the word 'cell' to refer to the basic unit of life when a sample of cork examined under a microscope reminded him of monks' monastic cells.

To investigate the effects of reduced air pressure on humans, he once sat under a bell jar while the air was pumped out.

As an architect, he helped rebuild London after the Great Fire and designed the Bedlam mental asylum, the London Monument to the Great Fire and the London College of Physicians.

Hooke's Law of Elasticity states that the deformation of a material is linearly proportional to the force causing the deformation.

HOOKE'S OTHER DISCOVERIES

Measurement of gravity using pendulums

Inverse square law describing planetary motions (demonstrated
   experimentally but not proven mathematically)

Nature of combustion

Binary star systems

Planet Jupiter's rotation

Light diffraction

Expansion of all matter when heated

Kinetic theory of gases

Number of vibrations corresponding with musical notes
   (anticipating Guiseppi Tartini's discovery of the wave nature
   of sound by eighty years)

Elliptical orbit of the Earth around the Sun

Planet Neptune (a hundred years before John Couch Adams and
   William Herschel's 'official' discovery)

Sun spots

HOOKE'S INVENTIONS

Universal joint

Marine telescope

Cross-hairs

Sash windows (first installed at Bedlam)

Anchor escapement in clocks

Circular flywheel in clocks

Anemometer (to measure wind)

Hygrometer (to measure humidity – after he examined the hairs
   on a goat's beard under a microscope)

Refractometer (to measure the refractive index of liquids)

Helioscope (for studying the sun)

Altimeter

False keel for ships

Wheel barometer

Equatorial quadrant (to aid astronomical observations)

Air gun

Marine chronometer (forgotten forerunner to John Harrison's
  design of 1761)

IDEAS AHEAD OF HIS TIME

Microdots

Synthetic fibres

Hypodermic needle (after studying stinging nettles and bee stings
  under a microscope)

Mercury amalgam, later used in dental fillings

Hypothesis that the Earth's magnetic poles were not fixed and were
  subject to reversal

Evolution (in a rudimentary form)

Respiration

Fossils

———

Sir Isaac Newton (1642–1727)

———

'Nature and Nature's laws lay hid in night:
God said, Let Newton be! and all was light.'

Alexander Pope

LIFE AND CHARACTER

Newton was born in Lincolnshire on the same day that Galileo died.

He was brought up by his grandmother after his father died and his mother remarried and moved away when he was an infant. The separation inflicted lasting damage on Newton's emotional health. As a child, he fantasized about burning his stepfather and mother alive in their house. He remained so insecure throughout his life that he would fly into a rage whenever his theories were criticized. He suffered a nervous breakdown in 1678.

Newton earned £2,000 a year as Master of the Royal Mint. He developed a hatred of counterfeiters and relished their execution.

He was the first scientist to be buried in Westminster Abbey.

NATURAL PHILOSOPHY

Newton considered himself a philosopher. His contribution to 'natural philosophy' was so revolutionary that it spawned a new science – modern physics. For most of his time at Trinity College, Cambridge, he was thought to be an average student. His most important work was undertaken at home in Lincolnshire while the university was closed for two years during the Plague.

He took a close interest in esoterica, from alchemy to the prophecies in the Book of Revelations. He chose an alchemical pseudonym for himself – 'Jehovah Sanctus Unus' (Jehovah, the Holy One) and tried to decipher the clues for creating the Philosopher's Stone that he believed were encoded into the Greek myths.

NEWTON AND HOOKE

Newton once wrote, 'If I have seen further, it is by standing on the shoulders of giants.' He was adamant that none of these giants were his contemporaries, and he often became hysterical when anyone suggested otherwise. He would brook no argument in the dispute with Gottfried Leibniz over who had invented calculus, and when another rival, Robert Hooke, mistakenly accused him of plagiarism, he was so incensed that to prevent further criticism he held back publication of his second great work, *Opticks* (1704), until after Hooke was dead. He then used his power as President of the Royal Society to seize the data gathered by John Flamsteed, the Astronomer Royal, so that he could use it in his own work, in which he later deleted all references to the man.

THE THREE LAWS OF MOTION
Elucidated in the Principia Mathematica (1687)

1. The Law of Inertia: An object remains at rest or at a constant speed unless a force is exerted upon it.
2. Any change in motion is proportional to the amount of force applied and the mass of the object. Force = mass x acceleration.
3. Every action has an equal and opposite reaction.

Charles Babbage (1791–1871)

'Propose to any Englishman any principle, or any instrument, however admirable, and you will observe that the whole effort of the English mind is directed to find a difficulty, defect or an impossibility in it.'

Charles Babbage

Babbage, the son of a banker, was a Professor of Mathematics at Cambridge University who invented the first computer, the Difference Engine, in 1822 and a year later the first programmable machine, the steam-powered Analytical Engine.

Lord Byron's daughter, Ada Lovelace, wrote the first computer programme for the Analytical Engine in 1843. It was designed to calculate Bernoulli numbers.

Babbage invented a system of coloured spotlights for use in theatres, but these were judged a fire hazard and never used. He also invented the cow catcher.

He once baked himself in an oven at 265 degrees Fahrenheit for five minutes in the interests of science. He survived, he wrote, 'without any great discomfort'. He was also lowered into Mount Vesuvius to take a closer look at the lava.

He stood for Parliament twice as a Whig candidate without success. He campaigned for Babbage's Act against his noisy neighbours, who responded by hiring stilt walkers, fiddlers and drummers to parade back and forth outside his window.

None of his designs for computers were constructed in his lifetime, despite £17,000 of public funding before the government pulled the plug. However, the Difference Engine was constructed in accordance with nineteenth-century tolerances at the London Science Museum in 1991. It worked perfectly.

Michael Faraday (1791–1867)

Faraday's father, a blacksmith, was often ill and unable to work. As a child, Michael sometimes received a loaf of bread that would be his only food for an entire week. His most important education came from volumes of the *Encyclopaedia Britannica* that he would deliver on his newspaper round.

As a teenager he performed his own experiments using a jerry-rigged electricity generator and won his first job in a laboratory after approaching the great chemist Sir Humphrey Davy.

He produced the first carbon and chlorine compounds, the first electric motor, discovered benzene and diamagnetism and propounded the view that space was filled with forces and fields rather than being an 'empty' container for material objects.

Faraday speculated that all the forces of nature, including gravity, were aspects of a single universal force into which they were translatable, the search for which continues to this day.

Queen Victoria gave him the use of a house at Hampton Court, but he rejected a knighthood.

Charles Darwin (1809–82)

DARWIN'S YOUTH

Darwin's maternal grandfather was the pottery magnate, Josiah Wedgwood. His paternal grandfather was the physician, Erasmus Darwin.

He was judged a failure at school in everything except sports. When he expressed an interest in chemistry, his classics-loving headmaster reprimanded him, and the other boys gave him the nickname 'Gas'. One day his father shouted, 'You care for nothing but shooting, dogs, and rat-catching, and you will be a disgrace to yourself and all your family.'

While he was a student at Cambridge University, his relationship with his girlfriend foundered because he spent too much time on his hobby – collecting beetles.

Darwin argued that cross-pollinated plants would produce fitter offspring than self-pollinators. In 1839, he married his cousin, Emma Wedgwood.

ON THE ORIGIN OF SPECIES

He formulated the Theory of Evolution by Natural Selection during his 1837–9 voyage circumnavigating the globe on HMS *Beagle*. He was only 22. But he did not publish *On the Origin of Species* until 1859. During this time he kept his views secret from the public for fear of the offence they might cause (his wife was horrified) and spent ten years studying barnacles. He said that expressing his theories felt 'like confessing a murder'. He was finally moved to publish when he received a letter from Alfred Russel Wallace, whom he realized was about to make a claim to the same theory.

He once attended a séance and was so offended by its outright charlatanry that he helped fund the prosecution of the medium, Henry Slade, in 1876.

The most famous portrait of Darwin shows him with a large, bushy beard, which he did not grow until he was 57 years old, whereupon friends failed to recognize him.

Darwin was agnostic on religious matters, although he was buried in Westminster Abbey.

Alan Turing (1912–54)

Turing was the founder of modern computer science and was responsible for the view that the human brain can be understood as a kind of digital computer.

CHILDHOOD

He was brought up in foster homes while his parents worked in India for the colonial administration.

When the General Strike of 1926 brought trains to a halt, Turing cycled 60 miles to his first day at Sherbourne School. His headmaster pronounced, 'If he is to be solely a Scientific Specialist, he is wasting his time at a Public School.' Trinity College, Cambridge, later rejected his application for a scholarship.

THE 'TURING TEST'

Under the 'Turing Test' for artificial intelligence, an examiner conducts a conversation through a remote terminal and receives two sets of responses – one from a human and the other from a computer. If he or she cannot tell which is the machine then, according to the Test, the machine possesses the ability to think. Despite an annual prize for the best attempt, no computer has ever succeeded in fooling an examiner in an extended test.

ENIGMA

During the Second World War, Turing helped to break the German Enigma codes at Bletchley Park. The nation later rewarded him with a conviction for gross indecency after his homosexual relationship with a man from Manchester was discovered. In lieu of a year's imprisonment, he submitted to a course of hormone injections designed to reduce the libido of sexual 'deviants'. Two years later he committed suicide by eating an apple laced with cyanide.

14

INDUSTRY, AGRICULTURE
AND COMMERCE

'The Tories in England had long imagined that they
were enthusiastic about the monarchy, the church and
the beauties of the old English Constitution, until the
day of danger wrung from them the confession that
they are enthusiastic only about rent.'

Karl Marx

'The people of England are never so happy as when
you tell them they are ruined.'

Arthur Murphy (1727–1805)

'Wealth, howsoever got, in England makes
Lords of mechanics, gentlemen of rakes;
Antiquity and birth are needless here;
'Tis impudence and money makes a peer.'

Daniel Defoe, *The True-Born Englishman* (1701)

The Bank of England

FOUNDATION

The Bank of England was founded as a private institution in 1694 by a Scotsman, William Paterson, to manage the government's debt. Subscribers were incorporated as the Governor and Company of the Bank of England in return for a loan of £1,200,000 charged at 8 per cent per annum.

The initial loan was required to fund William III's war against France in the Netherlands. The National Debt grew from £12 million in 1700 to £850 million by 1815.

The Bank moved to its present site in Threadneedle Street in 1734, by which time it had become the country's largest financial institution and a lender to other banks. The Bank's nickname, the Old Lady of Threadneedle Street, was coined by the cartoonist James Gillray after the Irish playwright Richard Brinsley Sheridan described it as 'an elderly lady in the city'.

Before the Bank of England was established, the nation's currency was stored in the Tower of London.

An Act of Parliament nationalized the Bank in 1946. Stockholders were compensated and the Governor reappointed to his post. It was granted the power to determine short-term interest rates in order to control inflation in 1997.

BANKNOTES

The Bank's first notes were handwritten on Bank of England paper and signed by a cashier. In the early eighteenth century, partially printed notes for completion by hand were issued in denominations from £20 to £1,000. Smaller notes were introduced progressively in times of war in anticipation of a gold shortage.

The first coloured banknotes were issued in 1928.

Banknotes issued by Scottish and Northern Irish banks have to be backed by an equal sum in Bank of England notes. Since there is over £1 billion of such notes in circulation, special million-pound notes are used for practical reasons. These never leave the Bank and bear no design.

The watermark was introduced to Bank of England notes in order to prevent fraud after Daniel Perrismore forged sixty £100 notes in 1695. He was fortunate to receive only a fine, for forgery was subsequently made punishable by death. The metal strip was added during the Second World War at a time when Germany was producing five hundred thousand forged notes a month.

THE GOLD RESERVES

The Bank manages the nation's gold reserves, but they were moved to the Treasury in 1931, when the United Kingdom left the Gold Standard. They would be moved to the European Central Bank along with the country's foreign currency reserves should Britain join the Euro.

A security lapse in the 1920s reportedly allowed a sacked Irish labourer to find his way into the vaults and urinate on the reserves.

HISTORICAL FIGURES ON BANK OF ENGLAND NOTES

£1	Isaac Newton	1978–88
£5	Duke of Wellington	1971–91
£5	George Stephenson	1990–2003
£5	Elizabeth Fry	2002–
£10	Florence Nightingale	1975–94

£10	Charles Dickens	1992–2003
£10	Charles Darwin	2000–
£20	William Shakespeare	1970–93
£20	Michael Faraday	1991–2001
£20	Sir Edward Elgar	1999–
£50	Sir Christopher Wren	1981–96
£50	Sir John Houblon*	1994–

* First Governor of the Bank of England.

Cockney Currency

'Lady Godiva'	£5
'Ayrton Senna'	£10
'Pony'	£25
'Ton'	£100
'Monkey'	£500
'Grand'	£1,000

The Pound Sterling

ETYMOLOGY AND EARLY HISTORY

The name stems from the pound of sterling silver used to mint a batch of 240 pennies in the Anglo-Saxon kingdoms in AD 775. They were coined to pay the Danegeld tribute to the Vikings.

Sterling became the national currency under Athelstan, the first undisputed English king, in AD 928.

After the Norman Conquest, the pound was divided into twenty shillings or 240 pennies.

In 1124, Henry I had ninety-four mint workers castrated for producing poor quality coins.

The symbols 's.' for shilling and 'd.' for pence derive from the Latin *solidus* and *denarius* used in the Middle Ages. The '£' sign developed from the 'l.' for *libra*.

THE FALL OF THE POUND

Between 1717 and 1914, sterling's value was defined in terms of gold rather than silver. Winston Churchill returned the country to the Gold Standard in 1925 at the pre-war exchange rate of $4.86 to the pound, which was roughly the level set by Sir Isaac Newton in the eighteenth century. In 1925, this represented a 10 per cent overvaluation, and the economic consequences led to the General Strike a year later. The Gold Standard was finally brought to a permanent end by the depression that followed the Wall Street Crash of 1929.

The Bretton Woods Agreement of 1944 marked the ascendancy of the US dollar over sterling. Although both were declared reserve currencies such that other nations were compelled to accept them in debt repayment, the dollar soon proved more popular than the pound in most cases.

Queen Elizabeth II's physical appearance on all denominations of the currency was 'updated' in 1968, 1985 and 1998.

THE POUND'S VALUE IN US DOLLARS

1791	$4.55	
1812	$3.62	(19th-century low)
1866	$6.88	(19th-century high)
1920	$3.66	

1926	$4.86	(following Churchill's return to the Gold Standard)
1932	$3.51	
1934	$5.04	(20th-century high)
1950	$2.80	(following Stafford Cripps's 30 per cent devaluation of 1949)
1968	$2.39	(following James Callaghan's 14.3 per cent devaluation of 1967)*
1976	$1.80	(forcing Dennis Healey to accept a rescue package from the IMF)
1980	$2.33	
1985	$1.30	(20th-century low)
1988	$1.78	
1998	$1.66	
2004	$1.83	

* The devaluation prompted Prime Minister Harold Wilson to assure the public: 'This does not mean that the pound here in Britain – in your pocket or purse – is worth any less...'

Source: Miami University, Economic History Services

DECIMALIZATION

Sterling was decimalized on 15 February 1971, before which it came in the following values:

2 Farthings = 1 Halfpenny
2 Halfpence = 1 Penny (1d)
6 Pence = Sixpence (a 'tanner') (6d)
12 Pence = 1 Shilling (a 'bob') (1/-)
2 shillings = 1 Florin (a 'two bob bit') (2/-)
2 Shillings and 6 Pence = 1 Half Crown (2/6)
5 shillings = 1 Crown (5/-)

20 Shillings = 1 Pound (£1)
21 Shillings = 1 Guinea (£1/1/-)

Introduction of Decimal Coins

1p	1971
2p	1971
5p	1968
10p	1968
20p	1982
25p	1972 (special issue only, to celebrate the Queen's silver wedding anniversary)
50p	1969
£1	1983
£2	1997 (1986 as a special issue for the Commonwealth Games)
£5:	2006 (special issue, for the Queen's eightieth birthday)

———

The Big Bang of 1986
The deregulation of the London Stock Exchange

———

CONSEQUENCES

1. Business is conducted by telephone and computer link instead of on the trading floor.
2. All firms became able to operate as both brokers and dealers.
3. Abolition of the minimum commission level.
4. Individual members lost voting rights in the Exchange.
5. Outside corporations are permitted to own member companies.
6. The Exchange became a Public Limited Company.

Sources of England's Wealth

Wool

Since the reign of Edward III in the fourteenth century, the Lord Chancellor has sat in Parliament on the Woolsack, stuffed with English wool – a symbol of what was once the chief source of the nation's wealth. (Today, the Woolsack is filled with wool from several Commonwealth countries as a gesture of unity.) In 1340, 30,000 sacks of wool were granted to Edward to finance the war against France.

Wool exports had risen to around 12 million fleeces per year by AD 1300, with a national flock of almost 20 million sheep. England dominated the wool trade in the Middle Ages, and Europe's textile industry was heavily dependent on English exports organized by the Cistercian monasteries in the northern counties. In 1326, foreigners were prohibited from travelling through the country to find the best prices. English wool could be imported legally to the continent only through the port of Calais.

The proceeds from wool enabled merchants to build the great 'wool churches' and 'wool houses' of East Anglia and the Cotswolds. (See 'Notable Wool Churches' in **The Church**.)

In 1275, an export tax was imposed on wool. 'The Great Custom' generated a significant part of the Crown's income.

Under a statue of 1556, anyone caught 'owling' – smuggling wool to France in the night – would have their left hand cut off and nailed up on display in a public place. Under George I, in the eighteenth century, this was changed to seven years' transportation.

SLAVERY

England's first slave-trading voyages between Africa and the West Indies were undertaken by John Hawkins in the 1560s. He was sponsored by Elizabeth I and his earliest slaves were sold to Spanish plantation owners.

Slaves were later used to man England's Caribbean sugar and tobacco plantations, and by the end of the seventeenth century the nation was the world's largest slave trader.

From 1698, when William III ended the Royal African Company's monopoly, to the ending of the slave trade in 1807, over 2,100 ships set sail on slaving voyages from Bristol alone. They transported around five hundred thousand Africans, whom they purchased from Arab and African traders.

TRADE

England dominated world trade after the successful naval wars against the Spanish and Dutch in the sixteenth and seventeenth centuries. By the 1680s, her colonies in America and the West Indies were sending home goods worth over £1 million a year. By the end of the eighteenth century they received 57 per cent of British exports and supplied 32 per cent of imports.

The extra-territorial legislation of the Navigation Acts effectively regulated the affairs of other sovereign states by requiring that British ships should conduct all commodity trade within the Empire.

THE INDUSTRIAL REVOLUTION

In the late eighteenth and early nineteenth century, England and the rest of the United Kingdom became the Workshop of the World.

Richard Arkwright built the world's first steam-powered mill in 1771.

Karl Marx's collaborator Friedrich Engels worked in his father's cotton mill in Manchester in 1842 when he was 23 years old. The plight of the workers there moved him to write *The Condition of the Working Class in England* (1845).

The Luddite movement began in 1811, when Nottingham's mill owners received letters from 'General Ned Ludd and the Army of Redressers' demanding the destruction of the machines that they believed threatened workers' jobs. An epidemic of vandalism spread across the country until it was put down by a combination of hangings, transportation to the colonies and action by the army.

In 1888, the first electrical power station opened in Deptford.

THE CITY OF LONDON

Stock dealers began trading in the Royal Exchange in 1698, and when they were thrown out for rowdy behaviour they began to conduct their business from Jonathan's Coffee House nearby in Change Alley. This burned to the ground in 1748, but the dealers built their own establishment, New Jonathan's, in Sweeting's Alley in 1771. The name was changed to the Stock Exchange, and their organization was formally regulated as of 1801.

The motto of the Stock Exchange is *Dictum Meum Pactum* ('My Word is My Bond').

The strength of the pound in the nineteenth century, backed by Britain's empire, led to the growth of London as the world's greatest financial centre. Today, more companies are listed on the London Stock Exchange than those of New York or Tokyo.

The business and financial services sector now accounts for more of the nation's GDP than manufacture and agriculture combined. The City alone generates more than a quarter of all corporate tax revenues.

Richard Arkwright (1732–92)

The pioneer of the Industrial Revolution was the youngest of seven children born to a Lancashire labourer. He never went to school and started out as a barber in Bolton before he was widowed. His second wife provided him with enough money to set up a business collecting human hair to make wigs.

On his travels he met the clockmaker John Kay, who had once worked with John Highs on a prototype spinning jenny, only to run out of funding some years before James Hargreaves's invention became famous. Arkwright plied Kay with drink and persuaded him to build and adapt several of Highs's machines without telling the originator.

In 1769, Arkwright patented a water-powered frame that could spin 128 threads of cotton at a time – compared to around a dozen for the spinning jenny. His patents were rescinded after Highs brought a court case against him in 1785.

Arkwright established the world's first steam-powered cotton mill in Cromford, Derbyshire, in 1771. The steam was used to pump water to drive the wheel. Arkwright built houses for the workforce, which he attracted by advertising for labourers with large families – the women and children would also work in the mill. He built another mill in Chorley, Lancashire, but it was burned to the ground by precursors of the Luddites.

By 1782 he employed five thousand workers in Derbyshire, Staffordshire, Lancashire and Scotland and had amassed a fortune of £500,000 (around £200 million in today's money).

Isambard Kingdom Brunel (1806–59)

LIFE AND ACHIEVEMENTS

Brunel was the son of a French engineer, a Royalist who had fled the Reign of Terror. His father sent him to France for his education and gave him his first job, helping to build the Thames Tunnel from Rotherhithe to Wapping. Completed in 1843, it was the world's first tunnel to be dug under a navigable river through soft earth.

He designed three great ships, each of which was the largest vessel in the world when it was launched. His first, the SS *Great Western*, was also the world's first steam-powered transatlantic passenger liner.

Brunel was appointed chief engineer for the Great Western Railway in 1833. He introduced the broad-gauge railway (50 per cent wider than standard gauge) that allowed for higher speeds, and built over 1,000 miles of track in the British Isles. He also helped design railways in Italy, India and Australia.

Brunel's critics warned that his Maidenhead Bridge would collapse when the first traffic crossed it. Completed in 1838, it is still the flattest and widest brick arch in the world.

When Bristol's Temple Meads Station was built in 1840, it was the largest single-span building in the world.

Brunel's Box Tunnel, on the route between Bath and Chippenham, was the longest railway tunnel in the world when it opened in 1841. Local rumour maintains that it was designed so that on Brunel's birthday the sun would rise to fill the tunnel opening precisely.

During the Crimean War, he designed a prefabricated military hospital and an armoured barge used in the attack on Kronstadt in 1854.

Brunel would smoke up to forty cigars a day while working on a project, and he has one in his mouth in his most famous photograph taken against the background of the *Great Eastern*'s anchor chains. The cigar was airbrushed out of the portrait when it featured on the cover of *The Life of Isambard Kingdom Brunel* by Emma Lynch (2005) lest it encourage children to take up smoking. More recently, in July 2006, Brunel University removed the cigar from a newly commissioned life-sized statue of the engineer. A university spokesman explained, 'The cigar would be too easily broken off. It's nothing to do with political correctness, it's for practical reasons.'

BRIDGES AND TUNNELS

Clifton Suspension Bridge
Maidenhead Bridge
Chepstow Bridge
Hanwell and Chippenham viaducts
Hungerford Bridge
Royal Albert Bridge
Paddington Station Bridge
Thames Tunnel
Great Western Railway Bridge
Box Tunnel

SHIPS

SS *Great Western* (1837)
SS *Great Britain* (1843)
SS *Great Eastern* (1858)

DOCKS

Bristol
Monkwearmouth
Cardiff
Milford Haven

STATIONS

Bristol Temple Meads
Paddington

The Railways

THE EARLY LOCOMOTIVES

Richard Trevithick built the first steam locomotive in 1804, but it proved unreliable and its designer died in poverty. The first practical design was developed by George Stephenson in 1814 for use in a colliery. The 'Blucher' could ferry 30 tons of coal at 4 mph.

Stephenson, the son of a colliery fireman from Newcastle upon Tyne, opened the first freight line from Stockton to Darlington in 1825 and the world's second earliest passenger line, from Liverpool to Manchester, in 1830.

At the grand opening of the Liverpool to Manchester Line on 15 September 1830, Stephenson's 'Rocket' ran over and killed the government minister William Huskisson, who had crossed the track to shake the hand of his political enemy, the Duke of Wellington.

The Rocket's maximum speed was 29 mph.

The first passenger line was the Canterbury and Whitstable Railway, which opened on 3 May 1830. Stephenson supplied the locomotive – the 'Invicta'.

The Railway Bubble

In the 1840s, 'Railway Mania' gripped the stock market as a speculative bubble followed over a thousand applications to build new rail links. The losses suffered by many investors prompted Lewis Carroll's line in *The Hunting of the Snark* (1876): 'They threatened its life with a railway share.'

The War of the Gauges

Stephenson rail gauges were 4 feet 8.5 inches wide (1,435 mm), whereas Isambard Kingdom Brunel built the Great Western Railway to a width of 7 feet 0.25 inches (2,140 mm). This led to 'The Battle of the Gauges' as the infrastructure expanded, which was eventually won by Stephenson's standard.

The railways were nationalized by Clement Attlee's government in 1947 and returned to private hands under John Major's in 1993.

The London Underground

The Metropolitan Line connecting Paddington to Farringdon was the world's first underground passenger railway, opening on 10 January 1863. Most of this route is now the Hammersmith & City Line.

The LU logo, featuring a blue bar set across a red circle, was designed by calligrapher Edward Johnston in 1913.

During 2004/2005, LU carried a record 976 million passengers.

Line Openings

Metropolitan Line	1863
Hammersmith & City Line	1863*

District Line	1868
East London Line	1869
Circle Line	1884
Northern Line	1890
Waterloo & City Line	1898
Central Line	1900
Bakerloo Line	1906
Piccadilly Line	1906
Victoria Line	1969
Jubilee Line	1979

* A branch of the Metropolitan Line until 1988.

FACTS AND FIGURES

Total number of stations: 275

Deepest lift shaft: Hampstead, 181ft/55.2m

Longest line: Central Line, 46 miles (60km)

Most stations: District Line, 60 stations

Longest escalator: Angel – 197ft/60m (vertical rise of 90ft/27.5m)

Busiest stations: King's Cross St Pancras, 77.5 million passengers a year. During the three-hour morning peak, 46,000 people enter at Waterloo.

Shortest distance between stations: Leicester Square to Covent Garden – 0.161 miles (0.26km), Piccadilly Line

Source: Transport for London

Deceased or Dormant English Car Marques
Some of their most famous models, and
current ownership of the marques

Austin	Allegro, Maestro, Mini	NAC*
Austin-Healey	Sprite	NAC
Hillman	Avenger, Imp, Hunter, Minx	Peugeot
Humber	Hawk, Sceptre, Snipe	Chrysler
Jensen	Interceptor, 541	Creative Group
Morris	Minor, Oxford	NAC
Reliant†	Bond Bug, Regal, Robin	see below
Riley	Elf, Pathfinder	BMW
Rover	Metro, 75	NAC
Sunbeam	Alpine, Talbot	Peugeot
Talbot	Horizon	Peugeot
Triumph	Dolomite, Spitfire, Stag	BMW
Wolseley	Six	NAC

* Nanjing Automobile Corporation.

† The yellow van driven by Del Boy Trotter in Only Fools and Horses is a Reliant Regal Supervan and not a Robin. The Reliant firm still exists, but rights to the Robin were sold to B&N Plastics in 2001, who produced the last vehicle the following year.

Unemployment Rates

North-East	7.6 per cent (worst in Middlesbrough – 12.4 per cent)
London	6.8 per cent (worst in Hackney – 16.4 per cent)
West Midlands	5.6 per cent (worst in Birmingham – 10.5 per cent)
North-West	5.1 per cent (worst in Liverpool – 11.1 per cent)
Yorkshire & Humberside	5 per cent (worst in Bradford – 8.2 per cent)
East Midlands	4.7 per cent (worst in Leicester – 8.5 per cent)
Eastern England	3.8 per cent (worst in Norwich – 9.1 per cent)
South-West	3.5 per cent (worst in Torbay – 5.6 per cent)
South-East	3.3 per cent (worst in Thanet – 9.8 per cent)

Source: TUC June 2006

Great Economists
And their signature ideas

DAVID RICARDO (1722–1823)

The Theory of Comparative Advantage, which justified *laissez-faire* economics and international free trade.

THOMAS MALTHUS (1766–1834)

The Principle of Population which, he wrote, 'is so superior to the power of the earth to produce subsistence for man, that premature death must in some shape or other visit the human race'.

WILLIAM STANLEY JEVONS (1835–82)

The Marginal Utility Theory of Value, according to which the value of a product to a consumer is inversely related to the number of those products he or she already owns.

ALFRED MARSHALL (1842–1924)

The notions of consumer surplus, quasi-rent, demand curves and elasticity.

JOHN MAYNARD KEYNES (1883–1946)

Deficit spending as cure for recession: 'If the Treasury were to fill old bottles with bank notes, bury them at suitable depths in disused coal mines which are then filled up with town rubbish, and leave them to private enterprise on the well-tried principles of *laissez-faire* to dig them up again... there need be no more unemployment.'

JOHN HICKS (1904–89)

The IS/LM Model for summarizing Keynesian economics and the Kaldor-Hicks Criteria for the efficiency of welfare allocation.

The Potteries

STOKE-ON-TRENT

In the late eighteenth century, the area of Staffordshire around Stoke-on-Trent became the centre of a newly industrialized ceramics industry and acquired the nickname 'The Potteries'. The foundations of this success were laid by the Irish painter Thomas Frye, who invented bone china in 1748 and set up a factory in Essex. The great

English potters of Staffordshire subsequently led the world with a combination of modern manufacturing methods and fine craftsmanship.

JOSIAH WEDGWOOD (1730–95)

'The Father of English Potters' was born in Burslem, Staffordshire. He was unable to operate a potter's wheel after a childhood bout of smallpox left him with a weakened right knee, which eventually resulted in the amputation of his leg. He turned to design work and set up his own business in 1759.

In 1766 he built the first industrial pottery factory, which he named the 'Etruria Works' after the area of Italy where ancient Etruscan porcelain was found.

Quality control was an important stage in Wedgwood's manufacturing process. He would patrol his factory with a stick and smash to pieces any work he thought was sub-standard.

His three most famous inventions were Queen's Ware (1762), Black Basalt (1768) and Jasper (1774). He also invented the pyrometer, for measuring oven temperatures.

Wedgwood was Charles Darwin's grandfather.

THE GREAT POTTERIES

Wedgwood	Stoke (1759)
Adams	Stoke (1769)
Minton	Stoke (1793)
Spode	Stoke (1770)
Royal Doulton	London (1815), moved to Stoke in 1877
Royal Worcester	Worcester (1751)
Denby	Derbyshire (1809)

A Short History of Farming

'The only thing the English have ever given European farming is mad cow disease.'

Jacques Chirac

FROM THE BRONZE AGE TO THE MIDDLE AGES

Rudimentary 'slash and burn' agriculture began in England around 4000 BC. Wheat and barley were the earliest main crops and livestock included sheep, pigs, cattle and goats. Hay was grown for animal feed from around 2000 BC.

Around 700 BC, crops included oats, tick beans, vetch, peas, rye and flax. Poultry included geese and ducks. The Romans found a patchwork of hedged fields when they arrived in the south-east of England.

Three-field crop rotation, with a cycle of cereal–beans–fallow, was developed before the Norman Conquest. The Normans introduced rabbits.

JETHRO TULL (1674–1741)

The man who revolutionized agriculture initially trained as a barrister at Gray's Inn, but opted instead to run the family farm in Howberry, Oxfordshire. It was not an entirely happy choice, as he resented the work and especially his labourers, who either refused or were unable to follow his instructions. After careful tutorials in how to plant seed efficiently in well-spaced rows, they would proceed in the traditional way of scattering the seed in random handfuls. In 1701, Tull invented a machine that would do the thinking for them.

The seed drill was a wheeled contraption that dug holes and set seed at regular intervals before covering them over with earth. All the operator had to do was tie it to a horse and refill it occasionally. Tull also invented the horse hoe for weeding fields. He published his ideas in a book, *The New Horse Houghing Husbandry*, in 1731, but they took another century to gain nationwide acceptance.

FOUR-FIELD ROTATION

The German four-field system of crop rotation, wherein the fallow year is replaced by a year of clover and a year of turnips, was introduced from Flanders by the politician and diplomat Charles Townshend in 1730. He was subsequently christened 'Turnip Townshend' for the zeal with which he promoted the method.

BREEDING

Selective breeding of livestock was introduced by Thomas Coke (1754–1842) and Robert Bakewell (1725–95) in the late eighteenth century. Coke held the country's first agricultural shows – the Holkham Shearings – on his estate in Norfolk. Bakewell bred sheep and cattle for meat rather than wool and labour, with the result that mutton became the nation's favourite meat for a time.

ENCLOSURE

The loss of common lands to enclosure caused widespread rioting and rebellion in the sixteenth century, including the Pilgrimage of Grace (1536) and Kett's Rebellion (1549). However, the need to feed a growing population led to the Acts of Enclosure passed between 1760 and 1830. Large landowners acquired more power in the countryside, while many smallholders and peasants were forced to seek employment in the new urban industries.

Corn Laws

The Corn Laws were brought in after the Napoleonic Wars to maintain high prices when cheaper imported grain became available. They were opposed by the middle classes, who saw them as a subsidy for aristocrats, and by the lower orders for their obvious effect on their ability to feed themselves. After a long public campaign by the Anti Corn Law League, the laws were eventually repealed in 1846 to help alleviate the Irish Potato Famine.

Agriculture today provides around 60 per cent of the nation's food yet employs only 2 per cent of the workforce.

15

THE CHURCH

'If there were only one religion in England, there would be danger of despotism, if there were two, they would cut each other's throats, but there are thirty, and they live in peace and happiness.'

Voltaire

Church Buildings

Oldest Cathedrals: Canterbury Cathedral was founded in 597, and Rochester Cathedral in 604. The oldest complete building is Ely Cathedral, finished in 1189.

Largest Cathedral: Liverpool Anglican Cathedral (consecrated 1924) at 104,275 square feet. It also has the world's largest organ, with 9,765 pipes.

Oldest Church: St Martin's in Canterbury has been in constant use since at least the sixth century.

Religious Affiliation in England (2001 Census)

Christian	71.7 per cent
No Religion	14.6 per cent
Not Stated	7.7 per cent
Muslim	3.1 per cent
Hindu	1.1 per cent
Sikh	0.7 per cent
Jewish	0.5 per cent
Buddhist	0.3 per cent
Other	0.3 per cent

Prominent English Saints

Alban (died c. 304): Became the first English martyr, whereupon, it is attributed, his executioner's eyes fell out.

Aldhelm (c. 639–709): Abbot of Malmesbury and Bishop of Sherbourne. Installed the first church organ in England in AD 700. He once preached a sermon for so long that his staff apparently took root and turned into a sapling.

Augustine of Canterbury (d. 604): Evangelizer of the British Isles.

Bede, the Venerable (672–735): Historian of the early English church.

Boniface (c. 675–754): Benedictine missionary to Germany, where he chopped down the Tree of Thor at Geimar and was martyred.

Dunstan (909–88): Abbot of Glastonbury exiled by King Edgar. Patron saint of goldsmiths, blacksmiths, locksmiths, musicians, lighthouse keepers and the blind.

Edmund Campion (1540–81): Jesuit martyred by Elizabeth I.

Edmund of Abingdon (c. 1180–1241): Presided over the ratification of the Magna Carta in 1237.

Edward the Confessor (c. 1003–66): Patron saint of kings, separated spouses and difficult marriages.

Hugh of Lincoln (1135–1200): Carthusian abbot who protected the Jews from mobs during the persecution of 1190–91. A swan guarded him while he slept. Patron saint of sick children and swans.

John Fisher (1469–1535): Bishop of Rochester martyred for opposing Henry VIII's divorce from Catherine of Aragon.

Osmund (d. 1099): Royal chaplain of William the Conqueror. Patron saint of the insane, the paralysed and those suffering from toothache.

Patrick (5th century): Patron saint of Ireland and engineers. Kidnapped and sent to Ireland as a slave.

Thomas Becket (1118–70): Archbishop of Canterbury assassinated by Henry II's knights.

Thomas More (1478–1535): Patron saint of civil servants, lawyers and politicians.

Swithin (c. 800–62): Patron saint of drought relief. According to legend, if it rains on St Swithin's day (15 July), then it will continue to rain for forty days.

Walburga (c. 710–79): Benedictine nun and missionary to Germany. Patron saint of mad dogs, plague victims, sailors and storms.

Wilibrord (658–739): Patron saint of epileptics.

___

The English Pope

___

Adrian IV (c. 1100–59, born Nicholas Breakspear) is the only Englishman to have become Pope.

After a cardinal was murdered during a riot in 1155, Adrian became the first Pope to put Rome under the Interdict, suspending public worship and withdrawing the sacraments from the populace.

He issued a papal bull giving Henry II dominion over Ireland, which the king then took by invasion in 1171. The authority was only to last for Henry's lifetime – a legal point that his heirs ignored.

The Nation's Favourite Hymns
Chosen by a Songs of Praise survey in 2005

------

1. 'How Great Thou Art' (Carl Boberg, trans. Stuart Hine)
2. 'Dear Lord and Father of Mankind' (John Whittier and Frederick Maker)
3. 'The Day Thou Gavest' (John Ellerton and Clement Scholefield)
4. 'Be Thou My Vision' (Dallan Forgaill, trans. Mary Byrne)
5. 'Love Divine, All Loves Excelling' (Charles Wesley and John Zundel)
6. 'Be Still, For the Presence of the Lord' (David Evans)
7. 'Make Me a Channel' (St Francis attrib. and Sebastian Temple)
8. 'Guide Me, O Thou Great Redeemer' (William Williams, trans. Peter Williams, and John Hughes)
9. 'In Christ Alone' (Stuart Townend and Keith Getty)
10. 'Shine, Jesus, Shine' (Graham Kendrick)

Notable Wool Churches

Demi-cathedrals built with the proceeds of England's wool industry in the Middle Ages:

St Mary's, Thirsk, Yorkshire
St Peter and St Paul, Northleach, Gloucestershire
St James', Chipping Campden, Cotswolds
Church of St John the Baptist, Burford, Oxfordshire
Church of St John the Baptist, Cirencester, Gloucestershire
St Nicholas', North Walsham, Norfolk
Holy Trinity, Long Melford, Suffolk
Church of St Peter and St Paul, Lavenham, Suffolk

The Church of England

'You simply couldn't write a novel like Graham
Greene's *The Power and the Glory* about a church built
on the conviction that anything can be settled over
a cup of tea.'

Jeremy Paxman, *The English* (1998)

'Alas the Church of England! What with Popery on one
hand, and schismatics on the other, how has she been
crucified between two thieves!'

Daniel Defoe, *The Shortest Way with the Dissenters* (1702)

There are over 16,000 C. of E. churches serving 13,000 parishes. Around a million people attend services on a Sunday, which is comparable to the number of English Catholics attending mass. A Church of England parish is the country's smallest unit of local government.

Since 1969, over 1,600 churches have closed – three times the number of new churches that have opened.

C. OF E. HIERARCHY

The clergy are comprised of deacons, priests and bishops. Deacons have the same role as priests except that they cannot administer holy communion. Bishops can ordain, confirm and consecrate churches. The monarch is the 'Supreme Governor' of the Church; the Archbishop of Canterbury is the head.

The Archbishop of Canterbury is considered *primus inter pares* – first among equals – in relation to the Archbishop of York. He is the leader of the Anglican Church worldwide and the thirty dioceses of southern England, while his colleague presides over the fourteen dioceses of northern England.

Rowan Williams, a Welshman, is the 104th Archbishop of Canterbury – the first to be appointed from outside the Church of England. His CV includes stints as Professor of Divinity at Oxford University, Bishop of Monmouth and Archbishop of Wales. He is also a Fellow of the British Academy.

John Sentamu, the first black Archbishop of York, is Ugandan. When he was a magistrate in his homeland under Idi Amin, he sentenced ten innocent people to jail to save them from being murdered by the tyrant's enforcers. He was also arrested and beaten up for sentencing one of Amin's cousins to five years. Sentamu remarked of C. of E. bureaucracy, 'When the last trumpet shall sound, a commission will be set up on the significance of the trumpet, the financial implications of that trumpet and for a report to come back in ten years' time.'

Women were first ordained as deacons in 1987 and as priests in 1994.

The Early Church

Christianity arrived in the second century with the Romans, though several writers in the Middle Ages claimed that the apostle Joseph of Arimathea brought the Gospel to the British Isles even earlier. The faith declined in the fifth century as Rome departed and the pagan Angles, Saxons and Jutes invaded.

In 597, Pope Gregory I sent the Italian monk St Augustine to convert the Saxon kingdoms, a feat that was achieved within ninety years. This was, however, his second attempt – having turned back in fear of the fierce Celts at the outset and been compelled by the Pope to try again. St Augustine is considered the first Archbishop of Canterbury.

England's first Christian martyr was St Alban, a Roman soldier who exchanged clothes with a priest he was protecting and was executed in the man's place in around AD 304. St Albans Abbey was erected on the spot and the town of the same name grew around it.

During the pagan period, the Celtic Church kept Christianity alive. However, Celtic practices were rejected in favour of Roman usage at the Synod of Whitby in 664. The synod also established the structure of the English Church, headed by two archbishops, of Canterbury and York.

Tudor Martyrs

John Foxe's Book of Martyrs (1563) detailed the gruesome deaths of 273 Protestants at the hands of Mary Tudor. It was displayed in churches around the country for propaganda purposes during the reign of Elizabeth I.

THE OXFORD MARTYRS

Nicholas Ridley and Hugh Latimer, the Protestant bishops of London and Worcester, were burnt at the stake in Broad Street, Oxford, in 1555. As the flames grew, the elderly Latimer called out, 'Be of good comfort Master Ridley, and play the man. We shall this day light such a candle by God's grace in England as I trust shall never be put out.'

Latimer was soon overcome by the smoke, but the fire burned more slowly on Ridley's side and the younger bishop suffered an agonizing death. Ridley's brother had tied bags of gunpowder around their necks, which was mistakenly believed to deliver a quick end when the flames reached it. However, gunpowder has no explosive power except when confined within a hard shell, so all it did was deliver horrific burns.

The third Oxford Martyr, Thomas Cranmer – the first Protestant Archbishop of Canterbury – was executed in March 1556 even though he recanted. Recantation was normally enough to save one from the stake.

MARTYRS BY REIGN
Numbers burned for heresy

Henry VII (1485–1509)	24
Henry VIII (1509–1547)	81
Edward VI (1547–1553)	2
Mary (1553–1558)	300
Elizabeth I (1558–1603)	4*

* Many more Catholics were executed, but for treason rather than heresy.

Methodism

The Methodists started out as a Christian group at Oxford University led by the Lincolnshire priest John Wesley (1703–91). Students gave them the name 'Methodists' for their methodical approach to study. They lived Spartan lives, fasting twice weekly and performing good works for prison inmates and the poor in lieu of entertainment.

The Methodists formally split from the Church of England in 1795, four years after Wesley's death. Like their founder, Wesleyan ministers and lay preachers would often spread the word in open-air sermons, which gained Methodism a strong following among industrial workers and farm labourers.

Despite their emphasis on acts of charity, most English Methodists derive their theology from the Dutch thinker, Jacobus Arminius, according to whom salvation is not dependent upon good works. They believe that salvation is a gift from God to those with faith.

Today, there are around 15 million Methodists worldwide.

16

LEGENDS AND FOLKLORE

'Why has not England a great mythology? Our folklore has never advanced beyond daintiness, and the great melodies of our countryside have all issued through the pipes of Greece. Deep and true as the native imagination can be, it seems to have failed here. It has stopped with the witches and the fairies. It cannot vivify one fraction of a summer field, or give names to half a dozen stars. England still waits for the supreme moment of her literature.'

Margaret in E. M. Forster's *Howard's End* (1910)

'The Hobbits are just rustic English people, made small in size because it reflects the generally small reach of their imagination.'

J. R. R. Tolkien (1892–1973)

King Arthur

THE LEGEND

King Arthur, despite his popularity in England, was neither a king nor English. The balance of evidence indicates that even if he existed he was a Welsh general who led the Christian Celts against the pagan Saxon invaders in the sixth century. Neither would he have looked at all like most of his clean-cut Hollywood representations – his name means the 'Bear Man'.

His symbols are the Red Dragon of Wales and the White Boar of Cornwall, where he may have been born.

The legend of a native enemy of the Saxons appealed to the Norman conquerors of England. The stories of Arthur had been kept alive in France by the Bretons, whom the pagan invaders had forced to flee to the Continent centuries earlier. They were retold as the medieval Arthurian romances, which added embellishments such as the Knights of the Round Table, Merlin, Camelot and the Sword in the Stone.

When Arthur died, his body was buried on the mythical island of Avalon. In 1190, the monks at Glastonbury Abbey claimed to have uncovered Arthur's tomb in their cemetery, but it is likely that this was a ruse to attract pilgrims after the abbey's existing relics were lost in a fire.

CAMELOT

Sir Thomas Malory, author of Le Morte d'Arthur, asserted that Camelot was located in Winchester, but his own publisher, William Caxton, disagreed and placed it in Wales. The earliest references to Camelot in literature mention Winchester as a separate city. Possible sites of Camelot include:

Carlisle
Cadbury Castle, Somerset
Tintagel Castle, Cornwall
Viroconium, now Wroxeter in Shropshire
Caerleon-on-Usk, Wales
Dinerth Castle, Wales

THE ROUND TABLE

The Round Table was said to seat 150 knights, including the king himself. Famous knights include:

Sir Galahad
Sir Lancelot du Lac
Sir Gawain
Sir Percivale
Sir Tor
Sir Kay
Sir Palomedes the
  Saracen
Sir Pelleas
Sir Tristram
Sir Morholt
Sir Lionell

Sir Bors
Sir Bedivere
Sir Lucan the Butler
Sir Girflet
Sir Yvain
Sir Erec
Sir Cador
King Hoel of Brittany
King Pellinor of the Isles
Sir Dinadan
Sir Mordred

Only the chaste and sinless virgin knight destined to recover the Holy Grail could safely sit in the *Siège Perilous* ('dangerous seat'). In early tales this was Sir Percivale, and later Sir Galahad. According to legend, Joseph of Arimathea brought the cup used by Jesus at the Last Supper to England, where it was hidden by the Grail-keepers.

The round table that hangs on the wall of the Great Hall in Winchester Castle was once believed to be King Arthur's, but radio-carbon analysis has dated the piece to the 1270s.

Sir Mordred, who betrayed his fellow knights, was the result of Arthur's incestuous relationship with his half-sister, Morgawse.

Arthur established four other knightly orders subordinate to the Round Table:

Queen's Knights
Knights of the Watch
Table of Errant Companions
Table of Less-Valued Knights

Fairy Folk

English fairies come in several varieties, not just the kind represented by Tinkerbell. Many are invisible, or go about their business in the dead of night when no one can see them. Some are invoked to frighten children into good behaviour, but they are also cited as the explanation of odd events from a broken saucer to a disabled child, and also for the mysterious appearance of what are probably ill-gotten gains. Perhaps the strangest acts accorded to them are those resulting in horses being found in the morning in their stables, sweating, exhausted and with tangled manes, when fairies are blamed for having ridden them all night.

Alternatively, much of fairy folklore may represent a kind of weak joke. Fairies were cited in the past in the same way that a modern driver who fumbles the clutch might blame 'lumpy petrol'.

After the English Reformation, the Church tried to portray fairies as demons, but according to Cornish legend, they were originally the angels who stayed neutral in the dispute between God and Lucifer. They were not wicked enough to be cast into hell, so were cast down to the earth instead.

WICKED FAIRIES

Abbey Lubbers: Also known as Buttery Spirits, these creatures inhabit religious houses and are blamed for tempting monks into drunkenness and gluttony.

Boggarts: Mischievous, invisible pixies that play tricks on travellers and householders, blamed by northern housewives for broken crockery.

Changelings: Fairies, also called 'oafs', who replace stolen human babies without the parents noticing. This has been used to explain children who seem healthy at birth but who later manifest mental or physical disabilities.

Goblin: Any small evil fairy.

Jenny Greenteeth: A water fairy rumoured to drag children into stagnant ponds. Her name probably derives from the weed or algal growth that would quickly overwhelm a small child who fell into a pond containing it.

Joint Eater: A greedy fairy that invisibly devours people's food in order to starve them. The victim constantly feels hungry despite eating large meals.

Queen Mab: A very small, malicious fairy who preys on midwives, pushing them into ditches and rivers at night and stealing babies.

At other times she merely spoils butter, tangles horses' manes and gives women blisters. She gets from place to place in a miniature coach drawn by insects.

Spriggans: Evil fairies said to be the ghosts of giants who guard buried treasure.

Will-o'-the-Wisp: A fairy who produces a flickering light to lead travellers astray on moors and marshes. Believers were unsure whether they really were a breed of fairy or the souls of unbaptized babies.

GOOD FAIRIES

Brownies: Helpful pixies who perform household chores in the night and bring luck to the householder. There is never more than one to a house. They must not be insulted or offended lest they turn into boggarts.

Gooseberry Wives: Protect gooseberry bushes from children, sometimes by taking on the appearance of a large hairy caterpillar.

Habonde: The queen of the fairies, who wears her hair in long dark plaits set off by a gold circlet inset with a star. Though an English monarch, she is also thought to have lordship over the fairies of France.

Hobgoblin: A fairy similar to a brownie who helps with household chores.

Hytersprites: Norfolk fairies conjured to frighten children from straying too far from home. They are also said to police the hanging of Christmas decorations, punishing householders who leave them up after Twelfth Night.

Robin Goodfellow: A fairy who can change his shape to frighten people and play practical jokes – for example, turning into a horse and throwing his rider in a river. Usually good-natured and often laughing, he also helps people around the house.

THE COTTINGLEY FAIRIES

The Cottingley Fairies were photographed with two teenage girls in 1917 and 1920. They were widely believed to be genuine – by, among others, Sir Arthur Conan Doyle, who reported on them for the *Strand* magazine. However, more than sixty years later the girls admitted that their fairy friends were, in fact, pictures cut out of fashion magazines, pasted on to cardboard and affixed to bushes. No one had thought to question why fairies should sport the latest Parisian hairstyles.

Mythical Beasts

COCKATRICE

A venomous serpent with the head and legs of a cock and the body and tail of a dragon, that could kill with a glance. The only way to kill it was by using mirrors. One knight from Essex is said to have defeated it by wearing armour fashioned from polished crystal, while another beast was defeated in Wherwell in Hampshire when someone lowered a mirror into its lair. The creature's reflection incited it to fight and kill itself.

Black Dogs

The devil in canine form, such as the Black Dog of Bungay in Suffolk, said to have rampaged through the village church killing and injuring those attending a service in 1577.

Dragons

Dragons featured prominently in Celtic mythology, and with the rise of Christianity in the British Isles, there was an impetus for tales to end with the death of the beasts. Dragon-slaying feats are sometimes attributed to the founders of prominent local families such as Sir Piers Shonks at Brent Pelham or Sir John Lambton. An eel thrown into a well by a young Lord Lambton in the Middle Ages grew up into a dragon while he was off fighting the crusades. It could not be killed, as severed parts of the beast would rejoin its body. It was only destroyed when the lord returned and faced it in the middle of a fast-flowing river, clad in armour covered in blades. As the dragon coiled around him it diced itself on the blades and the parts were carried away by the current before they could reform.

Gogmagog

A giant that lived in Cornwall when Brutus arrived on the island of Albion. According to legend, Brutus killed the creature and founded Britain.

Big Cats

Despite various newspaper reports of escaped pumas and panthers, no big cat has been killed or captured in England barring a small swamp cat that was run over in Hampshire in 1988. Rumoured sightings include:

The Surrey Puma, 1962–6
The Black Beast of Exmoor, 1983
The Beast of Bodmin Moor, 1994–5, was investigated by the
Department of Agriculture. A 'skull' was produced in July 1995, but
this was later found to have come from a leopard-skin rug.
The Beast of Essex, 1998, was said to have killed geese in Epping.

Photographs of so-called beasts have, in fact, shown normal moggies shot from deceptive angles.

Fourteen Notable Hauntings

Borley Rectory, Essex: The Rectory was built on the spot where Marie Laire, a seventeenth-century nun, was executed for fornication with a monk. In the early part of the last century it acquired a reputation as the most haunted house in England, as Marie harassed the occupants and scrawled pleas for help on the walls.

Corfe Castle, Dorset: A headless woman said to have betrayed the besieged Royalists in 1645 haunts the battlements.

Dunster Castle, Somerset: The castle's gift shop is haunted by a man dressed in green and a poltergeist that knocks souvenirs off their shelves. The spirit is said to have a particular dislike of the guidebooks on offer.

The Fleece Inn, Bretforton, Worcestershire: Former resident Lola Taplin, who died in 1977, is reported to take offence at patrons eating on the premises and occasionally dashes plates of sandwiches to the floor.

Ham House, Surrey: Fifteen ghosts, including the Duchess of Lauderdale (1626–98) – identifiable from her rose perfume – and several ghosts of dogs.

Hampton Court Palace, Surrey: Over twenty ghosts occupy the palace, among them Henry VIII and his wives Jane Seymour and Catherine Howard. Howard has been heard screaming for mercy.

Lyric Theatre, Shaftesbury Avenue, London: Murdered programme-seller Nellie Klute is said to turn up for work occasionally.

Lyveden New Bield, Northamptonshire: A figure thought to be Sir Thomas Tresham, who was implicated in the Gunpowder Plot of 1605, has been seen several times looking out from the upper windows of the unfinished Elizabethan house. There are no floors inside the building.

Newmarket Racecourse: Several riders have blamed the ghost of the nineteenth century's greatest jockey, Fred Archer, who committed suicide aged 20, for scaring their mounts during races. He has also been seen wandering through local stables.

Sawston Hall, Cambridgeshire: Mary Tudor is thought to haunt the hall's Tapestry Room.

Souter Lighthouse, Tyne and Wear: A deceased engineman from a local coalmine is said to occupy the lighthouse, where he annoys residents with his pungent tobacco.

Tower of London: Numerous headless figures, including Anne Boleyn, Sir Walter Ralegh and Lady Jane Grey, have been reported stalking the corridors.

Vine Street Police Station, London: The ghost of Sergeant Goddard, who hanged himself in one of the cells.

Windsor Castle: Charles I appears with his head intact, while Elizabeth I appears in a black shawl and George III haunts the Royal Library where he was sometimes confined during bouts of insanity.

OTHER CELEBRITY GHOSTS

Florence Nightingale	St Thomas's Hospital, London
George II	Kensington Palace
George IV	The Royal Pavilion, Brighton
Grimaldi the Clown	Theatre Royal, Drury Lane, London
Nell Gwynne	Salisbury Hall, Hertfordshire
Lawrence of Arabia	Cloud's Hill, Dorset
Boatswain (Lord Byron's dog)	Newstead Abbey, Nottingham

The English Roswell

In 1980, Lt. Col. Charles Holt, deputy commander of the United States Air Force base at Rendlesham, Suffolk, reported that military policemen had seen 'a strange glowing object in the forest...

described as being metallic in appearance and triangular in shape, approximately two to three metres across the base and two metres high. It illuminated the entire forest with a white light. The object itself had a pulsating red light on top and a bank of blue lights underneath... it was hovering or on legs. As the patrolmen approached, it manoeuvred through the trees and disappeared.'

A Ministry of Defence investigation proved inconclusive, but the story caught the imagination of several authors and journalists. However, in 2003, Kevin Conde, a former military policeman, revealed that the incident had been a practical joke he had played before he left the base to return to the United States. The 'spacecraft' was in fact a 1979 Plymouth Volare he had rigged with flashing lights and a distorted siren to frighten a gullible colleague on a foggy night.

Conde only discovered that the wheeze had entered UFO folklore when he happened to read the history of his old airbase on a USAF website years later. 'I was amazed,' he said. 'I had no idea about all this nonsense... I hate to be cynical, but when I see people making money out of this I have to ask myself if they are not nuts, what are they?'

Source: The Science of 'The Hitchhiker's Guide to the Galaxy', *by Michael Hanlon*

The Ravens in the Tower

According to legend, the astronomer John Flamsteed (1646–1719) once complained to Charles II that his work at the Tower of London was being interrupted by noisy ravens. He asked that they be culled, but the king was warned that if the ravens left, the White Tower would fall and disaster strike the realm. Charles ordered that at least six ravens be kept at the Tower thereafter. However, an academic study in 2004 found no references to the story earlier than 1895.

During the Blitz, German bombing reduced their number to a single bird, Grip.

One raven, George, was expelled in 1986 for chewing TV aerials.

Today, seven ravens with clipped wings are kept so that there is one 'spare' in case of an accident. Their names are Baldrick, Branwen, Hugine, Gwyllum, Hardey, Munin and Thor. The oldest is Hugine, at 24 years of age. Thor can mimic human speech.

They are fed on raw meat, eggs and biscuits, though this author has also seen one stalk and kill a pigeon.

———

Woodland Figures

———

ROBIN HOOD

He is thought to have lived in the twelfth century, when Sherwood Forest covered 100,000 acres rather than the 450 acres of today. The earliest surviving reference to the legend is William Langland's 1377 poem *The Vision of William Concerning Piers Plowman*. A gravestone said to be Hood's lies at Kirklees Priory, where he was killed by his cousin the prioress and Sir Roger of Doncaster.

Robin's Merrie Men
Little John
Maid Marian
Friar Tuck
Will Scarlet

Alan-a-Dale
Will Stukely
Much the Miller's Son
Gilbert of the Lily-White Hand
George-o-Green
David of Doncaster
Arthur-a-Bland
Right Hitting Brand

THE GREEN MAN

This pagan figure has been carved in relief into church buildings since the Middle Ages, typically in the form of a head emerging from foliage with vines growing out of his mouth.

JACK-IN-THE-GREEN

A traditional character in May Day celebrations – a villager dressed from head to toe in leaves and branches, whose role is either to encourage or ward off drunkenness.

HERNE THE HUNTER

A horned spirit that protects Windsor Great Park.

17
WARFARE

'We were not fairly beaten, my lord. No Englishman is ever fairly beaten.'

The Chaplain in George Bernard Shaw's *St Joan* (1924)

'When God wants a hard thing done, He tells it to his Englishmen... The Englishman is made for a time of crisis, and for a time of emergency. He is serene in difficulties, but may seem to be indifferent when times are easy. He may not look ahead, he may not heed warnings, he may not prepare, but when he once starts he is persistent to the death, and he is ruthless in action. It is these gifts that have made the Englishman what he is, and that have enabled the Englishman to make England and the Empire what it is.'

Stanley Baldwin

The Wars of the Roses (1455–85)

By the mid fifteenth century, Henry VI's weak rule had led to widespread anarchy in the countryside and failure against France in the Hundred Years War. His collapse into mental illness in 1453 led Richard Neville, Earl of Warwick (Warwick the Kingmaker), to set up Richard, Duke of York, as protector of the realm. Richard was first in line until the king's wife, Margaret, produced a male heir, Edward. Henry recovered his mind in 1455 and removed the duke from the royal council. Richard responded by declaring war on the House of Lancaster.

The fighting was conducted chiefly on foot. The only major cavalry charge took place at the Battle of Blore Heath in 1459, where Lord Audley was killed leading his Lancastrians into a massed volley of arrows.

The lower classes played little part in the wars. Most of the fighting was done by noblemen and their men-at-arms, tenants and retainers. There was no standing army at this time save for the garrison at Calais, which was cut off from the fighting.

It was customary after a battle to summarily execute captured noblemen while allowing the ordinary troops to flee. The overall death toll included nine dukes, one marquis, thirteen earls, twenty-four barons and the Prince of Wales. The wars so enfeebled England's great noble families that historians consider their conclusion to mark the end of the feudal period. The Tudor Age saw an increase in the power of the Crown over the land.

The houses of York and Lancaster were both descended from Edward III. Their badges were the white and red rose respectively.

Henry VII amalgamated the two colours in the Tudor rose when he married Elizabeth of York to unite the two houses.

THE MAJOR BATTLES AND THEIR VICTORS

22 May 1455	First St Albans	Yorkists
23 September 1459	Blore Heath	Yorkists
12 October 1459	Ludford Bridge	Lancastrians
10 July 1460	Northampton	Yorkists
30 December 1460	Wakefield	Lancastrians
2 February 1461	Mortimer's Cross	Yorkists
17 February 1461	Second St Albans	Lancastrians
28 March 1461	Ferrybridge	Yorkists
29 March 1461	Towton	Yorkists
25 April 1464	Hedgeley Moor	Yorkists
15 May 1464	Hexham	Yorkists
26 July 1464	Edgecote Moor	Lancastrians
12 March 1469	Losecote Field	Yorkists
14 April 1470	Barnet	Yorkists
4 May 1471	Tewkesbury	Yorkists
22 August 1485	Bosworth	Lancastrians (Tudors)
16 June 1487	Stoke	Lancastrians (Tudors)

The English Civil War (1642–51)

The war began in 1642 when, after five years of seeing his prerogatives slashed by the Long Parliament, Charles miscalculated by swarming into the Palace of Westminster with several hundred soldiers to arrest five MPs and a peer he accused of treason. They all escaped, but London was scandalized and the king was forced to flee the city.

The terms 'Roundhead' and 'Cavalier' were originally employed by the opposing sides as terms of abuse, though neither was widely used at the time. 'Roundhead' referred to the shaved heads of the London apprentices who supported the Parliamentarian cause.

The Roundheads presented themselves as the party of 'Englishness', which prompted the Celtic Welsh and Cornish to side with the king, whose support was strongest in the North and West. Charles also imported foreign mercenaries and Irish troops.

Parliament's initial leader was the Earl of Essex. Oliver Cromwell rose to prominence as the leader of the Ironside cavalry unit, with which he helped Parliament to victory at Marston Moor in 1644. Cromwell pronounced the cavalry 'honest, sober christians... honest goodly men'. The following year he defeated the Royalists at Naseby and Longport as vice commander of the New Model Army.

Thomas Fairfax ran the New Model Army as a meritocracy. Soldiers did not need high birth in order to become officers. There was a strong Puritan element, and some of the men would sing psalms on their way into battle.

After the surrender of Oxford, the Royalist capital, in June 1646, Charles was imprisoned at Hampton Court Palace, but he escaped and the war began anew. After Parliament's final victory at the Battle of Preston in 1648, the king fled in disguise to Scotland, but the Scots handed him over to the Roundheads.

The Rump Parliament was what was left after Pride's Purge, when Colonel Thomas Pride stormed Parliament to remove the moderate MPs who favoured the king's return to power. Charles was found guilty of treason and sentenced to death after trying to spark a war between the Parliamentarians and Scotland.

The Major Battles and their Victors

23 October 1642	Edgehill, Birmingham	Royalists
30 June 1643	Adwalton Moor, Bradford	Royalists
13 July 1643	Roundaway Down, Salisbury	Royalists
20 September 1643	Newbury, Berkshire	Draw
2 July 1644	Marston Moor, Yorkshire	Roundheads
27 October 1644	Newbury, Berkshire	Draw
14 June 1645	Naseby, Northamptonshire	Roundheads
17–19 August 1648	Preston, Lancashire	Roundheads

Charles I (1600–49, r. 1625–49)

Charles was a little over 5 feet tall (1.5 metres), with a stutter and a thick Scottish accent.

Charles the Ruler

The root causes of the Civil War were Charles I's 'high church' sympathies and his autocratic desire to rule without reference to Parliament. His abuses included arbitrary arrests and imprisonments, non-parliamentary taxation, the enforced billeting of troops and martial law. He was forced to call a Parliament to raise funds to put down a rebellion over his new Prayer Book in Scotland in 1637, but this backfired when, instead of granting him the money, MPs presented their own list of grievances. The king resorted to Catholic Irish troops, which further alarmed the Protestant Parliamentarians.

He adjourned Parliament in 1629 after the Speaker had been held down in his chair while three resolutions were passed condemning the king's behaviour. Charles ruled for the next eleven years without calling a Parliament.

He lived in Christchurch College, Oxford, during the Civil War.

CHARLES'S QUEEN

Henrietta Maria was both French and a Catholic. When she first came to England, she brought with her a retinue of one bishop, twenty-nine priests and 410 attendants, but Charles soon sent them back.

In 1641 she went as far as pawning the Crown Jewels to raise money for the king's army.

The US state of Maryland was named after her.

Sophia of Bohemia wrote after meeting Henrietta Maria that 'Van Dyck's portraits had so accustomed me to thinking that all English women are beautiful that I was amazed to find a small creature with skinny arms and teeth like defence works sticking out of her mouth.'

HIS TRIAL AND EXECUTION

At Charles's trial in Westminster Hall, he refused to recognize the legality of the court, describing himself as a 'martyr'. John Bradshaw, the presiding judge, had a special hat designed with reinforced metal plates inside to protect his head from Royalist missiles.

Charles was beheaded on 30 January 1649. He wore several layers of underclothes on his way to the block, as it was a very cold day and he did not want the public to see him shivering and mistake it for fear. Afterwards, members of the crowd were permitted to rush forward and dip their handkerchiefs in his blood, which was subsequently claimed to have effected miraculous cures.

The US states of North and South Carolina are named after the Latin form of 'Charles'.

Oliver Cromwell (1599–1658)

Cromwell grew up in Huntingdon, the small town for which he became Member of Parliament in 1628. He was distantly related to Henry VIII's Chief Minister, Thomas Cromwell.

CROMWELL THE PURITAN

Cromwell was wholly without vanity, and his fellow MPs noted that he dressed in dirty, scruffy clothes. He later told his portrait painter, 'I desire you would use all your skill to paint my picture truly like me... warts and everything.'

Cromwell underwent religious conversion and became a Puritan in 1634. Though his later rule allowed for greater religious freedom than the populace was used to, he cracked down on what he regarded as frivolous pleasures that offended his work ethic. Many sports were banned and theatres were closed down. Women were forbidden to wear brightly coloured dresses and cosmetics were prohibited. Puritan soldiers would patrol the streets and scrub the faces of anyone wearing make-up. He abolished Christmas festivities and soldiers would confiscate roast goose, plum pudding and even decorative holly. Swearing became a criminal offence that could lead to prison for persistent offenders.

CROMWELL THE GENERAL

Cromwell had no military experience prior to the Civil War, but proved a highly effective commander due to his determination and abundant common sense. As he said to his troops while fording a river, 'Put your trust in God, but mind you, keep your powder dry.'

Cromwell completed a bloody conquest of Ireland in 1649, having variously ordered and permitted the killing of several thousand civilians and surrendered soldiers at Drogheda and Wexford. He claimed these atrocities were retribution for the alleged Catholic massacre of Protestants in 1641 and were the 'righteous judgment of God upon these barbarous wretches'.

CROMWELL'S RULE

In 1653 Cromwell was appointed Lord Protector, the only commoner ever to be head of state. He dissolved the Rump Parliament, sending soldiers to 'help' MPs out of their seats. He then assembled the Barebones Parliament comprising 140 of the 'godliest' men in England, but he soon got rid of it when they demanded the abolition of tithing and an end to the national church system.

He turned down requests from colleagues to be crowned Oliver I after considering it for five weeks in 1657. He nevertheless carried out the offices of a king – appointing peers, living in the royal palaces and governing the country as an absolute ruler. He thought nothing of jailing men without trial and removing them to the Isle of Wight, the Scilly Isles or wherever they would be beyond the writ of habeas corpus. Finally, he appointed his eldest son Richard as his successor. 'Government,' he declared, 'is for the people's good, not what pleases them.'

He died in 1658 and was buried in Westminster Abbey, but Charles II later had his body dragged out, hung from a gibbet at Tyburn and decapitated.

Charles II (1630–85, r. 1660–85)

ESCAPE, RESTORATION AND REVENGE

Charles II was crowned King of Scotland in 1651 and led an army as far south as Worcester before he was defeated by Cromwell. He then hid in the boughs of an oak tree at Boscobel House for a day while Roundhead soldiers searched the woods below. After the Restoration, the Boscobel Oak became a tourist destination. So many parts of the tree were chopped off to make commemorative items that it eventually died, but it gave its name to England's numerous Royal Oak pubs.

George Monck, a leading Parliamentarian general, drove the Restoration of the monarchy in order to prevent anarchy. When Richard Cromwell lost the confidence of Parliament and abdicated in 1660, Monck called on Charles II to issue the Declaration of Breda, a document of goodwill that promised an amnesty and full payment of the arrears owed to the army. Charles returned to London in time for his thirtieth birthday.

Once on the throne, Charles insisted that fifty-nine regicides be tried for the death of his father. Many escaped, but the rest were hanged, drawn and quartered.

A statue at Newby Hall in Ripon, North Yorkshire, depicts a mounted Charles II trampling Oliver Cromwell into the ground. It was originally supposed to be the King of Poland trampling a Turkish soldier, but its intended customer – the Polish ambassador in London – could not afford to pay for it, so it was altered and renamed. This explains why Cromwell appears to be wearing a turban.

LOVE-LIFE

His marriage to Catherine of Braganza of Portugal in 1662 failed to produce an heir, but it was not for want of trying. The 'Merry Monarch' was a libertine who publicly acknowledged fourteen children by seven mistresses. What worried his advisors was that several of them were Catholic, including some French Catholics. The king's debauchery and foreign influences in the bedchamber were blamed for his foreign policy disasters. The Earl of Rochester quipped: Charles's 'sceptre and his prick are of a length/But she who plays with one may sway the other.' Several filthy rhymes deploring or celebrating the king's exploits were circulated. He was nicknamed 'Old Rowley' after a stallion known for breeding excellent foals.

The actress and courtesan Nell Gwynne was a more acceptable match. She was once mistaken for her rival, the Duchess of Portsmouth, while travelling through Oxford in her coach, whereupon she put her head out of the window and called out, 'Good people, you are mistaken – I am the *Protestant* whore.' She was said to have also secretly administered laxatives to another rival, Mary 'Moll' Davis, before the woman was due in the king's bedchamber.

Charles was notorious for rarely washing.

PLAGUE AND FIRE

In 1665, the Great Plague killed over seventy-five thousand people and a fifth of London's population. It was brought to an end in the capital only by the Great Fire of London in 1666, which destroyed over thirteen thousand houses along with St Paul's Cathedral.

TITUS OATES

In 1678, the so-called Popish Plot to assassinate Charles resulted in the judicial murder of over thirty innocent Catholics. The plot was fabricated by Titus Oates, a former Anglican priest dismissed from his parish for theft and drunkenness, who had infiltrated two Jesuit seminaries in Europe before he was expelled. Oates even implicated the queen. Charles proved Oates to be a liar before the Privy Council, but was unable to restrain the anti-Catholic hysteria that swept the country.

Charles sponsored the founding of the Royal Society, Christopher Wren's rebuilding of St Paul's and the Royal Hospital, Chelsea.

He converted to Roman Catholicism on his deathbed.

England's Adversaries

FRANCE

> 'The French are a logical people, which is one reason
> the English dislike them so intensely. The other is that
> they own France, a country which we have always
> judged to be much too good for them.'

Robert Morley, 1974

At the height of England's power, Henry II ruled more of France than the French king. His empire included Aquitaine, Anjou, Auvergne, Berry, Brittany, Gascony, La Manche, Maine, Normandy, Poitou and Touraine.

The last piece of France owned by England was Dunkirk, captured from the Spanish Netherlands by Oliver Cromwell in 1658. It was sold to the French by Charles II in 1662.

The nickname 'Frogs' originally referred to the Dutch – 'Nick Frog' – in the fourteenth century, since they were thought to inhabit marshland. It was transferred to the French during the Napoleonic Wars.

Oxford University's All Souls College was founded in 1438 to pray for all the souls of men who died in the wars against France. Its full name is 'All Souls College of the Faithful Departed'.

When Britain was allied with France during the Crimean War, the absent-minded English commander Lord Raglan found it impossible not to refer to the Russian enemy as 'the French' during briefings.

After almost a millennium of intermittent warfare, Lord Lansdowne and Paul Cambon, the French Ambassador, signed the Entente Cordiale on 8 April 1904. The agreement settled imperial disputes over Africa and Siam and recognized the right of free passage through the Suez Canal.

Wars with France

Norman Conquest (1066)
War of St Sardos (1324)
The Hundred Years War (1337–1453)
War of the League of Cambrai (1508–16)
Hapsburg–Valois War (1556)
Henry VIII's First Invasion (1513)
Henry VIII's Second Invasion (1522)
Henry VIII's Third Invasion (1544)
War of the Grand Alliance (1688–97)
War of the Spanish Succession (1702–13)
War of the Austrian Succession (1740–48)

Seven Years War (1756–63)
American Revolutionary War (1775–83)
French Revolutionary Wars/Napoleonic Wars (1792–1815)

Dishonourable mention: As the French army crumbled in 1940, the French government declined to sail its navy into British ports. Elements of it were shelled in their harbours by the Royal Navy to prevent them from falling into Nazi hands. Later in the war, the RAF bombed the Michelin tyre plant after the owners refused to sabotage production of high-quality tyres for the Wehrmacht.

SCOTLAND

> 'Sir, let me tell you, the noblest prospect which a
> Scotchman ever sees is the high road that leads him to
> England.'
>
> Samuel Johnson

Edward I stole Scotland's Coronation Stone, the Stone of Destiny or Stone of Scone, and installed it in Westminster Abbey in 1296. In 1950, four Scottish students managed to remove it – accidentally breaking it into two pieces in the process – and drove it back to Scotland, leaving it on the altar in Arbroath Abbey. The police recovered the stone and it was finally sent to a permanent home at Edinburgh Castle in 1996. It will be transported to England for future coronation ceremonies.

Between 1296 and 1482, the border town of Berwick-upon-Tweed changed hands thirteen times. It was put to siege and assaulted on more occasions than any other town in the world bar Jerusalem. Today, Berwick Rangers FC is the only English team to play in the Scottish Football League.

Wars with Scotland

English Conquest of Scotland (1295–6)
First War of Scottish Independence (1297–1328)
Second War of Scottish Independence (1332–57)
The Hundred Years War (1333–1453)
Edward IV's Invasion (1482)
War of the Holy League (1513) (James IV's invasion of England)
Henry VIII's Invasion (1542–9)
English Civil War (1650–51)

SPAIN

A major war between England and Spain was made likely in the sixteenth century by the civil war that broke out in France in 1562, meaning that both nations' traditional enemy was no longer a common threat.

Mary Tudor's widower, Philip II of Spain, offered to marry Elizabeth I in 1559, but she spurned his advances.

The world's oldest surviving alliance is between England and Spain's neighbour, Portugal. The Treaty of Windsor was signed in 1386 as 'an inviolable, eternal, solid, perpetual and true league of friendship'. It was invoked most recently in 1982 during the Falklands War, when Britain was given use of the Azores as a naval base.

The Armada, 1588

England and Spain had been effectively at war on the seas for some time in the form of sponsored piracy, but the final straw for Philip II was The Treaty of Nonsuch in 1585, under which England agreed to support the Dutch Revolt against Spanish rule.

Philip dispatched the Armada to secure the Strait of Dover and link up with the Duke of Parma who would bring thirty thousand hardened troops from the Netherlands.

The fleet comprised 130 vessels, 40 of which were large warships, carrying 8,000 sailors and 19,000 soldiers. But like the Battle of Britain, it was not quite the unequal contest that propagandists pretended. The English fleet defending the Channel was around the same size as the Spanish force, with the same number of ships-of-the-line. The English ships were also faster and better armed and their crews better trained.

The Spanish sought to exploit their infantry advantage but did not once succeed in boarding an enemy vessel. This was the first battle to be fought at sea exclusively with heavy guns.

Spanish losses were compounded by bad weather, and only sixty ships from the Armada returned home. Fifteen thousand men had been lost for only several hundred Englishmen, although most of those had succumbed to disease rather than enemy action.

Shipwrecked Spaniards who washed up on Irish shores were slaughtered as they landed, yet Oliver Cromwell was later to justify his massacres in Ireland partly on the grounds that the populace was eager to support any foreign invasion of England.

Wars with Spain
War of 1585–1604
Thirty Years War (1625–29)
War of 1654–60
American Revolutionary War (1779–83)
War of the Spanish Succession (1702–13)
War of the Quadruple Alliance (1718–20)
War of Jenkins' Ear (1739–42)*
War of the Austrian Succession (1740–48)
Seven Years War (1761–63)

French Revolutionary Wars (1796–1802)
Napoleonic Wars (1803–1808)

* The War of Jenkins' Ear was named after Robert Jenkins, a sea captain who claimed that Spanish coastguards had cut off his ear in 1731. He exhibited the ear at the House of Commons and the English public demanded restitution.

THE NETHERLANDS

In the seventeenth and eighteenth centuries, England and the Netherlands fought four wars at sea over the control of maritime trade.

The First Anglo-Dutch War (1652–4) began after the Parliament of the Commonwealth of England passed the 1651 Navigation Act as a direct challenge to Dutch shipping. Goods from Europe could be imported in English ships or those of the country of origin, while only English vessels could import goods from other continents. The stopping and searching of Dutch merchant ships became routine, and even those not bound for England were in danger if they carried French cargos.

England also demanded that all foreign vessels in the Channel salute Cromwell's warships. Those that did not show this mark of respect – some forty Dutch ships – were attacked. The next shots were fired over herring, as the navy took measures to prevent Dutch fishermen poaching in English waters.

The English admiral Robert Blake was wounded during his victory in the Battle of Portland in 1653, but during his recovery he wrote the seminal handbook on naval tactics *Fighting Instructions*, in which he emphasized the importance of fighting in a line of battle to maximize the power of broadsides. His successor George Monck used its precepts to defeat the Dutch at Scheveningen in July 1653.

The Second Anglo-Dutch War (1664–7) followed the capture of New Amsterdam and the seizure of the two Dutch trading posts in West Africa that were threatening the English hold on the slave trade. The war was a disaster. In June 1667 the Dutch fleet sailed up the Thames and the Medway to Chatham, destroyed four of the English navy's largest vessels and captured its flagship, the *Royal Charles*.

The Third Anglo-Dutch War (1672–4) was launched to aid Louis IX of France against England's future king, William of Orange. England's Lord High Admiral at the time was James, Duke of York, later to become James II and the man who fled before William during the Glorious Revolution. England made peace after four straight defeats.

The Fourth Anglo-Dutch War (1780–84) was declared by England after the discovery that the Dutch were secretly negotiating trade agreements with the rebellious American colonies. The conflict was a non-event as despite winning a small engagement off the Dogger Bank in August 1781, the Dutch were unable to bring a fleet to bear at all.

18

SPORTS AND PASTIMES

'The Englishman is seen at his best the moment that
another man starts throwing a ball at him.'

Vita Sackville-West

English Football

ANCIENT ORIGINS

Football is ultimately descended from the game *harpastum* brought to the British Isles by the Romans. Its rules are not known, but it seems to have been similar to Australian rules football.

Modern football evolved in England from the violent 'mob' football games that once engaged hundreds of participants in market towns and villages in the Middle Ages. Several public schools later created their own idiosyncratic versions and, when their alumni met at Oxford and Cambridge universities, attempts were made to standardize the rules. For the first few decades of its formal existence, soccer was a game for the upper classes while the working man preferred rugby.

MOB FOOTBALL GAMES

Violent, chaotic and dangerous, these have long been hated by the authorities and loved by ordinary folk. The 'pitch' can be several miles long with local landmarks or parish church portals for 'goals' and kick-off taking place in the main square. Often taking a whole day to play and sometimes involving the destruction of property, serious injuries and even fatalities, many mob games have been stamped out over the years. Edward II banned them in 1314, and several of his successors renewed the prohibition. The Police Act of 1840 put paid to several games. Those that survive do so either because they are the safest and gentlest or the most unruly, uncontrollable and unstoppable...

Ashbourne Royal Shrovetide Football: Played on Shrove Tuesday and Ash Wednesday with a decorated leather ball and two mills two miles apart to represent goals. Townsfolk are divided into two teams, the Upp'ards and Down'ards, according to whether they live above or below the Henmore Stream that flows through the Derbyshire town. In the nineteenth century, the game was relocated to open ground due to the damage caused by crowds rampaging through the streets.

Hallaton bottle-kicking contest: Played in Leicestershire on Easter Monday to a best-of-three format with three small wooden barrels rather than bottles, two of which are filled with ale. Players from Hallaton and Medbourne (outsiders are welcome to turn out for the Medbourne side) are first whipped up by scrambling for pieces of a large meat pie that is broken up and thrown into the throng. Goals are a stream and a hedge.

Haxey Hood Game: Held on 6 January in Lincolnshire to commemorate the day that Lady de Mowbray's red hood was blown off in the wind and thirteen local labourers chased after it. She is said to have granted each of them half an acre on the condition that they re-enact the scene for her amusement every year. Today it is played with a large rope and leather hood with groups of men scrimmaging between two pubs in Haxey and Westwoodside.

Hurling: A Cornish game still played in St Columb Major and St Ives. Played with a small silver-plated wooden ball that can be thrown or carried but not kicked. The St Ives version has been moved to the beach, but at St Columb Major it still begins in the market square.

THE FOOTBALL ASSOCIATION

The FA was founded in 1863, when representatives from twelve schools and clubs in the London area met at the Freemasons Tavern in Lincoln's Inn Fields. The code of rules they drew up was based on that of Cambridge University. F. W. Campbell, the delegate from Blackheath School, walked out over the issue of 'hacking', or kicking below the knee, which he saw as an essential part of the game. He argued that a prohibition would 'do away with all the courage and pluck from the game, and I will be bound over to bring over a lot of Frenchmen who would beat you with a week's practice'. The remaining eleven members agreed on the original laws of Association Football, or 'soccer'. They neglected to specify how many players should take to the field or for how long, which meant that one early match between Barnes and Crystal Palace involved nine men playing against fourteen for sixty minutes.

THE FOOTBALL LEAGUE

The first football club was Sheffield FC, founded in 1855. The oldest Football League club is Notts County, formed on 7 December 1864.

The Football League was formed in 1888. From the Midlands and Lancashire, its founder members were:

Aston Villa	Accrington
Derby County	Blackburn Rovers
Notts County	Bolton Wanderers
Stoke City	Burnley
West Bromwich Albion	Everton
Wolverhampton Wanderers	Preston North End

The inaugural championship was won by Preston North End, who were given the name 'The Old Invincibles' because they achieved this feat without losing a match. They also won the FA Cup that year without conceding a single goal. Most of the team were Scottish.

The most successful English club to date has been Liverpool, winning the League eighteen times, the FA Cup six times and the European Cup five times.

The first black professional footballer was goalkeeper Arthur Wharton, who signed for Preston North End in 1886 as a semi-pro and turned fully professional for Rotherham United in 1889. He took up his sporting career after training as a missionary and setting a new world record for the 100-yard (91-metre) dash. In retirement he became an alcoholic and died penniless after working as a labourer in a colliery for the last fifteen years of his life.

The maximum wage was abolished in 1961, when George Eastham went to court after Newcastle United refused him a transfer. Small clubs would thenceforth be unable to hang on to their best players, and Preston, Burnley and Blackpool would soon fall from the first rank of teams. Fulham's Johnny Haynes subsequently became the first £100-a-week footballer.

DISASTERS

In 1958, seven players from Manchester United's 'Busby Babes' team were among twenty-three fatalities in the Munich Air Disaster. Matt Busby recovered from injuries suffered in the crash and two of the other survivors, Bill Foulkes and Bobby Charlton, helped United to win the European Cup ten years later.

Thirty-eight people died as a result of English hooliganism in Belgium's Heysel Stadium in 1985, when Liverpool played Juventus in the European Cup Final. English teams were banned from European competitions for five years as a result.

Ninety-six people were crushed to death at Hillsborough Stadium in Sheffield on 15 April 1989, when the police opened a set of exit gates and five thousand fans eager to catch the kick-off surged through a narrow tunnel. Fences separating spectators from the pitch were removed and English stadia converted to all-seater venues as a result of the Taylor Report into the tragedy.

THE ENGLISH STYLE

Direct Play, otherwise known as the Long-Ball Game, 'kick and run' or the 'English' style of play, was officially endorsed by FA training manuals for many years. It was inspired by the studies of retired RAF Wing Commander Charles Reep (1904–97), who invented the statistical analysis of football in 1950 at a match between Swindon Town and Bristol Rovers. Reep discovered that most goals are scored from movements involving fewer than five passes and that the fewer the passes in an attack, the more likely it was that a goal would be scored. One notable disciple was Graham Taylor, who employed this thinking with great success at Watford and with rather less success as manager of the England team.

The FA Cup

HISTORY

The idea for the competition was dreamed up by the honorary FA secretary Charles Alcock in the offices of the *Sportsman* newspaper in 1871.

The inaugural tournament in the 1871–2 season was contested by fifteen sides. The final was played at the Oval in Kennington, where Wanderers – a team made up of former public schoolboys and university men – beat Royal Engineers 1–0 in front of a crowd of two thousand. Six hundred and forty-seven clubs entered in the 2005–2006 season.

The original trophy was stolen from the window of a shop in Birmingham in 1895, where it was on display after being won by Aston Villa. There have been four trophies in total.

The 1923 final was the first match to be played at Wembley Stadium. Bolton Wanderers beat West Ham United 2–0 before an estimated crowd of two hundred thousand. PC George Scorey on his white horse 'Billy' famously helped to keep order in the overcrowded stadium.

Playing for Manchester City against Birmingham City in the 1956 final, German goalkeeper Bert Trautmann was knocked unconscious in the seventy-fifth minute. No substitutions were allowed, but he recovered and was found to have completed the rest of the match with a broken neck.

In the nineteenth century, seven Scottish clubs played in the English FA Cup. Queen's Park were finalists twice and Glasgow Rangers lost to Aston Villa in a semi-final. Welsh clubs are still included in the competition, their last success being Cardiff City's win in 1927.

RECORDS

The only non-league club to win the cup was Tottenham Hotspur in 1901, when they beat Sheffield United 3–1.

The widest winning margin was Bury 6, Derby County 0 in 1903.

Two teams have won three times in succession: Blackburn Rovers (1884, 1885, 1886) and Wanderers (1876, 1877, 1878).

The only winning side to face top-flight opposition in every round was the Manchester United team of 1947–8. They beat Aston Villa 6–4 in the third round, Liverpool 3–0 in the fourth, Charlton Athletic 2–0 in the fifth, Preston North End 4–1 in the quarter final and Derby County 3–1 in the semis before overcoming Blackpool 4–2 in the final. None of United's games were played at home as Old Trafford was closed due to war damage.

The most prolific giant-killers have been Yeovil Town, who have beaten twenty Football League teams as a non-league side.

GREAT FA CUP UPSETS

1992: Third Round – Wrexham 2, Arsenal 1
The team that finished bottom of the league the previous year knocked out the league champions.

1988: Final – Wimbledon 1, Liverpool 0
The 'Crazy Gang's' captain and goalkeeper Dave Beasant becomes the first man to save a penalty in an FA Cup Final.

1984: Third Round – Bournemouth 2, Manchester United 0
Harry Redknapp's Third Division side beat Ron Atkinson's giants.

1980: Third Round – Harlow Town 1, Leicester City 0
The amateurs from the Isthmian League humbled the young Gary Lineker's team.

1973: Final – Sunderland 1, Leeds 0
Second Division Sunderland also knocked out top-flight Arsenal and Manchester City on their way to the cup.

1972: Third Round replay – Hereford United 2, Newcastle 1
Non-league Hereford beat a team that included the great Malcolm MacDonald.

1971: Fifth Round – Colchester United 3, Leeds United 2
Fourth Division Colchester were 3–0 up at one point against the league leaders.

The England Football Team

ORIGIN

The England team was established in 1870 and played the first official international football match against Scotland at Partick near Glasgow on 30 November 1872. The game ended 0–0.

England's first defeat to Continental opposition was a 4–3 loss against Spain in Madrid in 1929. However, they did not lose at home against a European team until they were beaten 6–3 by Hungary in 1953 – eighty-one years after their first international. England lost the return match in Budapest the following year 7–1, the team's heaviest defeat to this day.

THE BATTLE OF HIGHBURY

On 14 November 1934, Italy faced England at the Arsenal stadium in their first fixture since they had won the World Cup in Rome that summer. England – widely thought to be the world's best team – had not played in the tournament, and the match was billed as the 'real' World Cup Final. Mussolini offered each of his players the equivalent of £150 cash and an Alfa Romeo if they won. The England line-up included Stanley Matthews and seven Arsenal players – Frank Moss, George Male, Eddie Hapgood, Wilf Copping, Ray Bowden, Ted Drake and Cliff Bastin. Two minutes into the game, the Italian centre-half 'Luisito' Monti's foot was broken by a Ted Drake tackle, leaving the visitors to play on with ten men, as this was before substitutions were allowed. Incensed by what they regarded as a deliberate foul, the Italians made little attempt to play football for the rest of the first half as they endeavoured to injure as many English players as possible. The results included severe bruising, gashes, a broken nose and a broken arm. The FA considered withdrawing from all future international fixtures in protest at the violence. England survived to finish 3–2 up at the end, a score line regarded as inconclusive since Italy had played for so long with a man short and had had the best of the game once they began to concentrate on the ball. On the other hand, most of the English were finding it difficult to walk unaided by half-time. The Italian team are remembered in their country as the 'Lions of London'.

TOURNAMENT RECORD

England did not enter the World Cup until 1950. The FA was not a member of FIFA during the tournaments in 1930, 1934 and 1938, having resigned in 1928 over the question of payments to amateur players on international duty. In 1950, in Brazil, England failed to reach the knockout stage of the competition after suffering a humiliating 1–0 defeat to the USA.

The 1954 World Cup was held in Switzerland. England were knocked out in the quarter finals by Uruguay, losing 4–2.

In the Swedish World Cup of 1958, England again failed to progress to the knockout stage after drawing their group games against Austria, Brazil and the USSR.

In Chile in 1962, England were beaten 3–1 by Brazil in the quarter finals.

England failed to qualify for the 1974 World Cup, the 1976 European Championship, the 1978 World Cup, the 1984 European Championship and the 1994 World Cup. Technically, the same goes for the 1972 European Championship, but only four teams contested the finals.

England's Euro '96 anthem, 'Three Lions', was re-recorded by a German band as 'The Eagle on the Breast' and is now the official song of Eintracht Frankfurt.

TEAM RECORDS

The only England player ever to win the Golden Boot for the most goals scored during the World Cup Finals was Gary Lineker in Mexico in 1986.

England's record win is 13–0 against Ireland in Belfast in 1882.

Goalkeeper Peter Shilton holds the record for the most England caps, with 125 international appearances between 1970 and 1990.

The record goal scorer is Sir Bobby Charlton, with forty-nine goals in 106 appearances between 1958 and 1970. However, Jimmy Greaves has a strong claim to be England's greatest striker, with forty-four goals in just fifty-seven games between 1959 and 1967.

Viv Anderson was England's first black international, winning his debut cap under Ron Greenwood against Czechoslovakia in 1978. Paul Ince was the first black player to captain England in a full international against the USA in Boston in 1993.

The oldest player to represent England was Stanley Matthews, who played against Denmark in Copenhagen in 1957 at the age of 42 years and 104 days. The youngest was Theo Walcott, who was aged 17 years and 75 days when he made his debut as a substitute against Hungary in May 2006.

ENGLAND'S PENALTY SHOOT-OUT DEFEATS

2006 World Cup: vs Portugal (Quarter Final)
2004 European Championship: vs Portugal (Quarter Final)
1998 World Cup: vs Argentina (Second Round)

1996 European Championship: vs Germany (Semi Final)

1990 World Cup: vs Germany (Semi Final)

ENGLAND'S PENALTY SHOOT-OUT MISSERS

Stuart Pearce	World Cup Semi Final vs West Germany 1990
Chris Waddle	World Cup Semi Final vs West Germany 1990
Gareth Southgate	European Championship Semi Final vs Germany 1996
Paul Ince	World Cup Quarter Final vs Argentina 1998
David Batty	World Cup Quarter Final vs Argentina 1998
David Beckham	European Championship Quarter Final vs Portugal 2004
Darius Vassell	European Championship Quarter Final vs Portugal 2004
Frank Lampard	World Cup Quarter Final vs Portugal 2006
Steven Gerrard	World Cup Quarter Final vs Portugal 2006
Steven Carragher	World Cup Quarter Final vs Portugal 2006

ENGLAND MANAGERS
And how many matches they played, won, drew and lost

Sir Walter Winterbottom (1946–62)	P139 W78 D33 L28
Sir Alf Ramsey (1963–74)	P113 W69 D27 L17
Joe Mercer* (1974)	P7 W3 D3 L1
Don Revie (1974–7)	P29 W14 D8 L7
Ron Greenwood (1977–82)	P55 W33 D12 L10
Sir Bobby Robson (1982–90)	P95 W47 D30 L18
Graham Taylor (1990–93)	P38 W18 D13 L7
Terry Venables (1994–6)	P23 W11 D11 L1
Glenn Hoddle (1996–9)	P28 W17 D6 L5

Howard Wilkinson* (1999 & 2000)	P2 W0 D1 L1
Kevin Keegan (1999–2000)	P18 W7 D7 L4
Peter Taylor* (2000)	P1 W0 D0 L1
Sven-Goran Eriksson (2001–2006)	P67 W40 D17 L11

* Denotes caretaker manager.

Before 1946 the team was chosen entirely by an FA committee. The first manager to have complete control over the side was Sir Alf Ramsey.

ENGLAND PLAYERS SENT OFF

Alan Mullery vs Yugoslavia in Florence 1968

Alan Ball vs Poland in Chorzow 1973

Trevor Cherry vs Argentina in Buenos Aires 1977

Ray Wilkins vs Morocco in Monterrey 1986

David Beckham vs Argentina in Saint-Etienne 1998

Paul Ince vs Sweden in Stockholm 1998

Paul Scholes vs Sweden in London 1999

David Batty vs Poland in Warsaw 1999

Alan Smith vs Macedonia in Southampton 2002

David Beckham vs Austria in Manchester 2005

Wayne Rooney vs Portugal in Stuttgart 2006

The 1966 World Cup

'Look at the Germans! They're flat on their backs,
having massages. They can't handle you; not in extra
time...'

Alf Ramsey to his team after
90 minutes in the final

Four months before the finals, the gold Jules Rimet Trophy was stolen. A mongrel dog called Pickles later found it under a bush in South London in time for the tournament.

England's quarter final against Argentina was so violent that Alf Ramsey described his side's opponents as 'animals' and ran on to the pitch at the finish to prevent his players from swapping shirts with them. The Argentine captain Antonio Rattin, an especially grievous offender, was sent off by German referee Rudolf Kretlein for dissent. Kretlein did not understand a word of Spanish, but famously took offence at 'the look on his face'. Rattin refused to leave the pitch and had to be escorted to the changing rooms by police. He later became a far-right politician.

'Nobby' Stiles's real name was Norbert.

The final was played in front of 93,000 spectators and a further 400 million television viewers around the world.

At the time, England had never lost to West Germany.

Geoff Hurst became the first man ever to score a hat trick in a World Cup final. Hurst had replaced Jimmy Greaves, who was injured in the group match against France, but he kept his place after his team-mate had recovered. A decades-long dispute followed

England's third goal (Hurst's second), which hit the underside of the crossbar and then appeared to bounce in and out of the goal mouth. The goal was awarded after the referee consulted the 'Russian' linesman, the USSR's Tofik Bakhramov, from what is now Azerbaijan. In 1995, researchers at Oxford University concluded from computer analysis of television footage that the ball had not in fact crossed the goal line. However, the nearest England player to the ball at the time was Roger Hunt, who claims he knew that it was a goal – which is why he wheeled away in celebration rather than tap in the rebound. There was also controversy over England's fourth goal, which was allowed to stand even though a pitch invasion was in progress, prompting commentator Kenneth Wolstenholme's famous words, 'Some people are on the pitch. They think it's all over... It is now!'

THE ROUTE TO VICTORY

Group stage	England 0, Uruguay 0
Group stage	England 2, Mexico 0
Group stage	England 2, France 0
Quarter final	England 1, Argentina 0
Semi final	England 2, Portugal 1
Final	England 4, West Germany 2 (after extra time) (Hurst 19 mins, 100, 119, Peters 78) (Haller 13, Weber 89)

THE 1966 WORLD CUP FOOTBALL TEAM: WHERE ARE THEY NOW?

Gordon Banks: Forced to retire in 1972 after he was blinded in his right eye in a car crash. After working as a scout he played in the NASL alongside George Best for Fort Lauderdale Strikers before starting a company that distributed tickets for corporate events.

Bobby Moore: Played his last game for Fulham in 1977. When he wrote to the FA inquiring about the England managership following the departure of Don Revie that year, the FA reportedly did not bother to reply. He played for Seattle in the US soccer league before coaching Danish Third Division side Herning and then non-league Oxford City and Southend, which he saw relegated to the Third Division. He became sports editor of the *Sunday Sport* in 1986 and then commentator for Capital Radio before dying of bowel cancer in 1993 aged 51.

Martin Peters: Managed Sheffield United for less than a year before leaving and working in the insurance business with Geoff Hurst.

Geoff Hurst: After a career in the motor insurance trade, he is now Director of Football for McDonald's as well as a motivational speaker. He remains the only player to have scored a hat trick in a World Cup final.

Bobby Charlton: Managed Preston for two seasons. In 1990 he sold his company, Charlton Enterprises, for £3.5 million. He has also received an OBE, a CBE and a knighthood for his services to football. Joined the board of Manchester United in 1984 and remains England's highest-ever goal scorer.

Jackie Charlton: Starred in Shredded Wheat adverts before becoming an honorary Irishman as manager of the Republic of Ireland. Spends much of his time fishing.

George Cohen: Now raises money for cancer charities. His nephew, Ben Cohen, was a member of the team that won the 2003 Rugby Union World Cup.

Ray Wilson: Quit professional football in 1972 to go into the family funeral business.

Roger Hunt: Set up a successful haulage business and became a member of the pools panel, who predict the results of games called off due to bad weather.

Nobby Stiles: The memory of an unsuccessful stint in management at West Bromwich Albion was forgotten after his stewardship of the youth team at Manchester United, where he coached Beckham, Butt, Scholes, Giggs and the Neville brothers.

Alan Ball: Managed Portsmouth, Stoke, Exeter and Southampton before ending his career ignominiously at Manchester City. In 2004 his wife and daughter were both diagnosed with cancer, and he sold his winner's medal for £140,000.

On the thirty-fifth anniversary of the victory in 2001, Alan Ball remarked, 'I wish England had won since. For a start it would stop you wheeling us lot out and we could live in peace. I don't think players these days have the same hunger we did.'

Cricket

'Cricket civilizes people and creates good gentlemen.
I want everyone to play cricket in our country. I want
ours to be a nation of gentlemen.'

Robert Mugabe, President of Zimbabwe

EARLY YEARS

Cricket dates from the thirteenth century, when a primitive version was played by French shepherds against a tree stump or the wicket gate of a sheep enclosure, with a crook used as a bat and a stone as a ball.

The first county match was played between Kent and Surrey in 1709.

The County Championship was formalized in 1890, when it was contested by Gloucestershire, Kent, Lancashire, Middlesex, Nottinghamshire, Surrey, Sussex and Yorkshire. Surrey won the first three championships. The most successful club has been Yorkshire, with thirty championships.

The earliest cricketers bowled underarm. Overarm bowling was illegal until 1864. The style's immediate precursor and inspiration was 'roundarm' bowling, invented by Christina Willes, sister of Kent cricketer John Willes after she found that her skirts hampered an underarm action.

The first Australian side to tour England was a team of Aborigines coached by an Englishman, Charles Lawrence, in 1868. They played forty-seven matches, of which they won fourteen, lost fourteen and drew the rest. They also demonstrated a number of unique sports, including running races backwards, boomerang throwing and dodging cricket balls.

Eighteenth-century players commonly took to the field in tricorn hats, knee breeches and silk stockings. Predominantly white clothing became the norm only in the late nineteenth century.

Wisden Cricketers' Almanack was first published in 1864. Until 2003, two 'gentleman players' in top hats decorated its famous yellow cover. The change to a cover bearing the face of batsman Michael Vaughan prompted a heated debate on the letters page of *The Times*. Among the most sought-after editions of *Wisden* is 1916's, which includes the obituaries of W. G. Grace, C. B. Fry and Victor Trumper.

There are ten ways in which a batsman can get out: Caught, Bowled, Leg before wicket, Run out, Stumped, Handling the ball, Obstructing the field, Double hit, Hit wicket, Timed out. At the Oval in 1951, playing against South Africa, England's Len Hutton became the first player given out for obstructing the field in test cricket.

The Indian prince Kumar Shri 'Ranji' Ranjitsinhji played fifteen test matches for England between 1896 and 1902 and scored 989 runs.

THE MCC

Eighteenth-century aristocrats played cricket in White Conduit Fields in Islington, until they lost patience with the disorderly crowds that gathered to watch them play and gamble on the outcome. For the sake of exclusivity, they set up Marylebone Cricket Club with the help of founder Thomas Lord in 1787.

The first game, involving Middlesex vs Essex, was played on Dorset Fields (now Dorset Square). The MCC moved to its present home in St John's Wood in 1814, where the games drew so many spectators that stands had to be built to accommodate them.

Until 1864, the wicket at Lord's was prepared by allowing a flock of sheep to graze on its turf.

The MCC is the world's arbiter of the laws of cricket. In 1774, the width of the bat was restricted to 4¼ inches (108 mm) after Thomas 'Shock' White turned out for Reigate with a bat as wide as the stumps that made his wicket impregnable. In 1979, Dennis Lillee was banned from using his bespoke aluminium bat when the England captain Mike Brearley objected that it was damaging the ball.

There is an eighteen-year waiting list for MCC membership.

The first women's cricket club, White Heather, was founded in 1887, but women were not allowed to become members of the MCC until 1998, after the government threatened to cut off lottery funding if the club persisted in its 'sexist' ways.

THE ASHES

After the national side's first defeat on home soil, the *Sporting Times* ran a mock obituary: 'In affectionate remembrance of English cricket, which died at The Oval on 29 August, 1882. Deeply lamented by a large circle of sorrowing friends and acquaintances. RIP. NB – The body will be cremated and the ashes taken to Australia.'

England toured Australia that winter, and after a match at Sir William Clarke's estate outside Melbourne, Lady Clarke and her friends burnt one of the bails and presented the ashes to England captain, Ivo Bligh, in a miniature urn. After Bligh's death, the ashes were bequeathed to the MCC.

The Australian team does not traditionally get to take home the urn when they win the series, as it is rightly the private property of the Bligh family, who gave it to the MCC for safekeeping. The winner of the series instead receives a scaled-up replica in Waterford crystal.

W. G. GRACE (1848–1915)

Over a 43-year career in first-class cricket, Victorian England's greatest cricketer, William Gilbert Grace, scored 54,896 runs and 126 centuries. This was in an age when the poor state of many pitches made the bounce of the ball unpredictable. As a bowler he took 2,864 wickets.

His scores might have been even more impressive if it were not for his huge appetite – large lunches washed down with whisky made him sluggish at the wicket and bowlers tried to get him out during his 'digesting' period.

He played mainly for Gloucestershire and England, and in his last game at the age of 66 he scored sixty-nine not out for Eltham.

He was also known for his anger at the wicket and his gamesmanship. Clean-bowled first ball in one game, he refused to walk and took up his place at the crease for the next delivery. When the umpire insisted, Grace snorted, 'Play on! They've come here to see me bat, not you umpire.' For the toss he would use a coin with Queen Victoria on one side and Britannia on the other. Instead of 'heads' or 'tails' he would then shout 'woman'. A recent *Wisden* describes Grace as 'grasping', 'mercenary' and 'a shameless cheat'.

Grace was an amateur player and a medical doctor by profession. He employed locums at his practice in Bristol during the cricket season.

His face was used as God's in *Monty Python and the Holy Grail*.

C. B. FRY (1872–1956)

> 'Fry must be counted among the most fully developed
> and representative Englishmen of his period.'

> Neville Cardus

English sport's greatest ever all-rounder, Charles Burgess Fry, is best known for his cricket, but he also played football for England and jointly held the long jump world record.

He stood as a parliamentary candidate for the Liberal Party three times, and lost each time.

Fry was a delegate to the League of Nations on behalf of India for three years during the 1920s. He almost became King of Albania after the country's emissaries were sent out to find 'an English country gentleman with an income of £10,000 a year'. An amateur player who lived on the modest proceeds of journalism, endorsements and nude modelling, Fry fulfilled the first requirement but not the second.

Very handsome and fully aware of it, Fry liked to hold a classical Grecian pose after playing a shot. This behaviour tended to provoke the crowd into hurling abuse at him.

After a bout of mental illness, he became an admirer of Adolf Hitler, who sought his advice on running the Hitler Youth. Fry argued unsuccessfully that they should all take up cricket.

DOUGLAS JARDINE (1900–58)

Jardine long represented the low point of unsportsmanly conduct as the captain of the England team during the 'Bodyline' series against Australia in 1932–3. He instructed his fast bowlers to aim at the man rather than the wicket, so that the opposing batsmen were forced to defend their heads rather than their stumps and give away easy catches. When Harold Larwood felled Bill Woodfall with a ball to the chest, Jardine remarked, 'Well bowled, Larwood.' England won the series, and Harold Larwood later retired to Australia.

Jardine refused to speak to the Australian press not because he distrusted the media, but because he refused to speak to Australians as they were incapable of pronouncing the King's English correctly. He claimed to hate almost everything else about the country too. None of this was for effect. Once when a small boy asked to carry Jardine's bag, his hero snatched it back and roared at him with bared teeth.

IAN BOTHAM (B. 1955)

In 1977, Ian Terence Botham was in Melbourne after playing on a youth scholarship programme when he overheard Australia captain Greg Chappell disparaging the England team. Botham was so incensed that he punched Chappell and knocked him over a table before chasing him out of the room.

Against India in Bombay in 1980, Botham became the first player to score a century and take ten wickets in a test match.

Botham also played professional football for Scunthorpe United.

Against New Zealand in the Second Test in Christchurch in 1978, Botham deliberately got his team-mate Geoff Boycott run out after the Yorkshireman was felt to be scoring too slowly.

Botham was banned for a period in 1986 after he admitted having smoked cannabis on tour in New Zealand two years previously.

He never scored a century against the West Indies. However, their captain Viv Richards said that his friend Botham was the only person outside his family for whom he would stand up and risk physical injury.

He has raised over £5 million for charity on sponsored long-distance walks.

'Botham's Ashes'

During the 1981 Ashes series, Botham resigned the captaincy of England after a defeat and a draw in the first two tests. Midway through the Third Test at Headingley, England had been forced to follow on and trailed Australia by 221 runs. The situation was so hopeless that Ladbrokes offered odds of 500–1 against an England victory. With his team on 135–7, Botham said to the incoming Graham Dilley, 'Right then, let's have a bit of fun,' and went on to score 149 not out. England's lead was just 124, but Bob Willis bowled out the Australians for 111. It was only the second time a team had won a test match after being forced to follow on.

In the Fourth Test at Edgbaston, Australia were on 105–5, needing 151 to win, until Botham took five wickets for one run in twenty-eight balls. England won by twenty-nine runs.

At Old Trafford, he hit five sixes during an innings of 118, and England won the series 3–1.

Wimbledon

The All England Lawn Tennis and Croquet Club was founded purely as a croquet club in 1868, with tennis added in 1875. The game was originally called 'sphairistike' – Greek for 'playing ball' – but the name was dropped in favour of 'lawn tennis' as it was difficult to pronounce. Very little croquet has been played at the All England Club since the early 1880s.

The first Wimbledon champion was Spencer Gore in 1877. The Doubles competition and a Ladies' Singles tournament were added in 1884, when the latter was won by Maud Watson. The first champion from overseas was America's May Sutton in 1904.

The earliest 'stars' were the Renshaw twins, William and Earnest, who drew crowds of spectators on their way to winning thirteen titles between 1881 and 1889.

Since the All England Club moved to its present location in Church Road, Wimbledon, only two Englishmen have won Wimbledon singles titles – Arthur Gore and Fred Perry, the last in 1936. However, in August 1945 an Englishman serving in the US Army named Charles Hare won the United States European Championship on the old No. 1 Court. Women have been slightly more successful than men in recent decades, their last champion being Virginia Wade in 1977.

In 1949, Teddy Tinling, Wimbledon's official couturier, dressed Gertrude 'Gussy' Moran in frilly knickers that were visible under her skirt when she played in the Ladies' Doubles final. Fortunately, 84-year-old Queen Mary was unable to attend that day as she was confined to the palace by the heat. Nevertheless, a parliamentary debate ensued and Tinling was sacked.

In 1980, Bjorn Borg became the first man since the 1880s to win five Gentlemen's Singles titles back to back. William Renshaw won six between 1881 and 1886. In 1987, Martina Navratilova won her sixth successive championship. She won her ninth title in 1990. Pete Sampras and William Renshaw hold the record for Men's Singles titles, with seven wins each. Only two unseeded players have ever won a singles title – Boris Becker in 1985 and Goran Ivanisevic in 2001.

The 'cyclops' infra-red system for detecting foot faults was installed in 1980. The last year in which wooden rackets were used was 1987.

Centre Court and No. 1 Court are not used for the other fifty weeks of the year. The third largest court, No. 3 Court, is known as the 'Graveyard of Champions' due to the top-seeded players who have been knocked out there in the early rounds, including Pete Sampras and John McEnroe.

Every year around 60,000 lbs (27,000kg) of strawberries with 12,000 pints (7,000 litres) of cream are eaten at Wimbledon.

English World Heavyweight Boxing Champions

Bob Fitzsimmons	Undisputed	7/9/1892–17/3/1897
Lennox Lewis	WBC	14/12/1992–24/9/94, 7/2/97–22/4/01, 17/11/01–6/2/04
	WBA	13/11/99–29/4/00
	IBF	13/11/99–22/4/01
Michael Bentt	WBO	29/10/93–19/3/94
Frank Bruno	WBC	2/9/95–16/3/96

NB As in other categories, birthplace and parentage have been taken as the criteria for Englishness. Former WBO champion Herbie Hide, born in Nigeria, is not included while Lennox Lewis, born in London, makes the list although he was brought up in Canada and boxed for that country at the Olympic Games.

The Dangerous Sports Club

The club was set up at Oxford University in the mid 1970s by David Kirke, Chris Baker and Ed Hulton. It dispersed around the country when it was banned by college authorities in the late 1980s.

Kirke invented modern bungee jumping in 1979, when he tied a rubber cord to his ankles and leapt from Bristol's Clifton Suspension Bridge on 1 April. He was arrested and fined £100 for a breach of the peace. The stunt was based on the Pentecost Islanders' tradition of 'land jumping', in which tribesmen tie themselves to vines and then dive head first into sand from 80-foot (24 metre) wooden towers.

During the height of the club's popularity in the 1980s, many members were drawn from the public schools and the upper classes. Champagne and top hats featured in many of their stunts, which were often prohibitively expensive. A cocktail party was held on Rockall, a jagged rock 200 miles (322 km) out in the Atlantic, while the local authorities once prevented a group of enthusiasts from driving a double-decker London bus down a ski slope at St Moritz.

Their most famous member was Monty Python's Graham Chapman, whose involvement had mixed success. He failed to hang-glide over a volcano in Ecuador, and when he set off down a ski run in a gondola he was thrown over the side and pursued down the slope by the craft, narrowly avoiding serious injury. However, he managed to land safely after being thrown through the air over London's Hyde Park by a contraption used to launch fighter jets from aircraft carriers.

The club has arranged stunts for several Hollywood films, including the James Bond movie, *Goldeneye*.

Their emblem is a wheelchair.

Club Activities

Human catapult – with a medieval trebuchet*

Hang-gliding – over active volcanoes

Flying microlight aircraft – around Big Ben dressed in a gorilla suit

BASE jumping – Parachuting from Buildings, Antennae, Span (bridges), and Earth (cliffs)

Canyoning – Jumping down a series of waterfalls without a raft, wearing a life jacket and a crash helmet

Street luging – Lying face down on a surfboard and hurtling down long flights of concrete steps

Mountain zorbing – Rolling down slopes inside giant plastic spheres

Surrealist skiing – Creating sculptures and riding them down ski runs

Channel hopping – across the English Channel in the pouch of a giant inflatable kangaroo

* Nineteen-year-old student Kostadin Yankov was killed performing the feat in 2002 after he missed the safety net.

———

Country Sports

———

> 'The English country gentleman galloping after a fox –
> the unspeakable in full pursuit of the uneatable.'
>
> Oscar Wilde

The 'Glorious Twelfth' is the name given to the first day of the grouse-shooting season on 12 August.

The earliest kennel to specialize in breeding English foxhounds dates to 1676. The dogs are descended from the Talbot and Gascon foxhounds brought over from France by the Normans after 1066.

The hunting cry 'Tally ho!' on sighting the fox derives from the Norman French hunting exclamation 'Taïaut!'

England's oldest hunt is the Bilsdale Hunt in Yorkshire, established in 1668.

In 1891 the Humanitarian League was founded to campaign against foxhunting. In 2004 a parliamentary bill to ban hunting with hounds was passed by 339 votes to 155. Into 2006, the ban has largely been ignored in several areas, without penalty.

ENGLAND'S FIVE BEST TROUT STREAMS

Berkshire: The Kennet, Hungerford
Dorset: The Frome, Dorchester
Hampshire: The Itchen, Southampton
Hampshire: The Test, Portsmouth
Northumberland: The Till, Berwick-upon-Tweed

Rugby

HISTORY

Rugby, like soccer, is descended from the Roman game *harpastum*. The modern game was 'invented' in 1823 when William Webb Ellis picked up the ball and ran with it during a game of football at Rugby School.

The Rugby Football Union was formed in 1871, two months before the first international match between England and Scotland took place. Scotland won 4–1.

The League and Union versions split in 1895. Rugby Union teams have fifteen players, including a six-man scrum. Rugby League teams have thirteen, including an eight-man scrum. Rugby Union was an amateur game until 1995. Rugby League does not have an England team.

In the 2003 Rugby Union World Cup, Johnny Wilkinson scored ninety-eight of England's 307 points over the tournament.

ENGLAND'S RUGBY UNION WORLD CUP RECORD

1987 – Quarter Finals (Wales 16 – England 13)
1991 – Losing Finalists (Australia 12 – England 6)

1995 – Semi-Finals (New Zealand 45 –England 29)
1999 – Quarter Finals (New Zealand 44 – England 21)
2003 – Winners (England 20 – Australia 17)

RUGBY POSITIONS

1 2 3

6 4 5 7

8

9

10

11   12

13

14

15

1. Loosehead prop
2. Hooker
3. Tighthead prop
4. Left lock, 2nd row
5. Right lock, 2nd row
6. Blindside flanker*
7. Openside flanker*
8. Number 8

9. Scrum-half
10. Fly-half
11. (Left) winger
12. Inside centre
13. Outside centre
14. (Right) winger
15. Fullback

* The flankers switch positions depending on which side the ball is played
into the scrum.

Horse Racing

THE CLASSICS

The five English Classics are all contested by three-year-olds on the flat:

1. The Two Thousand Guineas (late April/early May, Newmarket, 1809–)
2. The One Thousand Guineas (late April/early May, Newmarket, 1814–)
3. The Oaks* (early June, Epsom, 1779–)
4. The Epsom Derby (June, Epsom, 1780–)
5. The St Leger Stakes (September, Doncaster, 1776–)

* The Oaks is a race for fillies only.

The Two Thousand Guineas, Epsom Derby and St Leger Stakes make up the 'Triple Crown'. This has been won fifteen times, most recently by Nijinsky II in 1970.

THE AINTREE GRAND NATIONAL

The first official Grand National steeplechase was contested in 1839 over 4 miles across country by seventeen ostensibly gentleman riders, though most were professionals. The winner was the 5–1 favourite, Lottery.

The 'Becher's Brook' water jump was named after Captain Martin Becher, who was thrown into the stream by his mount during the first ever race.

There are sixteen fences, all of which are jumped twice except for the 'Water Jump' and the 'Chair'. The latter is the tallest obstacle at

5 feet 2 inches (1.6 metres) preceded by a 6-foot (1.8-metre) ditch. A stone wall featured until 1844 when it was replaced by the 'Water Jump'.

The 1967 National was won by the 100–1 outsider Foinavon after most of the field was caught in a pile-up at the twenty-third fence. Foinavon was so far behind at the time that his rider Johnny Buckingham was able to plan a course through the mêlée.

Three other 100–1 outsiders have prevailed: Tipperary Tim (1928), Gregalach (1929) and Caughoo (1947). The hottest favourite ever to win was Poethlyn at 11–4 in 1919.

The record time in the race, 8 minutes 47.8 seconds, was set by Mr Frisk in 1990, carrying 10 stone 6 pounds (60 kg).

Only two greys have ever won: The Lamb in 1868 and 1871 and Nicolaus Silver in 1961.

Red Rum won a record three Nationals: 1973, 1974 and 1977. The horse is now buried at the Aintree winning post.

THE EPSOM DERBY STAKES

The first 'Derby' was run in 1890, when the winner was the 6–4 favourite, Diomed.

The race was named after the Earl of Derby, who won the privilege on the toss of a coin. Had he lost, the event would now be known as the Epsom 'Bunbury', after Sir Charles Bunbury.

Victorian parliaments adjourned for the day so that MPs and peers could attend the Derby.

In 1913, the suffragette Emily Davidson was killed when she threw herself in front of King George V's horse, Anmer.

Today, the course is 1 mile, 4 furlongs and 10 yards (2,423 metres). (Until 1784 it was just 1 mile long.)

Lester Piggott (b. 1935) rode a record nine Derby winners:

1. Never Say Die (1954)
2. Crepello (1957)
3. St Paddy (1960)
4. Sir Ivor (1968)
5. Nijinsky II (1970)
6. Roberto (1972)
7. Empery (1976)
8. The Minstrel (1977)
9. Teenoso (1983)

Morris Dancing

MEDIEVAL MORRIS

The first performance by 'moryssh dauncers' in England was in London on 19 May 1448. The troupe was paid the equivalent of 35p.

Morris dancing became popular in the sixteenth century after featuring in the court masques introduced by Henry VIII.

The word 'morris' comes from the French term for a dance, 'morisque'. It has also been suggested that the name 'morris' derives from 'Morisco', meaning 'Moorish', because the dancers would blacken their faces – a variant of morris dancing practised today by teams on the Welsh borders.

In 1599, the Elizabethan actor Will Kemp won a bet by dancing the 'Nine Dales Wonder' from London to Norwich during Lent, attracting crowds along his route.

THE MORRIS REVIVAL

The pastime had almost died out when the folksong enthusiast Cecil Sharp saw a dance in Headington in Oxfordshire on Boxing Day

1899. He initiated a morris revival under the auspices of the Victorian 'Merrie England' fantasy. Sharp organized dance lessons for young men and travelled the country to track down surviving teams, eventually founding the English Folk Dance Society in 1911.

In 1999, the Alford Morris Men of Lincolnshire were excluded from the official Morris Ring of England for allowing female dancers into their team.

THE SIX STYLES

Cotswold is the most common style, originating in the South Midlands, including Warwickshire, Northamptonshire, Gloucestershire and Oxfordshire. Groups of six or eight wave handkerchiefs while dancing.

Molly is an East Anglian style where the dancers wear outdoor work clothes and sometimes blacken their faces.

Welsh Border morris dancers in Hereford, Worcestershire and Shropshire wear long coats or tailcoats and bowler hats or top hats. Faces are blacked or masks worn and the performance includes stick clashing and shouting.

North West Clog dancing involves a procession of men from Cheshire or Lancashire wearing iron-shod clogs dancing in procession form.

Longsword is a Yorkshire variant in which six or eight dancers employ blunt swords and round off their act by joining the blades in a star formation.

Rapper is a kind of sword dance from Durham and Northumberland where five men wearing miners' breeches use a flexible steel blade to perform somersaults to the accompaniment of a fast jig.

ACCOMPANIMENTS

Each morris team features a 'Fool', usually the best dancer, whose job it is to interact with the crowd and enforce team discipline by doling out punishment with a pig's bladder tied to the end of a stick. There may also be a dancer dressed as an animal – usually on a hobbyhorse – or a dragon or unicorn – to entertain children in the audience.

Two instruments are used to provide a traditional musical accompaniment: the three-holed pipe or whistle and a drum, or tabor. Sometimes a 'squeezebox' or melodeon is also used, while Welsh Border dancers bring a full band.

MUMMING

Morris dancing is closely associated with mummers' plays, in which St George fights a Turkish knight until one of them is killed. A 'doctor' then appears and resurrects the fallen character with the help of a magic potion. The play also involves a jester and a man dressed up as a woman. Depending on the time of year, Father Christmas acts as the presenter. There is no record of such plays in this format before the eighteenth century.

APPENDIX

They Were Not English

T.E. Lawrence (Welsh)
Robert Adam (Scottish)
Ivor Novello (Welsh)
Lucian Freud (German)
Frank Auerbach (German)
William Herschel (German)
Ernest Rutherford (New Zealander)
Robert Boyle (Irish)
James Clerk Maxwell (Scottish)
Laura Ashley (Welsh)
Edmund Burke (Irish)
Ernest Shackleton (Irish)
Jacob Epstein (American)
Marie Stopes (Scottish)
Roald Dahl (Welsh)
Arthur Conan Doyle (Scottish)
Bertrand Russell (Welsh)